BRADFORD OF PLYMOUTH

BRADFORD
of PLYMOUTH

Bradford Smith

J. B. LIPPINCOTT COMPANY
PHILADELPHIA AND NEW YORK

Library of Congress catalog card number 51-11198

TO

MARY AND WILMER COLLINS

In whose debt I stand
with thankfulness and joy

CONTENTS

THANKS

Most of the library work for this book was done at or through the Williams College Library, the Bennington (Vermont) Free Library, and the Massachusetts Historical Society. I am especially indebted to Wyllis Wright and Miss Ethel Richmond of Williams, Mrs. Florence Moses of Bennington, Stephen T. Riley, Librarian of the Massachusetts Historical Society, and Mrs. Gladys Leslie, Librarian of Bennington College.

To Miss Jessie L. Knowlton of the Massachusetts State Library I am grateful for the rare privilege of examining the manuscript of Bradford's *Of Plimoth Plantation*. Miss Edna M. Werrey, Librarian of Pequot Library at Southport, Connecticut, graciously transcribed an original Bradford letter for me, while Isidore S. Meyer, Librarian of the American Jewish Historical Society, provided information about Bradford's knowledge of Hebrew. Most of all I am indebted to my wife, Marion Collins Smith, who lightened the labor and heightened the pleasure of a longish task.

B. S.

PROLOGUE

Although he has been dead nearly three hundred years, William Bradford has always seemed very close to me. I was raised on him, so to speak, by a mother who took pride in having him for an ancestor, who had read his book, and who managed to make him interesting to me even before I could read for myself. Before I was old enough to know better, I resolved that I would some day write a book about him, and during my college years I began to collect materials as I could find them. But only in the past three years has it been possible to devote time to what has become an even more interesting job than I had guessed.

It is always stimulating to come close to a great man. It is doubly so, somehow, when he has been neglected. And Bradford has been neglected. In the popular mind it is Miles Standish, John Alden and Priscilla Mullins who represent Plymouth, yet Bradford was its governor almost from its beginning to the end of his life. Warren has his cove, Priscilla her beach, Brewster and Carver their towns on the map of the Old Colony, yet there is no such memento of Bradford. Robinson, Brewster, Standish, Alden have all found biographers though offering far less material to a writer, yet Bradford has never had a full biography and even the two brief books that exist are now thirty and forty years old. Neither is in the modern sense a biography.

One deterrent may have been Bradford's great book itself, *Of Plimoth Plantation*—the source of almost all we certainly know about the Old Colony in its early years and the chief reliance of all who have retold the Pilgrim story. Somehow the necessity of such heavy borrowing may have prevented writers from building upon it a portrait of the man who made it. Or possibly Bradford is so nearly synonymous with Plymouth that no one has wanted to disentangle them.

It is true that we lack the sort of detail about Bradford a modern biographer likes to have. Yet while biographies are usually

9

developed from a wealth of hitherto unused material, it is equally exciting to extract a great man from the mystery of a past which has left little of such matter—to make him live by a reconstruction of scattered hints and materials which with patience can be pieced together to form a portrait. The story of William Bradford has to be written in this fashion. For though much is known of his times, his public acts and his effect upon his contemporaries, little is recorded of his personal life. To recapture the personality of this great and modest man from his works and acts and to project his influence upon American life is the purpose of this book.

That he was Plymouth's greatest man there is no doubt. His story is exciting because it is the story of America and because it curiously forecasts developments that were not to appear in full form for many years.

In an age of privilege he was a self-made man. While Boston was establishing a hierarchy he was trying to build in politics as in religion an earthly replica of the freedom Christ had promised. He was a thinker and a man of action, a writer of considerable charm, a linguist, farmer, business man, magistrate, diplomat and man of God. He belonged to an age when men did not have to channel their efforts as narrowly as they do now, and something of the largeness and scope and dignity with which this endowed a person clings noticeably to him.

As in Bradford, so in his little colony of Plymouth we see America in the making. The very smallness of things—after the first sickness only half a hundred were left alive—lends charm and makes for intimacy. Yet little Plymouth overshadows all other beginnings, and for good reasons. Not only in the appeal of its story but in the principles on which it was built it has an attractive force for us. Here yeoman England and commercial Holland are being transformed into something that will be called American. Here originate the civil marriage service, outright ownership of land (rather than the feudal types of tenure then current in England), a classless society in an age of rigid class distinctions, and government by free association of the governed. The Pilgrims proved that a community of families could survive in the new world and that it could live at peace with the surrounding Indians. Out of Plymouth came a system of government—the town meeting—which colored and enriched the bloodstream of American democracy and which continues a vital force to this day. Out of Plymouth came democracy in religion—the Congregational way. And out of Plymouth came that most valuable of a people's possessions—the myth, the credo which guides their best efforts and tells them, through an idealized memory of the past, what they ought to be.

In governments, says Bacon, "the first foundation or plantation is of more noble dignity and merit than all that followeth." Surely it was so with Plymouth, whose influence has been beyond all proportion to its size. And at Plymouth the influence of Bradford was beyond reckoning.

Though revered today as traditionalists, the Pilgrim fathers—a misnomer since most of the leaders were young men—were looked upon as radicals in their own day. They were radicals in religion and they were radicals in politics. They also, though it was not their own fault, had a fling at communism before going on to establish for us a pattern of private enterprise.

Attempts had been made before Plymouth to settle New England, but all had failed. Only one other English settlement had succeeded in the new world when the Pilgrims came, and the Jamestown settlers had once actually given up and started home for England when the arrival of reinforcements turned them back. Plymouth was the first permanent settlement begun by families. It was the first successful settlement made by men who intended to establish themselves and their posterity in the new world. And it was the first of the religious settlements. It was the example of Plymouth which, by making the common Englishman regard the new world as a place for permanent settlement, ultimately made North America English instead of French or Spanish.

Since Bradford was governor almost continuously for the first thirty-six years, the story of Plymouth is very largely his, and it lives for us today almost entirely through his engrossing book. In Bradford we watch the making of one of the first great Americans. Captain John Smith returned to England and remained English. Winthrop and the Boston leaders tried to re-establish place and privilege as they had known them in England. But Bradford groped toward the new world where all men, or at least all believers, might be free. This is an exciting thing to watch. It can be seen in his great book, though he was so modest that he is constantly hiding or ignoring his own part in the shaping of events. So it can be seen more clearly when highlighted as a story should be.

No man is complete within himself. No man fully lives except as he lives to serve and be a part of a social order, a community. Only a very fortunate man becomes so much a part of his community as to be almost indistinguishable from it. That was Bradford's fortune and his greatness. In him we may see a mature personality expressed in service to society and through a living, informing faith.

It is not too fanciful to speak of Bradford as the first American. Certainly he is, in the dignifying Emersonian sense, a representative man. So it should be profitable to have him come to life in our times and in our thoughts.

The present book is the first in a projected series of related narratives, all of which will be concerned with American communities that grappled with the great problem of harmonizing their economic and political concepts and activities with an overruling faith: in short, with the good life. Modern man is destroying himself in two ways—by regarding only his individual desires while shirking his social responsibilities; or by making himself a slave to the tyrannic community known as the nation-state. Freedom's crisis today is a double one, and freedom may be destroyed by slavery either to the selfish desires of the individual or by the brute slavery of the totalitarian state. It will not be destroyed if men understand that the mature personality is one which has found a way to harmonize its personal urges with the welfare of the community, if they are persuaded that a whole man is only one who fulfills himself in a serviceful life within a community, and if their faith in such a life burns bright enough to lighten the world: "a lanterne unto my fete and a light unto my path."

The Pilgrims knew this. Many Americans have known it and still know it. But in urban America there are too few who experience it. Unless means are found to widen their lives into the fellowship of working for goals beyond themselves, American society is facing downhill.

Among the communities I intend to present, through biography, social history, group biography or psychograph, are Oneida, the early Mormon settlements, New Harmony, Hooker's Connecticut, Roger Williams' Providence, and possibly the Shakers. An early book will be *Mission to Paradise,* an account of the lively events which followed the first coming of New England missionaries to pagan Hawaii in 1820. Somewhere, at the end of a trail whose length I cannot now measure, I hope to discover, and to share, the vision of that beloved community the search for which has been one of the great distinctions of our history and the heart of the American dream.

BRADFORD SMITH

Shaftsbury, Vermont
March 29, 1951

Since this book is a biography, not a novel, I have never put into Bradford's mouth a word for which I do not have chapter and verse. But since it is a biography, not a collection of documents, I have tried to bring Bradford to life by building from the available evidence descriptions of his thinking and feeling in situations that were important to his development as a man. If the historian is permitted to find trends and patterns by analyzing the day to day life of the past, the biographer has an equal right and duty to disclose the trends and patterns of an individual mind. That is what I have tried to do.

January 9, 1952

The Challenge

A YOUNG man, pale with a nearly fatal illness from which he has not yet recovered, stands on a knob-like hill of the New England coast looking out toward the sea. It is an April day in 1621, hot with the sudden youthful vigor of a New England spring, the sun's heat welcome to his weakened body. Not as good as wine, of which there is none left, nor as invigorating as food, of which there is little—but welcome.

The tang borne inland by the ocean breeze tickles his nostrils. He sniffs, then breathes deeply. He begins to feel better. Birds new to his eye burst into song among the branches. The thrust of awakening life in the soil is so strong that he can almost feel it in the soles of his feet. The birds, the salt breeze and the hot sun have made him suddenly aware that he is on the mend. The terrible lassitude of the sickness is beginning to leave him. His youth, his manly vigor begin to reassert themselves. He breathes deeply again, letting his chest rise high with the breathing. And to himself he barely whispers, to try the sound of it, "Governor William Bradford of Plymouth."

Then stepping around the unmarked graves on Cole's Hill (as it later came to be called), he starts down toward the beach, not minding the trembling in his legs now because he knows that it will soon be over.

It will need to be. At thirty-one, William Bradford is governor of a little group of Englishmen so weakened by disease and death

17

and lack of adequate food, so little prepared to get their living from the wilderness, so inexperienced, so unorganized and so incapacitated that a few Indians or another bout of disease could easily destroy them.

There is no ship in the harbor now. The *Mayflower* has sailed for England after staying five months to see the little group settled. The tiny village of Plymouth—nothing more than a few miserable huts of wattle and daub with thatched roofs and wooden chimneys lined with clay—fronts a wilderness of ocean with England two or three hazardous months away. Behind it stretches a wilderness even less known and explored, full of imagined perils and unimagined wonders. Except for a few thin trails of exploration, it is a wilderness no European has seen.

Wilderness, then, before and behind; weakness within. Of the hundred and two people who had arrived with the *Mayflower* the previous November, only fifty-six left alive. Only nineteen men, of whom again a mere handful are entirely well.* So few and so weak, against all that wilderness. Among the dead are the first governor, John Carver, the wives of Miles Standish and Edward Winslow, the entire family of Christopher Martin who has inconsiderately departed leaving the colony's finances in a chaotic state. The dead include all of the Mullins family except Priscilla, whom legend is to cherish as the heroine of the Pilgrim story. They include Bradford's young wife Dorothy.

The grandeur of the phrase, "Governor William Bradford of Plymouth," fades a little as the young man reflects on the shrunken size of his charge. Yet for an orphan without wealth or birth or influence—for a man of plain yeoman stock to become any sort of governor in the year 1621 is a thing of note. That he should have been chosen above all the rest—even above older men like Cooke or Allerton or Fuller their doctor—is a mark of favor for which he thanks God. Because he knows, within himself, that it is a charge of which he is capable. They have trusted him, and he will fulfill the trust.

Governor Bradford! What would they say now, those chiding neighbors at Austerfield, those prying and jealous villagers, if they knew that the boy they had tried to shame for his stubborn

---

* Only three couples remained unbroken after the first sickness. Four families were entirely wiped out.

religious unorthodoxy was a governor? Or what would Dorothy have said, if she had lived to see it?

A sudden twitch of the face he cannot control comes with the thought of Dorothy his wife. A mere child of sixteen she had been at their marriage seven years ago, still in the flowering of her womanhood when the *Mayflower* had brought her with him to the new world but a few months back. Yet after surviving all the horrors and indignities of that dangerous and crowded voyage, she had lived but a few days. Drowned—fallen overboard, they said—while he was away on a trip of exploration.

How had she fallen? How could it have happened so that there was no one about to save her? Had the strain of the voyage unsettled her mind?

Perhaps now, as his strength begins to come back and his lusty manhood feels the need of her, he reflects that drowning had at least spared her the miseries of the general sickness, from which twelve of the twenty women had died. Since God had seen fit to take her earlier, could he pretend to write a better fate for her, or to wish that she had lived only to suffer as these other women had suffered before they died?

So now he was alone again—as he had been alone in his orphaned childhood. (His son John was still in Holland, and was not to come to Plymouth for several years.) Yet not alone. For now, as at Austerfield, the brotherhood of the church enwrapped him. As in his childhood, this sanctified family would take the place of the natural family he lacked. It had then received and mothered him as a child. Now, in return, he must nurture it as a man. The people knew, for they had chosen him governor, they knew he had the qualities to lead them, to be like a father to them. Their choice of him was instinctive, having the wisdom of instinct. Now, with his strength returning, he knows it too.

Coming to the beach, he makes sure that the shallop is secure, stands a moment looking at the ocean, then turns toward the few little huts that are Plymouth. For no easy reason he grins. Then he starts up the hill, feeling stronger in his legs than he has felt in many days.

The urgency of what waits to be done strikes him with sudden force, and this in itself he knows to be a sign that he is mending. He begins to run over in his mind the things he must see to, placing them in categories and mentally assigning the proper men to each job. Chiefest of duties, of course, is the planting, and everyone must work now at that. Thanks to Squanto's guidance, the Indian corn is already being sown, a few alewives to each hill so as to make the ground yield its fruit. He had wondered at first about that, for so far as he could recall the Bible provided no such precedent for planting. Yet the many hazards of the brethren (he has no name for the religious group which, meeting first at Scrooby in England had gone on to Holland—the "Pilgrims" never did get a name for themselves) had taught him that God's Providence was never the worse for vigorous human aid.

After planting, homes must be built. They must be sturdy English houses of plank, not these miserable huts of clay and reeds and grass, so crowded that a man can have no decent privacy with his wife. Then there must be defenses against the Indian. Though the Lord has mercifully preserved them through their defenselessness, and though they have signed a treaty of peace with Massasoit which has been not only preserved but carried out with an excess of fraternizing which severely gnaws into their food supplies, still there will be no reasonable safety until they have a fort and a stockade.

There is the fishing to be so organized that they can both feed themselves and send salt fish to the merchant adventurers in London. Already this plan has sadly miscarried by the failure of the *Speedwell* to make the voyage, for she was to have been the foundation of their economy—in fishing, in trading with the Indians along the coast, in carrying their produce back to London for credit and for needed manufactures and supplies. It was no plan of the Leyden people to subsist on the labor of their own hands. They had planned to be merchants, trading and selling for profit.

Lacking capital, they had bound themselves to labor in the interest of the merchants who financed them, until their debt was paid. To accomplish this the product of their labor was poured into a common storehouse, their needs doled out from a common supply. Plymouth, therefore, began as a communist society. There is nothing more instructive in our history than the changes that took place in this little communist village as it shaped itself to become, unknowing, the pattern for a great democracy.

Then there is a whole government to be organized. Their patent is from the Virginia Company and they have settled in New England. They have nothing to bind them but the paper signed on board the *Mayflower*—the compact in which they promise to abide by such laws as they shall make for themselves.

As for the members of the Leyden church, they had needed no such compact. They were already bound in a most solemn and binding covenant, that of the church itself. It was for the strangers on board—and they made the majority—the folk sent over by the merchant adventurers that a signed compact was needed. Men like Billington, who already showed signs of giving trouble. Or men like John Alden—young, promising well—who would in time become leaders.

There were half again as many strangers as brethren. Only forty-one (including fourteen children) of the Leyden congregation had come over, out of the total hundred and two men, women and children who reached America. Only three of these —Brewster, his wife, and Bradford himself—can be traced back to the original church at Scrooby in England. Only twenty of the Leyden folk survived the first sickness. Of the forty-one men who signed the Mayflower Compact but eighteen survived, and only six of these were from the Leyden congregation—Bradford, Brewster, Winslow, Allerton, Fuller and Cooke. Yet the Leyden influence remained the dominant one, largely because of Bradford.

Planting, building, trading, governing—these are some of the plans that run through William Bradford's lively mind as he comes up from the beach to the houses, noting as he approaches the fields who is working, who loiters, and who spends his energy seeming to work while accomplishing nothing.

"Master Bradford, may I have another shovel from the store?"

"The women would have the day's portion measured out, that they may get on with their cooking."

"We are run out of seed. What would you have us plant next?"

He finds that these questions, and many more like them, which yesterday tired him today have the stimulus and savor of wine. The people look to him, they rely on him, they trust him. And with God's help, he will be worthy of the charge.

"The spring now approaching," he writes in his history *Of Plimoth Plantation,* one of the great and greatly neglected classics of American literature, "it pleased God the mortalitie begane to cease amongst them, and the sick and lame recovered apace, which put as it were new life into them: though they had borne their sadd affliction with much patience & contentedness, as I thinke any people could doe. But it was the Lord which upheld them, and had beforehand prepared them: many having long borne the yoake, yea from their youth." *

He feels that new life in himself this April morning, he senses it in the men. The memory of the many dead, the memory of Dorothy, and of John Carver who had been stricken in the field so that he never spoke more, the memory of the perilous voyage, and of the insults of a godless crew, then of the explorations for a place to settle—being literally frozen stiff in spray-drenched clothes in an open boat, lying in the open in midwinter and eating cold food and marching in the rain and being so miserably sick that death itself would have been a relief—all these memories cannot wipe out the fact that they have survived. The discomforts, the hazards, the memories are nothing. Life itself is the treasure, and they have preserved it.

* Quotations from Bradford and other contemporary writings are given verbatim wherever possible, except that contractions have been spelled out. Thus the definite article is always rendered *the* and not *ye*—which incidentally was *never* pronounced with the *y* sound. *Y* merely stood for the old Anglo-Saxon letter "thorn" which represented the sound of *th.*

"A Lanterne unto My Fete"

THE baptismal entry can still be seen in the parish register at Austerfield:

19 March 1589   William Bradford *

It is the only entry of world-wide interest destined to be made in the records of this very small English village, and it gives us the only information we have of the approximate birthdate of one of the most influential founders of American democracy and the American way of life. In an age of high infant mortality, baptisms were early. Therefore, though we shall never know the exact date of William Bradford's birth, we can safely place it within a few days of March 29, 1590.

In the little hamlet of Austerfield on the southern border of Yorkshire, the Bradfords were people of consequence. For several generations their wills had indicated the possession of extensive lands, animals and personal belongings—even to such luxuries as feather beds and, in a time when the common folk used wooden tableware, silver spoons. Not forks. No Englishman at this time used a fork.

* Under the Old Style calendar then in use in England the year did not begin until March 25, so according to our reckoning Bradford was born in 1590. Bradford's baptism, after making a ten-day correction also necessary in converting Old Style to New, was therefore on March 29, 1590. Since the Old Style was used throughout Bradford's life, however, it will be retained in this book, the period from January to March 25 being rendered thus: 1620/1.

Thus when William Bradford's great-great-grandfather Peter of Bentley-cum-Arksey died in 1542/3 he had willed "to Robert my son children every one of them a yewe lambe." This sentence, and the act behind it, brings a dead page to life, letting us see as in a shaft of sudden light the desire of that good old man to pass on to the future his love of husbandry, his tender regard not only for his grandchildren but for those ewe lambs on which his wealth was founded.

How simply and how beautifully this bequest symbolizes the English yeoman!—his shrewdness, his pride of ownership, his dependence on natural increase as the source of wealth, his sense of value, his pastoral outlook. Peter Bradford, in that simple phrase of his, was leaving more than a ewe lamb to each grandchild. He was bequeathing a way of life. Handed down with little change through four generations to William Bradford, it supplied the groundwork on which, in 1620, the beginnings of a new nation were to be based.

The English yeoman was proud of his status. Though occasionally rising to the rank of "gentleman," most yeomen preferred to remain as they were. For one thing, it cost less. If you were a gentleman or a knight you were taxed more and oftener. Though contemporary writers sometimes accused the yeoman of being too grasping, there was a general feeling that he was the backbone of England, the "pith and substance of the country." The yeoman was thought to live well, to keep a good house and a good table, and to work hard to increase his wealth. He was an ambitious, aggressive, land-hungry small business man.

The circumstances of the time favored his land hunger. Crown and monastery lands were for sale. Forest, waste and fen awaited clearing—and at a time when the increase of city populations was causing a rise in food prices. He was therefore, like Shakespeare, an active agent in the enclosure movement, pushing his fences out here and there into formerly waste land where he thought he could get away with it, and sometimes even ploughing up the king's highway.

One thing a yeoman could not have—land that was wholly and absolutely his. The dead hand of feudalism still lay on any property he called his own, and even over lands that he considered his, the right of a lord of the manor extended. Of the many types of land tenure three were most common—knight service, which involved the obligation of armed service; copyhold in which the death of the holder might terminate the tenure or the rent might be arbitrarily raised; and socage, the best form of tenure, often involving no more than such nominal annual payment as a pepper corn, a nutmeg, or a red rose.

So along with his land hunger, the yeoman had to suffer a sense of never quite satisfying his appetite. The sword of a dead feudalism hung over his table—with consequences to be seen in Plymouth Colony.

Land hungry and land loving—this was the stock of which William Bradford came.

Like great-great-grandfather Peter (the earliest of William's ancestors who has been certainly traced), the succeeding generations had shown sound business sense and practiced good husbandry. For each was possessed of lands and houses not only in one town, but in two or three. Grandfather William (the two generations preceding our American Bradford were also Williams) bought property in Austerfield, Bawtry, and Misson, the latter over the border in Nottinghamshire. Since our William was an only son, his inheritance would have been considerable.

Besides the Bradfords, the only family of any importance in Austerfield was the Hansons. Since young William's father had married Alice Hanson, William was as well born as anyone in Austerfield could be. But neither family claimed to be anything more than yeoman. So the Bradfords of America who trace their ancestry back to Governor William and then sport a coat of arms are deluding themselves. The Bradfords of Austerfield were not nobility; they were much better. They were sturdy tillers of the soil who labored for what they had. They were producers.

From the name, which means a broad ford, the Bradfords generations before must have lived by a river wider than the little Idle that runs through Austerfield. Sometimes the name was written Bradfourth, as for instance in recording the death of young William's father. In those days men seem to have liked variety in their spelling—a tendency still strong in many a schoolboy and almost as many grownups.

Old Peter Bradford would have thought it appropriate that his great-great-grandson should be born in lambing time, when all the household was busy with the care of this natural increase on which the wool-growing yeoman's prosperity depended. As the lambs often needed nursing, the young heir of the household —even though he was a first-born son—probably had to share the family's attention with the creatures of the sheepfold, and may have been warmed at the same hearth with them.

At his birth the reawakening year had already brought its increase of tasks to the household around him. The ploughing and manuring and pruning in a well-ordered farm were done before lambing time. Next came the "stirring" of the land before sowing grain, the scouring of ditches, the planting of gardens. By May, when the young master had begun to take an interest in things beyond the scope of his own touch, the lambs were weaned. In June came the shearing—a busy time when the yard was full of workmen clipping and washing. In that class-conscious era the difference between a clipper and a washer was clearly marked by what the master gave each for his dinner—ale, bread and cheese for the clippers; a mixture of boiled milk, crumbled white loaf, ale and nutmeg for the washers.

Often thereafter must the youngster lying in his cradle have watched his mother combing and carding the soft wool—and no doubt have got his own hands into it and been punished, as little able as any child to understand why it is wrong to touch, to explore, to experiment.

Through July haying and August harvest and the fall tasks of threshing, cider making and slaughtering, young William grew like the young of any time or place—learning to use his hands, to laugh, and to delight and provoke his parents with all the winsome and disgusting animal traits of infancy. Then as the months passed he learned, like any child, how to creep, to totter, to walk; to borrow the language of his elders.

Since the "hall" of a yeoman's house was a room of all purposes, the baby would have been from the beginning part of the life of the household. No separate nursery, no quiet room or hushed voices for him. In the hall was a long table with benches, a cupboard and a chest. These seem to have been standard. There may have been a chair or two—even a tapestry on the wall. These were luxuries, and in Austerfield only the Bradfords and Hansons would have had them. The fireplace was cluttered with spits, andirons, trivets—for the cooking was also done in the hall. Even to have a fireplace was somewhat of a novelty, for in the early part of Elizabeth's reign they had been rare even in homes considered well to do. In the homes of the poor, fires were still built in the middle of a room or against the wall if the wall were of stone. The smoke had to get out through the open lattices which served for windows, glass being then as rare as fireplaces.

Young Alice Bradford, William's mother, would not have done any elaborate cooking. She roasted her meat or boiled her pottage before an open fire, and what the diet lacked in variety was made up in the quantities of beer or ale consumed.

Beyond the meat, bread, ale and cheese which formed the staple, testimony conflicts as to the amount and kind of vegetables consumed in yeoman households. In southern England vegetables of many kinds were eaten while in some northern areas they were scarcely grown. In any case most of the vegetables familiar to us were known then—radishes, pumpkins, cauliflower and cabbage, cucumbers, carrots, parsnips, turnips, beets, asparagus, onions, lettuce, spinach, as well as artichokes and even tulip bulbs. Years later, when Bradford was responsible for the welfare of that band of Pilgrims in the wilderness, the only vegetable he mentions as having been planted the first season was peas—and they never matured. Yet this proves nothing, for he had been too long separated from his old home to have brought seeds from it. In a poem written after many years at Plymouth, he names a wide variety of vegetables grown and eaten there.

Whether Alice Bradford served many vegetables or not, she doubtless made butter and cheese from the milk of the cow or two belonging to the household. The meat and dairy products on her table would not have been very different from those of today. Even Chaucer's poor widow had had her bacon and eggs.

The manners that accompanied the eating of this fare can be guessed from an etiquette book of the day which advised against spitting on the table, blowing the nose into the napkin, throwing bones under the table or picking the teeth with a knife.

Though two meals a day were all the townsman ate—dinner at eleven or twelve, supper at five or six, in the country men ate their early pottage before starting the day's work.

By the time young William had reached the crawling stage he had grown familiar with the rest of the house—the parlor with its best bed, the room where the dairy work was done, the brewhouse where his mother made the large quantities of beer or ale consumed by the household. Also, as he entered the crawling stage, he was in danger of approaching the end of his life. Infant mortality was high in those days, and for a reason that seems to have been overlooked.

The Elizabethan housewife covered her floor with rushes. They were replaced or covered with new ones now and then, but the idea of a clean floor does not seem to have been present even in well-run households. Down into the rushes seeped bits of food, spittle, vomit, dirt from shoes intimate with the barnyard, and sometimes the excrement of man or beast. This was the platform offered to the Elizabethan youngster at his crawling age. Is it any wonder that he often failed to survive?

Yet young William met the test. So did his sister Alice, born three years before him. Another sister, Margaret, had been buried the day after her baptism, in 1585/6. There were no other children.

Though William did not escape the ordeal of the rush floor, he did manage to be born in an age which seemed to those who lived in it one of real luxury by contrast with what had gone before. As late as 1628 a chimney was still a thing you willed separately from the house. So was the wainscoting of the hall. One of the things most impressive to the older generation was the remarkable change in the appearance of towns and villages during the early reign of Elizabeth as chimneys began to go up. Another was the change from wooden spoons and bowls to pewter. Houses were coming to be built more and more of stone rather than thatch and rough plaster. And people, even plain farmers, were no longer sleeping in straw with a log for a pillow, but actually climbing up into beds. Even feather beds were not beyond the means of a well-to-do yeoman.

Young William, as he crawled about among the rushes, would not have found his way too much obstructed. For furniture was still a rare commodity. Even the castles of the great had but few chairs, and those who inhabited them often carried their furniture with them when they traveled. Needless to say, sanitary and bathing arrangements were either absent or of the most primitive sort.

Yet William survived. When he was big enough to get up off his hands and knees he tottered into the yard to watch his father and the hired workmen going out to the fields with barn manure or coming in with the plough at the end of the day. He no doubt chased the ducks and was spanked for it, fell into the pigsty and otherwise made intimate contact with the hazards of country life. This childhood in the country was to have its importance later. The men and women who reached Plymouth in New England survived. No one knows how many thousands died in the earlier attempt to settle Virginia. But we do know that most of them had lacked any experience of raising their own food.

In the Bradford household, however, as in Yorkshire generally, the raising of food for the table was only a sideline to the raising of wool. The demand for English wool in Europe, chiefly the Low Countries, was the foundation of the yeoman's prosperity —at least in this part of England. Many yeomen also went into the cloth and clothing business—an item of significance in view of Bradford's trade during his stay in Holland.

William would have watched his mother carding the wool or spinning it into thread. Though the weaving and fulling were generally not done in the household, some of the Bradford wool would come back from the weaver in the form of cloth to be made into clothing. For though the yeoman did not produce all, he still produced much of what he required in his own home.

We would have a more intimate picture of Bradford's early home life if we could be sure that the place in Austerfield now known as the Bradford house was surely the one he grew up in. It is easily possible, but it is not proven. In any case that part of it which is old enough to qualify must be very like the house young William knew. It is of stone, solid and substantial, unimposing as to size, undecorated—severely functional in its uncompromising squareness of wall, its determination to keep out the weather and stand forever, but to make no pretense of anything else.

The growth of an individual is outward, from himself as center. The infant starts by exploring himself—his hands, feet, ears, then the things his hands can grasp, then what he learns to focus on, and finally what he can crawl or walk to. By the summer of 1591, when the first major event took place in William's life, he would have been old enough to get beyond the household and to see something of the little hamlet, full of his own kin whether Bradfords or Hansons, to which he belonged.

Most of the buildings of Bradford's day, being of wattles, thatch and rough clay, have not survived. Even the land has changed. For in Bradford's youth the country around Austerfield was marshy, its thickets full of wild fowl. Where fields are now, forests covered the land or moors overgrown with heather stretched their fingers down into the bogs. Of grazing land there was a good deal, but the complete patchwork of neatly tended fields with their intersecting hedges of hawthorn was yet to come.

As the fenny land was contained and held in by the surrounding moors, so the moors were compassed and gathered in by low rolling hills within eyeshot on either side. Even the landscape had a pastoral quality in this land of flocks, held gently within its bounds by a shepherding hand.

The sixteenth century was not sentimental about landscapes, preferring to translate real country life into a ridiculous convention of courtly swineherds and mincing milkmaids who were only courtiers in disguise. So it may never have occurred to Bradford to worship nature in Wordsworthian style. Yet a feeling for the land must have been strong where the family had been so long wedded to it. Bradford who, as we shall soon see, was a sensitive child, must have had the feeling his contemporary Shakespeare expressed in *As You Like It:*

> And this our life exempt from public haunt
> Finds tongues in trees, books in the running brooks,
> Sermons in stones, and good in everything.
> I would not change it.

Not that Austerfield was a Utopia. No village is too small to have its quota of poverty, misery and drunkenness, and England in Elizabeth's day seems to have excelled especially in the last. To be sure, in this little hamlet near the border of the shires of

Nottingham and Lincoln and close to Sherwood Forest the Robin Hood tradition was still strong. But the "merrie England" we like to believe in was for the majority a place of toil, disease, and early death, with small regard for personal liberty.

Though the village life had its sports—attractive to us for their quaint names of quarterstaff, barleybreak, tilting at the ring and running at quintain, and its feasts and festivals, these were occasional. The toil was continuous.

There was, as perhaps in village life everywhere, a strong sense of neighborhood. Yeoman wives had to serve as nurse, physician and counselor to families in need. The men—those who could write—gave service as real estate agents, lawyers, witnesses and scribes. To be esteemed a good neighbor was important to the yeoman, who was in and of the village where the squire was only its patron. This sense of stewardship young William acquired unconsciously as he trotted into humble kitchens with his mother, watched her administer some simple country remedy or carry food to the needy. Equally strong in its influence would be the family's praise of a good workman and its scorn for the shiftless and idle. There were no subtleties in such an outlook, but there were no deceptions either. When Bradford found himself responsible, years later, for setting the tone of a new community he did not have to reflect; he had merely to draw upon his earliest experiences.

Austerfield was a hundred and fifty miles from London. In 1590 this distance was a more effective barrier than the earth's circumference today. The Great North Road in spite of its grand name was nothing but a narrow horse path frequently infested with highwaymen. No one in Austerfield had ever been to London. Even the Bradfords, well to do as they were by local standards, would not think of making the trip unless some strange and unexpected crisis should cast them out of the village orbit. And this, they would say if they ever thought about it, simply could not happen.

Yet the things that were happening at the court in London were to do exactly this to William Bradford.

To draw a fair picture of Elizabethan England is a difficult matter—difficult because the age embraced so many contrasts,

but difficult too because we have been reared on a romantic notion of the era which is far from the truth. We think of Shakespeare, of Raleigh and Essex and Bacon, of Marlowe and Spenser
and Donne. Good Queen Bess and merrie England, boar's heads
and yule logs and spiced ale, extravagance in dress and language
and manners persuade us that this was a golden age. We forget
that while Shakespeare's plays were being performed, the audience discharged their urine into a barrel sunk in the ground of
the pit until the odor became so offensive that calls to burn
the juniper, thus disguising rather than expelling the smell,
would drown out the voices of the actors. We forget that the
gallant Raleigh was a pirate and a gangster who had gained the
queen's favor through his ability to stamp out opposition by
wholesale murder. We ignore the fact that the great philosopher
Bacon like everyone else had to fawn and beg for a meager
government post to sustain him. Everyone remembers that Marlowe died in a ditch after a drunken brawl, but few recall that
Spenser, while writing his beautiful if long-winded praise of
Elizabethan England in the *Faerie Queene,* was also recommend-
ing that the Irish be obliterated. Merrie England was not so jolly
for the thousands of unemployed, many of them ex-soldiers, or
for the desperately poor who, forced to steal, were punished with
a cruel indifference to suffering and disregard for human life
which we find it hard to understand. (In justice to that age,
we should perhaps admit that the atomic bombs dropped on
Japan probably killed and maimed more people than Elizabeth
throughout her whole reign.)

For trifling offenses men had their ears cut off or their noses
slit—or both. The pages of the court records drip with the blood
of those maimed by judicial order, while capital punishment
was decreed for hundreds of crimes. Statesmen, fearing the pressure of population upon food supply, looked upon the death
penalty as a convenient way of keeping the nation within bounds.

To be sentenced to a prison term was almost as severe as a
death sentence, since the prisons were so foul, so disease-ridden,
that few could survive an extended stay. With nothing but filthy
straw to lie on, with no provision for human waste, no heat, and
indifferent or positively rotten food, the strongest man soon
succumbed. Many innocent men, thrown into jail on mere sus-

picion, died without ever coming to trial. Elizabeth's jails were
not much better than Hitler's gas chambers.

Meanwhile "broken men" by the thousands—and women too
—wandered about with no employment, no home, and no hope.
The rising price of wool had led many landholders to dispossess
their small tenant farmers in order to use the land for their own
flocks. Victims of a changing economy or of debilitating war
service or disease, they turned to beggary or crime. No one had
a remedy for these situations. Because the homeless were many
they were feared, and because they were feared they were severely
punished when caught.

Even the common folk who had work were not a great deal
better off. Toil, disease and early death were often their lot, and
drunkenness too often their chief recreation.

As for those who should have known better and who had the
means to order their own lives, affairs were not much better.
Peers of the realm, by special dispensation from Elizabeth, were
given "benefit of clergy"—that is, freed from the jurisdiction
of the courts—when convicted of highway robbery. As a special
law to this effect was passed, it apparently was needed. Indeed,
the chief justice of England, John Popham, is supposed to have
indulged occasionally in highway robbery before being elevated
to his high office.

The law gave no protection to an innocent man. He might be
thrown into jail at the pleasure of a high officer, tortured, and if
brought to trial denied the assistance of counsel or the right to
confront his witnesses. The judge held his job at the pleasure of
the crown, while the jury well knew that they would be punished themselves if they gave a verdict contrary to what the queen
desired. Rammed onto pikes on London Bridge were rows of
the rotting heads of men summarily tried for treason. Com-
moners who attempted to get redress for a wrong done them by
a nobleman found themselves thrown into a dungeon where no
legal process could get them out. Even officers of the courts were
handled in this way if they attempted to discharge their duties.
Though England was internally at peace, there was little sense
of security when a man might be thrown into jail and left to
die there simply for having offended someone with influence.

This was the counterpart of Elizabethan splendor.

As for the much-vaunted learning of the age, the European scholar Bruno, visiting England in 1583, met most of the reputed scholars but found few who were willing to accept the theory then widely understood in Europe that the earth revolves about the sun. He thought the students at Oxford ignorant and ill-mannered, spending most of their time in drinking and fighting.

To the Elizabethan, life was full of unexplained events, of chance rather than cause. Demons and ghosts were as real to him as, to us, are molecules and electric waves. He knew nothing, naturally, of the true causes of many physical ailments. He did not even know that the blood circulated by the action of the heart. To him any unusual behavior of the natural world, such as storms and earthquakes, was a warning from God. He accepted the theory of divine right of kings so unquestioningly that, if he happened to be at court, he bowed and scraped even to the vessels in which the queen's supper was to be served. The world was still full of vast unknown spaces, and the presence of this great unknown must have had an effect on his outlook.

The Elizabethan age was one of surprising contrasts—of a noble literature and an ignoble worship of royalty; of great courage and large deceptions; of expansion and discovery abroad with cruelty and suppression at home.

The queen embodied in herself many of these contrasts. She loved display—her wardrobe contained two thousand gowns, yet she allowed her most loyal ministers to grow impoverished in her service while showering her amorous favorites with enriching monopolies which, covering everything from wine and salt to steel and smoked herring, drove prices up and strangled trade. She had a reputation for shrewdness, yet the only consistent aspect of her policy was its vacillation. She demanded absolute fidelity in her courtiers yet was not above sacrificing them to save herself. She was both queenly and shameless, strong and irresolute, learned and foolish. Her faults epitomized the age that bears her name.

This larger world was still unknown to the child William when at the age of sixteen months, before he was old enough to take the measure of it, death visited his household. On July 15, 1591, William Bradfourth, as the church register spells it, was buried in the churchyard. This was young William's father, and since he had been only seven years married he must still have been a very young man. Which of the many prevalent diseases carried him off we do not know.

So young William grew up with no memory of his father.

This in itself need not have been a crushing handicap in an age accustomed to early deaths. Young William had several uncles and at least one grandfather to fall back on. But when he was only four his mother, marrying again, sent him to live with his grandfather William Bradford. Then within two years (1596) his grandfather died. For a year his mother had charge of him again until her early death. Finally, when still only seven years old, the lad was put in charge of his uncles, Robert and Thomas Bradford.

There is no doubt that these changes had a profound effect on the boy. They are probably the original source of his religious awakening at the age of twelve, and consequently of his large contribution to the history of the American continent. If his mother had kept him with her, he would have found a way to compensate for the loss of his father, but then she had renounced him too—for so it would have seemed to a four year old. Twice robbed, he then lost the grandfather on whom he had learned to rely as a father, and shortly after that his mother—this time for good.

A child of William's sensitive perceptions could not have lost much time discovering that in the household of his uncles he was without a champion. That peculiar twist which makes people regard an orphan as an inferior—almost as if he were somehow to blame for his disability—would have made itself clearly felt. There is no reason to suppose that William's uncles, however fair, were any different from the other men of their age. They would have regarded a child as a somewhat subhuman species, and rather than make allowances for the inner wound his orphanage had left, they no doubt exacted more from him for that very reason.

This, then, accounts for the "soon and long sickness" which according to Cotton Mather was William's childhood lot. It also accounts for that forbearance, tolerance, and sensitivity toward others which were marked traits of his later life.

When the basic character is strong, a wound may often prove a benefit.

Was it perhaps because he was puny and sickly that the family decided to educate him? In Elizabeth's time there were plenty of men better off than the Bradfords who could not read or write. At least as late as 1547 their number had included peers of the realm. Shakespeare's father, though a high bailiff, could not write his name. When men of such prominence did not know their letters, knowledge was but caviar to the general.

William Bradford's clear uncluttered prose and his beautiful hand, remarkable in a time when embellishment and confusion both in grammar and in penmanship were the fashion, give proof of early gifts in this direction—gifts which his uncles must have had the sense to recognize. Knowing the value to any yeoman family of a member who could reckon, write out deeds, examine titles and otherwise attend to the family business instead of relying upon a stranger, they may have decided to use him as the family's man of letters. Other advantages too came to the man who could read. The ability to read was regarded in court as a proof of belonging to the clerical class. Any rascal or criminal who could demonstrate his "clergy" by reading from a book could thus avoid punishment in the temporal courts, since he was then subject only to church law. This is the original "benefit of clergy."

But where did William get his schooling?

Whether Austerfield had a "dame school," or whether the class was conducted by a clergyman or craftsman we do not know. Schools of the time were formed around some person, whether dame or cleric or merchant, who was willing to pass his knowledge on and make a bit on the side. The study of reading began with a hornbook—a kind of board with a handle, its letters preserved by being placed under transparent horn. Beginning with ab, eb, ib, ba beb, bi bob, and other equally practical noises, the student went on ultimately to something that made sense—if he got that far. Going through a reader completed the curriculum.

Such a school, of ten or a dozen youngsters of varying ages, probably provided all the formal education ever received by one of America's outstanding historians and magistrates. Yet this did not prevent Bradford from growing up to know several languages including even the ancient Hebrew.

Somewhere the boy found books, though books in this age were rare. Perhaps he got them from the Reverend Mr. Silvester of near-by Alkley, who had an English and a Latin library. Since reading and writing were still to a large extent confined to the clergy, it is natural that much of the literature was theological. This would in part account for Bradford's early interest in religion. At his death, Silvester left his library to a grammar school at Rossington. Since this was but three miles from Austerfield, it is just possible that Bradford attended it.

Among the popular titles of the day were Foxe's *Book of Martyrs*, the *Praise of Folly* by Erasmus (translated into English in 1549), the Bible, works on astrology and a guide book for country justices by one Dalton.

That Bradford read the first three is beyond doubt; that they shaped his thinking, beyond question.

Erasmus' book with its richness of classical allusion first opened to this country boy a sense of the past and of the great world beyond the comfortable circle of hills that surrounded him. Its keen criticism and sharp style were later to influence his own writing.

Equally exciting to his young fancy was that huge tome of Foxe, twice as long as Gibbon's *Decline and Fall* and many times as full of blood and agony. Here was the fear and hatred of Roman Catholicism, "the whore of Rome," which filled the minds of Englishmen who could still remember the persecutions under bloody Mary. Here was the noble adherence to a principle in the face of death, so dear to the idol-hungry mind of youth. And here, indeed, one of the principal heroes was a Bradford—John Bradford, burned at the stake because he would not disavow his faith.

William would have wondered whether that man from neighboring Lancashire could have been kin to him. It would not have been hard for him in any case to identify himself with such a hero. Indeed, he could scarcely have avoided it. For Foxe too he must have had a kindred feeling, for the author of this immensely popular book had been born in near-by Boston (Lin-

colnshire)—the place where a few years later young William was
to be imprisoned after the failure of his first attempt to escape
into Holland.

The "soon and long" sickness that afflicted Bradford in his
youth had begun in the collapse of security and certainty resulting from the deaths of his father, mother and grandfather. But
it is easy to see how, subconsciously, the boy would have continued it as a defense against the surrounding rude world of
dunged field and dumb beasts, and the frank talk of men who
in Shakespeare's phrase got their living by the copulation of
cattle. How crude a world this seemed to a youth who had been
devouring the Bible and Foxe!

Despite his frailty, William was set to tending sheep. And like
any young idealist who has discovered a world through books,
he welcomed the solitude. The long hours alone with his flock
may even have given him an opportunity to get on with that
reading of the Bible which continued for the rest of his life.
What a reading that must have been, with Foxe behind him to
give it perspective, the blue English sky overhead pierced with
the shrill sweet music of the lark, the yellow flowers of the gorse
seeming to soak up the golden sunlight as it fell, and the sheep
grazing around him as in the very book he was reading.

To be a shepherd then must have seemed like entering into
the biblical past, becoming one with David and Isaac and Joseph.
How then could he have kept the sting from his eyes and the
fullness from his throat when with the woolly flocks all about
him he read from his Geneva Bible:

> The Lord is my shepherd; I shal not want.
> He maketh me to rest in grene pastures, and leadeth me by
> the stil waters.
> He restoreth my soule, and leadeth me in the paths of right-
> eousnes for his Names sake.
> Yea, thogh I shoulde walke through the valley of the shadow
> of death, I wil feare no evil: for thou art with me: thy rod and
> thy staffe, they comfort me.
> Thou doest prepare a table for me in the sight of mine adver-
> saries: thou doest anoint mine head with oyle, and my cup run-
> neth over.

Douteles kindenes and mercie shal follow me all the dayes of my life, and I shal remaine a long season in the house of the Lord.

Both the age and his own time of life led the boy to consider very literally what he read. And there was not a phrase in this perfect poem which did not speak to him directly, and to his own condition. For here, as he guarded his own sheep—some of them without doubt the descendants of the ewe lambs bequeathed by that good old man, his great-great-grandfather, the Lord guided him through the miracle of His Book while he sat in a green pasture beside the still waters of the Idle. That stirring of the soul which belongs by right to every adolescent had begun. Already he had been led through the valley of the shadow of death, and from the indignities and loneliness of orphanage he had begun to find relief. The house of the Lord should be his home.

"Thy worde is a lanterne unto my fete," he read, turning the pages, "and a light unto my path."

Lowering the book he could look out across the woolly backs that surrounded him and up the gentle slope to the peak of a low hill. Then for a moment he would *be* in ancient Palestine. He would scarcely have been surprised if the bush before him had burst into fire.

His uncles, good hardy yeomen, shook their heads over his peaked looks which even long days with the flocks had not overcome. How could they know that this was a paleness not of weakness but of strength—the paleness of the idealist, the thinker?

William Bradford was no weakling. He survived ordeals that would have killed most men, and did kill many. Now, as he approached young manhood his uncles were about to be treated to a sample of that strength in a way that would amaze, anger and confound them.

"A Grain of Mustard Seed"

THE explosive force that shot young William Bradford out
of the little northern hamlet where he seemed destined to
spend his whole life was religious. It was the same force which
was to rob Charles the First of his head, to settle the wilderness
known as New England, and to establish a way of life which
still affects the conduct of the American people. It was a force
which came early and with intensity into William's life.

The loss of his parents and his grandfather had made young
William a shy youngster, turning in upon himself. And turning
inward had, as with any gifted child, the result of opening up
unsuspected caverns of the mind, creating desires and surmises
only half defined which were satisfied only with the discovery
of the miracle of the written word.

That William was a good student and a quick learner we
know from the impressive knowledge of languages and literature
he later managed to acquire, in spite of a life burdened with
labor both for himself and others. Cotton Mather tells us that
at twelve he was already a student of the Scriptures. But where
did he get this knowledge? Probably not from his parish church,
for in his day the churches of England were filled with men incapable of preaching. Even cooks and stewards were preferred
to livings by masters who wanted to pocket the income.

Yet the Bradfords were, and always had been conformers. So
young William was marched off to church every Sunday with

the rest of the family, there to hear the service which the queen had decreed as the religion of her people. Back in old Peter's time the king had been Roman Catholic, so Peter had been Catholic. "I bequeath my soul to god Almighty and to owre ladie saint Marie," he had written in his will. Catholicism had lingered well past King Henry's reign in northern England. Grindal, when first going down to his province as Archbishop of York in 1570, reported that the people still observed old Romish feasts and festivals. By the time William was born in 1590 the Roman rites had of course given way to the somewhat equivocal Anglican practices under the very equivocal Elizabeth. And Bradford might have spent the rest of his life listening to the Anglican service if it had not been for one of those accidents which so frequently change the course of history. To Bradford, of course, it would not have seemed an accident, but a Providence of God.

Somewhere, somehow, he met a young fellow of his own age who had been going to church at Babworth where Richard Clyfton was preacher. For sixteen years Clyfton had been preaching Puritan principles there. Bradford was persuaded to go and hear him. And from that moment, the course of his life was changed.

But who was the boy who took him there, and how did they meet? To these questions there is no answer, for Cotton Mather who is the only source of our information tells us no more. Since Babworth was eight miles from Austerfield it is likely that the other boy lived at some distance from Bradford and possible that they met as shepherds somewhere in the fields between the two villages.

William at this time must have been a pale youth, still suffering from the effects of his "soon and long sickness." It may indeed have been this friendship, with its consequences, which effected the cure of a condition obviously psychosomatic. Clearly it was one of those boyhood friendships that come with the awakening of the mind, or awaken it; a sudden discovery of mutual interests, a sharing of confidences which have never been shared before, an awakening of that social part of the personality which yearns for the reassurance that one's inner feelings are not unique and peculiar but general and universal, and

therefore capable of being shared. Forced in upon himself by
circumstances, William must have begun in this friendship
that widening of the personality, that turning outward without
which there can be no maturity. And we know that he continued this outward turning with its capacity for wider service
to the end of his life.

Already an avid reader, Bradford must have been hungry for
talk about the things he read. Not only was his new companion
a sounding board for the long thoughts he had so far kept to
himself; he knew where further light could be had.

So, on a Sunday morning, the two boys walked together to Babworth to hear Richard Clyfton. Bradford was entranced. This
was the doctrine he had half dreamed of. Clyfton, "a grave and
fatherly old man," as Bradford called him in later years, was a
sound and interesting speaker. But even more important than
what he said must have been the personal impact he made on
William. Knowing what we know of Bradford, the key to his
willingness to walk sixteen miles every Sunday is found in the
word "fatherly." Bradford was still seeking a father substitute.

Clyfton, religion, and the new friend had a wonderful effect
on William Bradford. In that reaching out which belonged to
his years he had touched something as firm as rock and as large
as life. An emptiness had been filled. The loneliness of orphanage had suddenly disappeared. He had a friend and a faith. He
had the pleasure of flouting the uncles against whom his childhood had built up a deep resentment, and a means of flouting
them that was morally acceptable. His revolt—the revolt any
adolescent must go through in order to grow up—had the sanction of religion. It was not negative but positive.

This crisis of growing up is the pivot on which maturity turns,
and those who like Bradford manage to pull it off successfully,
positively, become adults while those who achieve it negatively
or incompletely live a lingering childhood for the rest of their
lives. The struggle cured Bradford of his childhood sickness—
a sickness which had arisen from the lack of any positive faith,
person or symbol to tie to. The fatherless Bradford was still hungry for fulfillment, still looking for an anchor. Religion brought
the sublimation of those early desires and furnished a positive
motivation which lasted to the end of his life. Thus did Bradford

enter on his "holy, prayerful, watchful & fruitful walk with God, wherein he was very exemplary."

No one young enough to remember the adolescent yearning for purity, for an idol worthy of worship, for a secure nest for the spirit can fail to sense what happened to young William Bradford, or to understand how the longing for certainty, for assurance, for knowledge was satisfied by the authority of the Bible and of the able preacher who expounded it.

The discovery of religion was more than a spiritual exercise for this fatherless young man; it was an acceptance of self. From loneliness and weakness William Bradford had worked his way out of the cocoon of inward-looking adolescence to an awakening which would mean sharing and serving. In other words, he had grown up.

When his uncles learned where he had spent his Sunday, they were furious. They forbade him to attend church at Babworth, or to associate with such "fantasticall schismatics" as attended there. The Bradfords were looked up to as leaders in their little village, and they did not propose to have one of their number dishonor the family by any commerce with radicals.

But on the next Sunday William was missed again from the family pew in Saint Helen's at Austerfield. And he continued to be missing in spite of every threat his uncles could think of. The emergence of this unsuspected strength in the nephew they had considered a weakling caught Robert and Thomas off balance. They did not know how to deal with it. They must have tried the usual tricks—ridicule, appeal to pride, to what was owed to the family, to the memory of his dead parents. They accused him of ingratitude and stupidity. But events were to make them wonder whether—horrible thought—they could be wrong.

When William Bradford went across the fields to Babworth instead of going to his parish church at Austerfield he was stepping into the midst of a controversy which had been in the making not only since Henry the Eighth had made himself free of Rome, not only since Wyclif, "morning star of the Reformation," had preached the right of direct access to God through faith and through knowledge of His holy word, but one inherent in the Christian faith. Was religion a matter of unchalleng-

able authority or of individual conscience? Was the institution
or the person to determine belief? Was the church a man-made
thing capable of error, or must it be accepted without correction
as the determinant of all religious matters?

When King Henry declared his independence of Rome, he
provided a pattern of conduct which could just as well be used
against him and his successors. For if Henry could separate from
Rome, why might not other bodies of believers separate from
Henry?

The analogy would not have occurred to Henry, of course.
To him there could be no comparison between the actions of a
king and those of his subjects. It was a well-established principle
that the subjects followed the religion of their king. Obedience
in this regard was taken as much for granted as obedience to the
secular laws of the realm. Henry was no believer in religious
liberty. The very notion would have been abhorrent to him,
had he been able to understand it. The idea of freedom in
thought whether religious or otherwise had yet to be fought for
—and won by much expenditure of blood.

Yet Henry had begun a course which would give the subjects
of his successors an opportunity. The Roman monolith had been
broken. From its parts still smaller pieces could more easily
be chipped. With no intention of doing so, Henry had opened
a path for the Reformation in England and for the ultimate
triumph of democracy over monarchy. For in separating from
Rome he had willynilly attacked the principle of authoritarianism. He had struck a blow at the stability of a system based upon
hierarchy and changelessness. Once that system was attacked, his
own authority was threatened. Not at once, but in time.

Conflict was held off for a while by the reforming principles of
young King Edward, or actually of the bishops—Cranmer, Rid-
ley, Hooper and Latimer—who led the Anglican church in the
direction of the Calvinist Protestantism that was spreading across
the continent of Europe. Had Edward lived, much of the conflict
that followed might have been avoided. A liberal policy in religion would have satisfied the Puritans. But the obstructive
attitude of Mary, Elizabeth and James was such that the Puritans
had to fight for political strength in order to gain the religious
reforms they yearned for.

Under bloody Mary those who would not recant their non-Roman beliefs were barbarously burned, hanged or dismembered, their bodies hacked to pieces with the axe, the bloody remains thrown into baskets, the heads stuck up on London Bridge as if they had been guilty of some inhuman crime.

Foxe's *Book of Martyrs*—favorite reading in Bradford's day, perhaps as much for its bloody realism as for its sanctity—tells the story in all its frightful detail. Though bloody Mary was an amateur compared with Hitler and his gas chambers she opened a wound which has not healed in England to this day, and which tinges with suspicion the attitude of English-speaking countries toward the church of Rome. Yet long before the persecutions of Mary, Englishmen had been struggling to win wider freedom in religion, and long before Luther began his work on the continent Englishmen had suffered and died for it. As far back as 1165 thirty weavers in the diocese of Worcester were summoned before the council of Oxford for their independent thinking. William of Occam, born about 1270, was excommunicated for his attacks on papal supremacy. Separated churches on the Congregational pattern are known to have existed at least as early as 1553. Within forty miles of Bradford's birthplace Puritans were killed during the so-called Pilgrimage of Grace in 1536.

But of all the early Protestants, the greatest was Wyclif (c. 1320–1384), who lighted the way even for Luther. Wyclif taught the immediate dependence of the individual upon God—a relationship which did not need the interference of the priest or even the presence of the sacraments. He also taught the supreme authority of the Bible. To carry his doctrines to the humblest he chose poor or simple priests to be itinerant preachers, and to bring the Bible within the reach of all he began a translation into English which marks the beginning of English prose literature. His followers, the Lollards, walking the lanes and highways of England in their long red robes of coarse wool, preached Wyclif's message to the common folk and established that firm tradition of resistance to authority, worldliness and greed in the religious establishment to which the Puritans and Separatists of the seventeenth century by right belong. The Lollard books, multiplied by the slow process of transcribing, were widely distributed. Like all reformers, the Lollards were hounded and persecuted by those in power.

This movement of Wyclif's met with a wide acceptance among the people. Then under the boy king, Edward the Sixth, government itself accepted the desire for reform and co-operated with it. But Elizabeth's reign made it clear that two different ideas of reformation were at work in England—one arising out of a popular demand for a decent clergy and a church which would purge itself of the greed and ignorance and evil living of which many of its priests were guilty, the other arising out of a need to reconstruct the political bases of the religious establishment from the ruler's point of view. The conflict between these two attitudes carried one king to the block and kept England at war within herself for nearly a century.

Essence of the Protestant movement was the desire to do away with all the walls that had been raised by church and priests between the individual and God. The priesthood, elaborate liturgies and ceremonials, costly vestments and buildings, the church's concern for temporal power and wealth, man-made dogmas and doctrines nowhere found in the Bible—all these were what the Protestant wanted to sweep away, restoring that intimate contact with God which the Old Testament patriarchs had.

Students often wonder why the Pilgrims placed so much emphasis on the Old Testament. One reason was that in their hatred of all intermediaries and their desire to escape from the Roman Catholic system with its priests, saints, and set forms, even Jesus seemed a wall between them and their God.

It was just here that Luther struck his hardest blow against Rome. Against the Roman view that man cannot reach God sacramentally except through a priestly mediator Luther set the assertion of the priesthood of all believers. This, together with his insistence on church services in the vernacular and the elevation of the sermon to a place of major importance, was his chief gift to the religious revolution. Calvin, insisting that the officers in a church are to be elected by the people, gave political form to the essentially democratic idea that all who believe are equal before God. These major contributions to Protestantism lie behind the Puritan and Separatist movements.

But neither Calvin nor Luther thought of a church as something separate from the state. To Luther the state was divinely ordained, and its magistrates should represent the whole body of believers. To Calvin it was essential that every member of the state be subject to the discipline of the church. This system he actually established in Geneva, from which it was copied in other parts of Switzerland as well as in Scotland and parts of France. In this respect the Pilgrims, or Separatists, though they derived from Calvin departed radically from him.

Puritan—Presbyterian—Separatist—Pilgrim: before going any further it may be as well to clear up these terms.

Puritanism in England was essentially a movement within the established church for the purifying of that church—for ministers godly and able to teach, for a simplifying of ritual, for a return to the virtues of primitive Christianity. There was nothing revolutionary about the main body of its doctrine. It accepted the medieval view of a world in which man was the center, and though it may have said that man was made in God's image it tended to think, rather, of a God made in man's. It believed literally in the two "cities" of God and the devil and in the constant struggle waged between them and made apparent in the human struggle between body and soul. It believed that man having fallen through Adam was redeemed through Christ. Its innovating principle was in the idea that the Bible, rather than any established religious hierarchy, was the final authority. Therefore every man, every individual, had direct access to the word of God. It was the Puritan's aim to reconstruct and purify not only the church, but individual conduct and all the institutions men live by.

Like any movement of importance, Puritanism is too complicated a thing to be summarized in a brief paragraph. Its adherents were both conservative and radical. "For long nourished together, their discords concealed, in the furnace of the Civil War they fell apart, the Presbyterian and Independent, aristocrat and Leveller, politician and merchant and utopian gazed with bewildered eyes on the strange monsters with whom they had walked as friends."

Leader of the Puritans during the age of Elizabeth was Thomas Cartwright (c. 1535–1603). His chief opponent was Archbishop

John Whitgift, once a fellow at the same table with him in Cambridge. Whitgift had him removed from his posts at Cambridge and made it necessary for him several times to escape to the continent because of his teaching that the Scriptures were a sufficient guide to the proper form of church government. From exile Cartwright brought home the idea of church government which was to become Presbyterianism. While church and state were to be independent in administration, and church members were to have a share in the selection of their officers, one national church was to include all. Cartwright's influence thus made English Puritanism essentially Presbyterian. It also meant that purifying the church would have to await the action of civil authority.

There was, however, a body of men who saw that if they had to wait for Elizabeth to act, they would wait a long time. They conceived of a quicker way to purify the church—by withdrawing from the state church and establishing a separate congregation of like-minded believers. This was the solution brought forward by Robert Browne in 1580, and this was Separatism.

In Elizabeth's day Separatists were treated as agitators. A mob in Fleet Street kicked one as if intending to kill him. Said an observer: "And I confess it had been no matter if they had beaten the whole tribe in like manner."

The men we know as Pilgrims were Separatists—regarded by most decent people in their time as revolutionaries, radicals, a threat to the state. These radicals are the men we now revere as the staid, conservative, bed-rock founders of our nation. Time changes all things.

Robert Browne (1550–1633) was a singular character who, after discovering the one practical, immediate way to reform the English church, ended by returning to it, an apostate to his own principles. Yet Browne was the first religious democrat. Civil magistrates, he argued, have no right to meddle in spiritual affairs. All men who believe in Christ are equal before him. The English church is too corrupt, too subject to the civil authority, to offer any hope of reform. By insisting that all men must by law belong to it and attend its services, the English church condemns itself to being a body full of the ungodly, from which true believers are bound to separate. A true church, on the other hand, is one made up of true believers, joining themselves together under God by a covenant and watching over and exhorting each other. Its only officers should be those named in Scripture—pastor, teacher, elders, deacons and widows or deaconesses. Nowhere in the Bible is there any authority for bishops or state-controlled churches. The sole authority over a true church is Christ Himself, with Whom the union is sealed in the Lord's Supper.

This was indeed democracy in religion. It was such dangerous doctrine that Browne had to run off to Holland. In 1583 two men were executed merely for possessing his books. The Pilgrims deeply resented being labeled Brownists, as they resented being called democrats—another bad name in that day. "It is very injurious," Bradford complained, "to call those after his name whose person they never knew, and whose writings few if any of them ever saw, and whose errors and back-slidings they have constantly borne witness against."*

Nonetheless, Browne gave the Pilgrims their basic doctrine —that men have a right to worship as they please, in a church of their own forming and without interference from the civil authority.

It is worth noting, since the Pilgrims were to be so strongly influenced by the life of Holland, that Browne himself had picked up the first seeds of his doctrine from the Dutch Mennonite woolen workers in Norwich, where he preached. At this time there were a hundred thousand Netherlanders living in the British Isles, most of them skilled craftsmen who were required by law to take an English apprentice into each household. Thousands of English soldiers and merchants had also been in Holland. The Dutch influence on religious reform in England was therefore widespread.

Something, however, Browne must have gained from the atmosphere of Cambridge, that seedbed of Puritanism and reform from which came William Brewster the Pilgrim, John Greenwood, Francis Johnson, John Penry, John Robinson and many other men who were linked with the history of the Pilgrims. Greenwood went from Cambridge to be chaplain to Lord Rich in the same lordly hall at Rochford, Essex, where Anne Boleyn

---

* The original of this *Dialogue* having been lost, it exists only in modern spelling.

had lived before she caught the eye of King Henry. A few years later Greenwood was the recognized head of the Separatists in London, for which crime he was promptly thrown into jail.

While Greenwood was in prison a young man who had been living the frivolous life of the court happened one day to be walking with one of his companions through a London street on a Sunday—this story we have from William Bradford's *Dialogue* (1648)—when

> he heard a preacher at his sermon very loud, as they passed by the church. Upon which Mr. Barrow said unto his consort, "Let us go in and hear what this man saith that is thus earnest."
>
> "Tush," saith the other, "What! shall we go to hear a man talk?"
>
> But in he went and sat down. And the minister was vehement in reproving sin, and sharply applied the judgments of God against the same; and, it should seem, touched him to the quick in such things as he was guilty of, so as God set it home to his soul, and began to work his repentance and conversion thereby.

Inquiring further regarding this religious teaching, Henry Barrow was sent to Greenwood in prison, and while in talk with him there in 1586 was himself made a prisoner. The remainder of his short life (1550?–1593) was spent in jail, where he wrote the pamphlets which made him in a sense the father of English as contrasted with American Congregationalism. While accepting Browne's Separatist views, he urged a compromise between rigid Separatism and rigid Presbyterianism in the shape of a democratically chosen assembly of elders to join together and regulate the separate churches.

After being held for years in the filthy jails of the period, these two good men were tried—and of course found guilty—of "devising and circulating seditious books." The next day, March 24, 1593, they were taken to Tyburn as if for execution, and then carried back to jail again. A week later they were again taken to the gallows. This time the ropes had been placed about their necks before they were again reprieved and returned to jail. No thoroughly satisfactory explanation of this cruel treatment has ever been given, though it is possible that Burghley, the Lord treasurer, may have been trying to save their lives.

On April sixth they were hurried again, early in the morning, to the place of execution and put to death. It has been claimed that this action was one of malice on the part of the bishops who were angry at Parliament for refusing to make it a felony to maintain any opinions against the ecclesiastical government.

Even more inhuman was the treatment meted out to John Penry (1559–1593), suspected of writing the Martin Marprelate tracts which with high-spirited humor and satire attacked the anti-Puritan prelates of England. Penry was brought before John Popham, the lord chief justice who had once been a highwayman. He was convicted of sedition and hanged, cut down while still alive, drawn and quartered, the bloody remains being carried away in a basket after the manner of those happy days under good Queen Bess.

Why were such noble and sincere church reformers treated like criminals?

Because independence in religion *did* threaten monarchy, and the monarchs knew it. Although the Puritan and Separatist leaders were both strenuous and sincere in their protestations of loyalty to the crown, the principles they advocated were bound to be a danger to absolute rule, as they proved to be a few years later. The charges of sedition and treason, though they seem to us today ridiculous and indefensible abridgements of human freedom, were in a sense justified if you accept the principle of absolute monarchy.

Puritanism and Separatism did carry a very strong and very dangerous political import, as events proved. As Hume puts it, "The precious spark of liberty had been kindled, and was preserved, by the Puritans alone; and it was to this sect . . . that the English owe the whole freedom of their constitution."

But the Puritans still assumed that a church should be national, as had Luther and Calvin. This was a long way from freedom in religion. The Separatists were radicals who believed in that manifest impossibility, freedom of religious faith. What this did to their politics when they came to the new world we shall see later on.

Meanwhile Elizabeth and James persecuted the leading Separatists as cruelly, if not as frequently, as bloody Mary had persecuted anti-Catholics. Since the crown was still the highest authority in spiritual as well as in temporal matters, religious

dissent and civil sedition were indistinguishable. It was under
Elizabeth that Barrow, Greenwood, Penry and many other sincere Christians were martyred.

The reforming ministers and laity looked with hope toward
James when the shrewd, profligate, scholarly and profane Bess,
ironically known as the Virgin Queen, finally departed this life
in 1603. James came from Scotland where the accepted Presbyterianism gave indication of a more liberal kingly attitude
toward religion. James was known to fancy himself as a scholar
and theologian. James would surely look with favor on the Puritan movement.

Confidently a group of eight hundred and twenty-five of the reforming clergy signed a petition to James shortly after his ac-
cession to the throne. They humbly begged that what they regarded as popish vestiges be removed from the Anglican service.
They requested, among other things, that the sign of the cross
be omitted in baptism, that cap and surplice be discontinued,
that the ring be dropped from the marriage service, that bowing
at the name of Jesus be stopped. They asked that the ministry
be limited to men godly and able to preach and that the custom
of appointing to church livings men who rarely or never visited
them be ended.

The Millenary Petition (so called because nearly a thousand
clergymen had signed it) was received by Jamie with a flat no.
He had suffered enough, he let it be known, from the Presbyterians in Scotland. The Anglican church, with its acknowledgment of the monarch as supreme head, suited him very well
and he would have no meddling with it.

If the Millenary Petition had been accepted, the day of mo-
narchic power might have been somewhat lengthened. But James
made the usual mistake of the man in power—refusing to grant
concessions, attempting to stamp out the spirit of freedom, and
thus only stirring up an issue larger and more formidable than
the one he at first had to deal with. For by being too rigid to yield
anything to the just complaints of the Puritans, James forced
them to get political power in order to enjoy the religious latitude they wanted.

James was shrewd enough to see the threat to monarchy that
lay in any liberalizing tendency in religion. The monarch who

had invented a new form of torture for witches (he split the fingernails and thrust needles beneath them) was not likely to be squeamish in his handling of dissenters. He was shrewd enough to know that of all dissenters the Brownists held the greatest threat to his arbitrary power. Had not their leader written that civil magistrates as well as religious leaders should be chosen with the consent of the people?

Yes, James would know what to do with Separatists wherever he found them.

If William Bradford's attendance at Richard Clyfton's services had angered his guardians, there was worse to come. For Clyfton, even though a Puritan, was a pastor of the established church. But Babworth was not the only center of religious awakening. The leaven of dissent, planted by Dutch Anabaptists living in the area, was also working in other near-by towns. In 1602 a group had begun to meet in Gainsborough, about twelve miles from Austerfield. And in 1606 with the arrival of another Cambridge man, John Smyth, as pastor, it gave up all hope of reform within the Anglican church and became a separate church on Brownist principles.

When William became a member of this congregation, his uncles redoubled their efforts to prevent his disgracing the family. Other members of the family jumped to their support. They were rewarded, Mather tells us, with sudden death—an outcome which Bradford certainly and perhaps even some of his remaining relatives would have regarded as a sign from God. From this time on he was allowed to worship as he wished.

The distance to Gainsborough soon proved too much of a trip for those living around Austerfield. So the group split in two, the smaller part meeting at Scrooby which was within easy walking distance of Bradford's home. The revered Richard Clyfton was called to be the pastor of this group. It must have taken more than average courage for this learned man, who had spent his life in the Anglican church, to throw in his lot with the despised Separatists. He soon gained as an assistant a young man, John Robinson, who was to become the most distinguished of the Pilgrim religious leaders.

Mainstay of the Scrooby group was William Brewster, the man

above all others who most influenced Bradford's life. Brewster
had attended Cambridge, he was old enough to have been Bradford's father—how often in his youth Bradford seems to have
been attracted to such men!—and he was a man of influence in
the community. Postmaster in a day when the job meant responsibility for the royal mails, living in the large though even
then decaying manor house of a bishop, and with an exciting
past, Brewster easily became a hero to the young man whose
search for a father had also brought him a way of life.

To young William Bradford, who had never traveled more
than a few miles from his birthplace, Brewster's past was romantic. While still in his teens he had become a sort of personal
secretary to Sir William Davison, one of Elizabeth's chief diplo-
mats. Living in London and in the midst of the court, he had seen
all the great men of the time. He had gone to Holland with his
master when Elizabeth decided to send at least token aid to the
Dutch Protestants who were so bravely fighting for religious
freedom against the massed forces of mighty Spain. He was entrusted with the great keys to the gates of Flushing when they
were handed to Davison as security for the loan granted by Elizabeth. Perhaps his proudest moment in that day of rather child-
ish splendors was the time when, returning to London with his
master, he was allowed to wear the great gold chain presented
to Davison by the Dutch.

If Davison's career had thereafter run smoothly, Brewster
would no doubt have remained in London and William Bradford would never have emigrated to America. But Davison, after
being rewarded for his work in Holland with the post of principal secretary of state in charge of foreign affairs, soon became the
scapegoat in one of Elizabeth's most perfidious acts. When she
chose to throw upon him the responsibility of having had her
cousin Mary Queen of Scots beheaded, he bore her unjust accusation like a loyal retainer. Brewster went with him when he was
committed to the Tower, cared for him during his two years of
imprisonment, and then apparently in disgust at court life returned to his boyhood home at Scrooby where he took over the
duties of postmaster at his father's death a year later. This was
the year of Bradford's birth, and Brewster was still in his twenties.

Comfortably fixed in a government job with an assured salary, why did Brewster choose to meddle with religion?

According to Bradford, Brewster was "first seasoned with ye seeds of grace and vertue" at Cambridge, that hotbed of religious controversy and breeding place of most of the eminent Puritans and religious radicals of the time. His master Davison had also been an avowed Puritan, and had shown an interest in promoting Brewster's own religious life. The intimate view he had had of Hollanders risking their lives and everything they owned for religious liberty was no doubt a factor. All these influences helped to make Brewster, in spite of his dependence on the royal pocketbook, a dissenter.

It was not long after 1606 that the meetings began in Scrooby, only two miles from Austerfield. Thus at sixteen, or perhaps seventeen, began for Bradford the relationship which was to be the longest and most influential in his life. If Mary Queen of Scots had not had her head chopped off, William Bradford would probably have spent his life as an obscure yeoman in an obscure English hamlet. It was Brewster who brought out his latent qualities.

William Bradford was in his teens, William Brewster just entered upon his forties. Somewhat sickly yet with a sturdiness beneath, young William was immediately attracted to this man. With the sure grip of instinct, he bound himself to the most important, the most congenial person he had met in all his life. The bonds were never broken until Brewster's death nearly forty years later.

The story of the exceptional youngster doomed to life in a very unexceptional hamlet is too familiar to need emphasis, except that we can scarcely conceive today of the isolation and ignorance of a village like Austerfield. Genius early recognizes itself—that is perhaps one of its tragedies; and Bradford must soon have discovered his intellectual loneliness without knowing either the cause or the cure. This emptiness the companion who led him to Babworth had helped to fill. But it was Brewster—father, teacher, man of the world—who filled it completely.

Brewster knew the answers to the questions Bradford had been asking himself. Brewster could lend him books, guide his read-

ing, tell him what the world was like beyond Austerfield and
Scrooby and Babworth. A man of position and experience beyond anyone else in the neighborhood, Brewster could offset the
attempts of Bradford's uncles to turn him from his religion. If
Brewster, living in the bishop's manor and bailiff of the episcopal estates round about, could be a dissenter, what did the opinion
of a couple of ignorant farmers matter? If the king's own representative was willing to risk his position to hold these forbidden
meetings for worship—and in the bishop's own hall—what could
dissuade his admirer from following him? Is it not even likely
that Bradford enjoyed the challenge, the sense of companionship
that came of sharing with Brewster the danger of these meetings?
For nothing, as those who have been through war or natural disaster know, can so bind one man to another as the sharing of
danger.

This was Bradford's substitute for a tie of blood. This was
what bound him to Brewster, finally, in a bond as strong as that
of father and son. In Brewster Bradford found that mixture of
excitement with nobility which his soul longed for. Child of his
age, Bradford could scarcely have failed to value highly all the
things that elevated Brewster to a place of prominence and respect—his official positions, his education, his travels and his
personal contact with the great. What Brewster sanctioned must
therefore be noble, choiceworthy. Better still, to the adolescent
in search of adventure, what Brewster practiced promised excitement. This was more than escape from the toilsome farm
life which one of Bradford's intellect must have chafed at. This
was escape to something positive. There was a goal. And Brewster,
with his wide knowledge of affairs, his experience on the continent and his first-hand view of the war between the Spanish and
the Dutch, must have made Bradford see that the little congregation at Scrooby was part of a larger contest in which men
were even then shedding their blood.

Fortunately we have Bradford's own estimate of Brewster.
Since men are likely to praise the virtues which they would
like to find in themselves, it tells us something of Bradford,
too.

"He was wise and discreete and well spoken," says Bradford,
"having a grave and deliberate utterance, of a very cherfull

spirite, very sociable & pleasante amongst his freinds, of an humble and modest mind, of a peaceable disposition, under vallewing him self & his owne abilities, and some time over valewing others; inoffencive and inocente in his life & conversation, which gained him the love of those without, as well as those within . . . He was tender harted, and compassionate of such as were in miserie . . . In teaching, he was very moving & stirring of affections, also very plaine & distincte in what he taught."

Bradford now attached himself to Brewster, and was in many ways in the same relation to him as Brewster had been to Davison. The evidence from Bradford's later life proves that Brewster did his work well. He had the intelligence to recognize ability in a youngster—a somewhat rare trait in adults, who for the most part think of the young as inhabiting a different world from their own and consequently make the ungracious error of treating them by rules which make no more sense for children than they would for adults.

From Brewster William Bradford probably learned to read Latin, and Brewster was probably William Bradford's substitute for a formal education. Even if Bradford went to the grammar school at Rossington, he would not have learned much more than the mechanics of Latin. For in their teaching of Latin the grammar schools of the day restricted themselves to a painful concentration on grammar, so that most scholars gained little but a cordial hatred for the subject and unless they went on to a university never discovered the glories of the classical literature at all. Studying under Brewster, William would not have sat from seven in the morning until five at night all the year through as grammar school boys had to do, and Brewster's university training as well as his own urge to learn would have led him on to Latin literature.

Brewster had the wisdom to draw out the boy's ability and put it to work. Without Brewster, Bradford's innate abilities would probably have dried up for lack of use, leaving him to live out his years unknown in an unknown hamlet, tending the offspring of the kine bequeathed by good old Peter Bradford.

And when the boy who had first led him to Babworth and Richard Clyfton became "a wicked apostate," William was too firmly established to be turned aside from his own course which now lay so clearly before him.

The "soon and long sickness" was over. In Brewster he had a father, in the little congregation a mothering family, and in his heart certainty and a goal.

So the little group of Separatists at Scrooby, in Bradford's felicitous phrase, "shooke of[f] this yoake of antichristian bondage, and as the Lords free people, joyned them selves (by covenant of the Lord) into a church estate, in the felowship of the gospell, to walke in all his wayes, made known, or to be made known unto them, according to their best endeavours, whatsoever it should cost them, the Lord assisting them."

The Scrooby meetings were usually held in the bishop's manor house where Brewster made his home, "and with great love he entertained them when they came, making provission for them to his great charge." They had to be held in as much secrecy as possible, for unauthorized religious meetings, as the martyrdom of Barrow, Greenwood, Penry and others had shown, might carry very severe consequences. King James, in one of the boyish rages which in those days seem to have been a kingly prerogative, had sworn that he would make all his subjects conform, "or I will harry them out of the land." What happened when this little group tried to leave the land is, in view of James' threat, interesting.

Just what was in the Separatist doctrine which infuriated James?

Most books about the Pilgrims fail to make the fairly obvious point that it was the politics rather than the theology of religion which occupied them. The Separatists added nothing to theology. Yet in church polity they created a revolution.

It was not until they reached the new world, where they could shape things to their own liking, that they were able to carry out their notions of the proper relationship between religion and government. But in the act of separating from the church of England they exposed their central belief—that the church *is the people*. This, the reverse of the theory that *l'état c'est moi*, was bound to get them into difficulty.

"The king," John Robinson argued, "indeed is to govern in causes ecclesiastical, but civilly not ecclesiastically, using the civil sword, not the spiritual, for the punishing of offenders." It is not surprising that this sweeping away of the doctrine of royal supremacy should have infuriated James. What the king in fact resented was the attempt to make him subject to law or regulation of any kind, or to restrict his power. It took several generations, a beheading and a civil war to bring this about, and the Separatists were the spearhead of the attack.

It is this which entitles their church to be thought of as the nursery of democracy. Those who like to believe that religion is the opiate of the people must admit that religion also provides the revolutionary force which sweeps away old orders and establishes new. No one can study the history of the Pilgrims without concluding that American democracy had its rise in a religious movement.

In Bradford's day democracy was a fighting word, and to call a man a democrat was as much of an insult as questioning his legitimacy. Robinson in his published works is always defending the Separatists against the stigma of being democrats. Yet it was the essential democracy of the primitive Christian church which appealed to the group Bradford had joined, and for what it promised they were willing to suffer exile, poverty, perhaps death.

These earnest Christians could find no warrant in Scripture for the massive, splendid, and barbaric structure which had been erected upon the simple teachings of Christ, and which dared to call itself His church. They could find no bishops, popes, cathedrals, robes of gold brocade, indulgences, or bread turned into virtual flesh in the Bible. The church they found there was simple in the extreme, without distinctions of rank and emphasizing the supreme value of every individual before God. It was without elaborate paraphernalia or man-made ritual. This was the church they wanted to reinstitute. It would be essentially a church of laymen, hence democratic. It would be a church based upon biblical authority, not overlaid with man-made inventions.

But the Bible had very little to say about how such a church should be organized. Practically the only useful passages were

I Corinthians xii 28, I Timothy v 17 and Romans xii 6–8. And these did not do much more than suggest that there should be elders, teachers, and widows to look after the poor. Indeed, the emphasis seemed to be altogether on the corporate nature of the church, the "body of Christ" in which all members were equal.

This was one essential of a true church—that its members should be equal. The other was that they should be freely joined together in a covenant, not forced in as the Anglican church forced all the people of England, the good with the evil. Such a church would be like a family in the closeness of the bond which bound the members together and in the concern which each felt for the other's welfare. In practice this concern led to admonishments of conduct that resembled family bickering to a marked degree!

In such a church, power rested with the whole body though government might be delegated to a group of officers. Small wonder that Jamie didn't like it!

This distinction between the power and the government of a church was the brainchild of the Pilgrims' distinguished pastor, John Robinson. Robinson had joined the Scrooby congregation as an ordinary member, coming over from Sturton le Steeple to which he had retired after arriving at views too advanced for the Anglican church. He too was a product of Cambridge University and had been influenced, like Brewster, by the advanced views of William Perkins. Persuaded by John Smyth to join the separation, he soon became teacher of the Scrooby group, a position second to that of minister. When Clyfton left the group in Holland, Robinson stepped into his place.

Of the several Separatist groups, all but the one we know as the Pilgrims were split apart by internal dissensions and broken by disputes either personal or theological. That the Pilgrims survived this hazard is largely Robinson's doing. Bradford gives us the best picture we have of the man's character in his first *Dialogue*. He was "learned and solid of judgment," says Bradford, "with a quick and sharp wit, a tender conscience, very sincere in all his ways, a hater of hypocrisy and dissimulation, very plain with his best friends, courteous, affable, sociable, an acute and expert disputant, very profitable in his ministry and comfortable to his people."

But the quality which raised him above the other religious rebels of his time was his tolerance. Plymouth and the Pilgrims are popularly associated with a sternly intolerant creed, an error which arises from confusing Boston with Plymouth. But the Pilgrims had been taught by a man who could say:

"There is hardly any sect so antichristian or evil . . . in which there are not divers, truly though weakly led, with the spirit of Christ in their persons, and so true members of his mystical body. With whom to deal rigorously for some few aberrations of ignorance or infirmity, were more to please Christ's enemy than Christ."

This tone of reason and moderation informs much of Robinson's published work. It was rare in a day of bitterly fought religious controversy.

The other quality of Robinson which is precious to us because of its effect on the Pilgrims and on American life is his essential democracy. Robinson tried hard to hide or deny it, but it shows forth in every important point he makes. The power to call a minister rests with the whole church, that is, with the people. The power to form a church is theirs. "The liberty granted to the people for the choosing both of deacons and elders . . . was an ordinance eternal, and perpetual." The power to "prophesy," that is to speak on religious matters, belongs to all the people and not to the minister alone. The Pilgrims arranged their religious services so that all who wished could speak.

These ideas are of a very different quality from the ones upon which Boston was founded. They continued to guide the Plymouth church though Robinson never came to the new world. They were fed to the brilliant young Bradford at his most impressionable age, and through him and the other Plymouth leaders they became a part of America.

While Bradford was finding in Brewster the father he had never had, and in the tightly knit little group of worshipers at Scrooby a substitute for the family he lacked, the prisons of London were crammed with innocent people whose only crime was the sincerity of their Christian faith. Without benefit of habeas corpus, they had been thrown into jail by any bishop who suspected their nonconformity. There they might lie for months or even years without being brought to trial, many, as Bradford said, "perishing by cold, hunger, or noisomeness of the prison." In the first *Dialogue* which is one of his most interesting works he speaks of sixty persons "being made close prisoners, allowing them neither meat, drink, fire nor lodging, nor suffering any whose hearts the Lord would stir up for their relief, to have any access unto them; so as they complain that no felons, traitors, nor murderers in the land were thus dealt with." Families of those imprisoned were often left without support and without the privilege of seeing the prisoner.

It was not even necessary to commit an overt act of separation from the church of England to be severely punished. George Cotton, for hearing a portion of Scripture read in a friend's house, was thrown into prison for twenty-seven months without being brought to trial. If a man's family should refuse to attend church, he could be thrown into jail merely for harboring his own kin.

Separatists who were thrown into prison begged that they might have at least equal treatment with Catholics by being allowed to take the oath of allegiance and thus be freed from prison. Although certain judges were willing to do this, the bishops for the most part prevented it. To them, as to the monarch, the danger of freedom was greater than that of authoritarianism. They wanted for themselves not only the absolute authority exercised by the Roman church but absolute political authority too. And they were more willing to take a chance on a subject who subjected himself to that kind of authority than to one who denied it.

In order to convict imprisoned Separatist preachers the bishops were willing to go beyond the bounds of fair play. In London forty-two preachers were employed as detectives to visit the prisoners, engage them in conversation and try to lure them into saying something that could be used as evidence against them.

The threat of such treatment hung all the time over the little group at Scrooby, whose meetings for worship could scarcely be kept secret in a village of two hundred where the arrival of strangers every Sunday would be sure to arouse curiosity and where Brewster especially, as bailiff and postmaster, would be a subject of village gossip.

The blow was struck toward the end of 1607 when five members of the Scrooby church were summoned before the Ecclesiastical Commissioners of the province of York. One of the summoned was Brewster. The charge was being "disobedient in matters of religion." Already he had given up the postmastership, probably under pressure. Was it not likely that he would next be driven out of the manor house which belonged to the very diocese which was now examining him?

Clearly there was no more safety in England for those who would worship according to conscience rather than according to law. But where could they go? And how could they escape?

"Conflicts & Sharp Beginings"

FOR many years Englishmen had sought refuge on the continent when their religious beliefs were at odds with the current policy of their ruler, and the roll of those who had fled in search of religious freedom reads like a *Who's Who* of England's spiritual leaders.

So in Bradford's time whole congregations were going into voluntary exile in Holland where they could worship according to belief rather than according to law. There was the congregation organized in 1587 by John Greenwood which, after his execution and that of its other leaders Barrow and Penry, had fled to Amsterdam. The Gainsborough congregation under John Smyth, to which Brewster and Bradford had for a time belonged, had made its escape to Holland in 1607.

With Brewster's arrest, fine, and the loss of the postmastership it was clear that the little group at Scrooby would soon be destroyed. Brewster's position had not protected them from signs of open hostility on the part of neighbors who shared the hysteria felt throughout the land over the Separatists—a feeling fostered by countless sermons from Anglican pulpits.

Men never show their primitive origins so clearly as in their attitude toward the minority in their midst. It does not seem to matter whether the minority differs in politics, religion, social customs, skin color, race or national origin so long as it offers the majority what it is looking for—a scapegoat. In India it was the

Untouchables, in Japan the Eta, in Nazi Germany the Jews, and in our own South the Negro. Men need a symbol of their own guilt, an outlet for their own frustrations, a goad to consolidate their social order. The minority provides all of this. In persecuting that minority men satisfy the blood lust of their primitive origins, expiate their own guilt, and feel as if they were drawn closer to each other by the very act of expelling or wounding the non-conformist.

The Scrooby group were now the victims of this ancient group hysteria. "The worke of God was no sooner manifest in them," Bradford tells us, "but presently they were both scoffed and scorned by the prophane multitude . . . and the poore people were so vexed with apparators, & pursuants, & the comissarie courts, as truly their affliction was not smale . . . They could not long continue in any peaceable condition, but were hunted & persecuted on every side, so as their former afflictions were but as flea-bitings in comparison of these which now came upon them. For some were taken & clapt up in prison, others had their houses besett & watcht night and day, & hardly escaped their hands; and the most were faine to flie & leave their howses & habitations, and the means of their livelihood."

It needed strong persecution indeed to separate these earth-rooted yeomen from fields and farms which had nourished their families as far back as they knew, from the husbandry which was their only trade, from English their only language. Yet despite all hazards, they decided toward the end of 1607 to go over into Holland.

If the decision had been hard for men of mature years, it was hard enough for William Bradford, now a young man of seventeen.

Since his first meeting with the Gainsborough congregation he had come more and more under Brewster's influence until the relationship had grown to be like that of father and son. Is it, by the way, an understandable omission that in his book, *Of Plimoth Plantation,* he mentions only once and then casually the Brewster son who was only three years his junior? In any case, he looked up to Brewster as to a father and must have leaned heavily upon his advice when deciding to go with the group to Holland.

Heir to his father's estate, young Bradford was no pauper, yet if he left England before reaching his majority he might lose all.

What stormy scenes he may have had with his guardian uncles, or whether he got Brewster to intercede for him we do not know. Probably they had by this time given up any hope of controlling him, and were glad to have him leave since he had become a disgrace to the family. In January 1607/8 William's sister Alice died at the age of twenty. She was the last of his immediate family, the last strong tie of affection which had bound him to his home. He was free to go now. But he did manage to keep a hold on his patrimony. What happened to it in Holland is another story.

Once the Scrooby group had decided to leave England, their troubles had just begun. For though James had thundered that he would harry unbelievers out of the land, he was careful to see that none should succeed in getting out if they were bold enough to try. Men do not really want to lose the scapegoat they persecute, for if they were rid of it they would only have to find another.

Even a respected Englishman who wanted to go abroad had a hard time of it. He had to prove that he was widely acquainted with England, or Lord Burghley would tell him to visit his own country before traipsing off to spend good English pounds abroad. He had to satisfy his creditors, make his will and receive the Lord's Supper. Then he might be allowed to go. But not the Separatists; they must remain and be persecuted.

Yet by one means and another Clyfton, Brewster, Robinson, and a few more of the most ardent managed to dispose of their property and set out on foot for Boston with their families. With them went William Bradford.

One of the most interesting old towns in England, Boston must have seemed a marvelous place to the young Bradford. Among its many ancient buildings the guildhall and the great church of St. Botolph would have impressed him most, the latter with its magnificent tall tower then known to mariners the world over as "Boston Stump"—a landmark which could be seen far out to sea. Yet we find nothing of this in his own account, which steers close to the main events and generally omits the little, personal things we would give so much to know.

A few years later there would start out from Boston and its vicinity a group of Puritans of good family and some wealth who would establish in the new world a new Boston which would eclipse the old. But if any of them saw or recognized the poor Separatists when they were captured and made "a spectacle & wonder to the multitude," and if they later identified them in the new world, they left no record of it.

All accounts of the Pilgrim departure into Holland depend upon William Bradford's, written some twenty-two years later. Any retelling seems by comparison so derivative and second-hand that I prefer to print here in full the second chapter of that neglected masterpiece of American literature, Bradford's *Of Plimoth Plantation*. For concision, clarity of narrative, choice of the right word and beauty of rhythm it will bear comparison with any similar piece of writing either of Bradford's age or our own. Yet Bradford had but a few years of indifferent schooling. How many college graduates, how many professional writers whose work appears in millions of copies can hold a candle to the work of this yeoman's boy, acquainted only with "the inocente trade of husbandrey"?

Of their departure into Holland and their troubls ther aboute, with some of the many difficulties they found and mete withall.

Being thus constrained to leave their native soyle and countrie, their lands & livings, and all their freinds & famillier acquaintance, it was much, and thought marvelous by many. But to goe into a countrie they knew not (but by hearsay), wher they must learne a new language, and get their livings they knew not how, it being a dear place, & subjecte to the misseries of warr, it was by many thought an adventure almost desperate, a case intolerable, & a miserie worse then death. Espetially seeing they were not aquainted with trads nor traffique, (by which that countrie doth subsiste,) but had only been used to a plaine countrie life, & the inocente trade of husbandrey. But these things did not dismay them (though they did some times trouble them) for their desires were sett on the ways of God, & to injoye his ordinances; but they rested on his providence, & knew whom they had beleeved. Yet this was not all, for though they could not stay, yet were they not suffered to goe, but the ports & havens were shut against them, so as they were faine to seeke secrete means of conveance, & to bribe & fee the mariners, & give exterordinarie rates for their passages. And yet were they often times betrayed (many of them), and both they & their goods intercepted & surprised, and therby put to great trouble & charge, of which I will give an instance or tow, & omitte the rest.

Ther was a large companie of them purposed to get passage at Boston in Lincolnshire, and for that end had hired a shipe wholy to them selves, & made agreement with the maister to be ready at a certaine day, and take them and their goods in, at a conveniente place, wher they accordingly would all attende in readines. So after long waiting, & large expences, though he kepte not day with them, yet he came at length & tooke them in, in the night. But when he had them & their goods abord, he betrayed them, haveing before hand complotted with the serchers & other officers so to doe; who tooke them, and put them into open boats, & ther rifled & ransaked them, searching them to their shirts for money, yea even the women furder then became modestie; and then caried them back into the towne, & made them a spectackle & wonder to the multitude, which came flocking on all sids to behould them. Being thus first, by the chatchpoule officers, rifled, & stripte of their money, books, and much other goods, they were presented to the magestrates, and messengers sente to informe the lords of the Counsell of them; and so they were comitted to ward. Indeed the magestrats used them courteously, and shewed them what favour they could; but could not deliver them, till order came from the Counsell-table. But the issue was that after a months imprisonmente, the greatest parte were dismiste, & sent to the places from whence they came; * but 7. of the principall were still kept in prison, and bound over to the Assises.

The nexte spring after, ther was another attempte made by some of these & others, to get over at an other place. And it so fell out, that they light of a Dutchman at Hull, having a ship of his owne belonging to Zealand; they made agreemente with him, and acquainted him with their condition, hoping to find more faithfullnes in him, then in the former of their owne nation. He

---

* Bradford was one of these.

bad them not fear, for he would doe well enough. He was by appointment to take them in betweene Grimsbe & Hull, wher was a large comõne a good way distante from any towne.* Now aganst the prefixed time, the women & children, with the goods, were sent to the place in a small barke, which they had hired for that end; and the men were to meete them by land. But it so fell out, that they were ther a day before the shipe came, & the sea being rough, and the women very sicke, prevailed with the seamen to put into a creeke hardby, wher they lay on ground at low-water. The nexte morning the shipe came, but they were fast, & could not stir till aboute noone. In the mean time, the shipe maister, perceiveing how the matter was, sente his boate to be getting the men abord whom he saw ready, walking aboute the shore. But after the first boat full was gott abord, & she was ready to goe for more, the mr. espied a greate company, both horse & foote, with bills, & gunes, & other weapons; for the countrie was raised to take them. The Dutch-man seeing that, swore his countries oath, "sacremente," and having the wind faire, waiged his Ancor, hoysed sayles, & away. But the poore men which were gott abord, were in great distress for their wives and children, which they saw thus to be taken, and were left destitute of their helps; and them selves also, not having a cloath to shifte them with, more then they had on their baks, & some scarce a peney aboute them, all they had being abord the barke. It drew tears from their eyes, and any thing they had they would have given to have been a shore againe; but all in vaine, ther was no remedy, they must thus sadly part. And afterward endured a fearfull storme at sea, being 14. days or more before they arived at their porte, in 7. wherof they neither saw son, moone, nor stars, & were driven near the coast of Norway; the mariners them selves often despairing of life; and once with shriks & cries gave over all, as if the ship had been foundred in the sea, & they sinking without recoverie. But when mans hope & helpe wholly failed, the Lords power & mercie appeared in ther recoverie; for the ship rose againe, & gave the mariners courage againe to manage her. And if modestie woud suffer me, I might declare with what fervente prayres they cried unto the Lord in this great distres, (espetialy some of them,) even without any great distraction, when the

---

* Dexter places this at Stallingsborough.

water rane into their mouthes & ears; & the mariners cried out,
We sinke, we sinke; they cried (if not with mirakelous, yet with a
great hight or degree of devine faith), Yet Lord thou canst save,
yet Lord thou canst save; with shuch other expressions as I will
forbeare. Upon which the ship did not only recover, but shortly
after the violence of the storme begane to abate, and the Lord
filed their afflicted minds with shuch comforts as every one cañot
understand, and in the end brought them to their desired Haven,
wher the people came flockeing admiring their deliverance,
the storme having ben so longe & sore, in which much hurt
had been don, as the masters freinds related unto him in their
congrattulations.

But to returne to the others wher we left. The rest of the men
that were in greatest danger, made shift to escape away before the
troope could surprise them; those only staying that best might,
to be assistante unto the women. But pitifull it was to see the
heavie case of these poore women in this distress; what weeping
& crying on every side, some for their husbands, that were caried
away in the ship as is before related; others not knowing what
should become of them, & their litle ones; others againe melted
in teares, seeing their poore litle ones hanging aboute them, crying for feare, and quaking with could. Being thus aprehended,
they were hurried from one place to another, and from one
justice to another, till in the ende they knew not what to doe with
them; for to imprison so many women & innocent children for no
other cause (many of them) but that they must goe with their
husbands, semed to be unreasonable and all would crie out of
them; and to send them home againe was as difficult, for they
aledged, as the trueth was, they had no homes to goe to, for they
had either sould, or otherwise disposed of their houses and livings. To be shorte, after they had been thus turmolyed a good
while, and conveyed from one constable to another, they were
glad to be ridd of them in the end upon any termes; for all were
wearied & tired with them. Though in the mean time they (poore
soules) indured miserie enough; and thus in the end necessitie
forste a way for them.

But that I be not tedious in these things, I will omitte the rest,
though I might relate many other notable passages and troubles
which they endured & underwente in these their wanderings &

travells both at land & sea; but I hast to other things. Yet I may not omitte the fruite that came hearby, for by these so publick troubls, in so many eminente places, their cause became famouss, & occasioned many to looke into the same; and their godly cariage & Christian behaviour was such as left a deep impression in the minds of many. And though some few shrunk at these first conflicts & sharp beginings, (as it was no marvell,) yet many more came on with fresh courage, & greatly animated others. And in the end, notwithstanding all these stormes of oppossition, they all gatt over at length, some at one time & some at an other, and some in one place & some in an other, and mette togeather againe according to their desires, with no small rejoycing.

Bradford and Brewster were among those who stayed "to be assistante unto the women" when their plans for escape fell apart the second time. Finally in August 1608, the last of those whose determination still held arrived in Amsterdam. It had been a thorough winnowing. Perhaps it was as well, for in the trials ahead only the strong could survive. Several times before the move to America this group was to be tried again on the anvil, until what remained was true metal.

One more indignity remained for young William Bradford, who after staying to help the women and children arrived in Middelburg, Holland, only to be seized as a fugitive from English justice on the accusation of a passenger. The false report was soon straightened out and he was cleared, but for a lad of eighteen he had had his share of "conflicts & sharp beginings."

He too was being shaped by the forge of experience and on the anvil of destiny.

"Delightefull Societie &
Spirituall Comforte"

BY a strange conspiracy which has lasted for three hundred years, the Dutch are regarded as a joke in America—with good humor for the most part, but with the notion that they can scarcely be taken seriously. Washington Irving is in part responsible for this. We think of Rip Van Winkle and Ichabod Crane and *Knickerbocker's History of New York* when we think of the Dutch—of men impractical or easily overwhelmed by ghosts or shrews, of men devoted to heavy food, heavy drinking and the rather humorous sport of bowling.

Yet Irving did not make this attitude, though he popularized it. He picked it up from its English origins, even from the English language itself. For our tongue is full of unconscious degradation of the Dutch. When someone speaks with disagreeable frankness we say he talked like a Dutch uncle. When an invitation fails to carry with it the offer of a free meal we call it a Dutch treat. A furtive departure is Dutch leave. A Dutch bargain is a cheat, a Dutch auction is no bargain at all, a Dutch concert is a musical horror. Dutch courage is the kind derived solely from a bottle, and only the incredible can beat the Dutch—that is, can exceed their gift for lying.

Although some of this hostility was originally directed toward the German, who in vulgar speech is a Dutchman, the practical effect has been to make us think of the Netherlanders as a rather inferior folk—and this in spite of the fact that they are racially more closely akin to the English than the Scotch, the Irish, or any other continental people.

Where did the prejudice get its start?

At least as far back as Shakespeare's time Elizabeth's courtiers showed a marked distaste for the thrifty, trade-conscious Dutch. Her be-laced and be-ribboned dandies thought themselves well above men who valued a fine painting more than a brocaded doublet, or who preferred to make rather than to consume, to use time rather than to waste it. The war between England and the Netherlands in 1666, when the Dutch fleet sailed up the Thames and threatened London, furthered in England a tendency to belittle what could not be surpassed. Then the defeat of the Dutch in America, and the conversion of New Amsterdam to New York, completed the formation of an attitude which is with us yet.

The result has been a misreading of history, a misinterpretation of the foundations and sources of American life which has lasted to this day. Ask any well-informed person where America got its ideas of government, the secret ballot, religious liberty, freedom of the individual and the rights of man and he will name England. He was taught this in school, and learned errors die hard. As a rule he believes it so passionately that fact cannot shake him. Yet the fact is that many of the basic political and social benefits which we think of as characteristically American came to us not from England but from the Netherlands. American history was shaped by the flight of a little group of persecuted Christians from England into Holland. And Holland (as well as the Netherlands generally) until long after the Pilgrims had come to America was England's guide and teacher in almost everything which has made her great.

The Netherlands led all of Europe in commerce and manufacture. In the weaving of all sorts of cloth, from fine linen to heavy velvet and brocade, she was supreme, as well as in the manufacture of crockery, metal goods, in sugar refining—indeed in all branches of industry. Ignoring the thundered prohibition of mighty Spain, she had built an empire of trade throughout the Orient. The wealth resulting from her skill and energy had made her cities the jewels of the continent. Yet this wealth was not spent upon idle show, but on schools, on hospitals, and on charity in the fine, warm original sense of that word.*

The children of these fortunate provinces went to schools supported by the state. There was hardly a Netherlander who could not read and write—and this at a time when few even of the ruling class knew their letters in England. Even the modestly well to do knew mathematics and the classics and could speak several European languages. The Netherlands were far ahead of the times with their hospitals, their orphan asylums, their homes for the aged and for invalided soldiers. They dressed plainly, but adorned their homes with choice paintings and cultivated the art of music. Their fields were the richest, their cattle the finest in the world. They were industrious enough to lead Europe in business, resourceful enough to have snatched their very earth from the sea, and brave enough to have fought the greatest power of the age, mostly single-handed, over a period of forty years. Their successful revolt against tyranny marks the beginning of the political and social world we know today. In fact, the Netherlanders of the seventeenth century were two hundred years ahead of the rest of Europe, not only in culture and commerce, but in their concept of government and of the rights of men. From such a country the Pilgrims came to Plymouth in New England. There is scarcely a fact in American history of more consequence, as there is scarcely one whose significance has been more neglected.

The fugitives from Scrooby arrived in Holland just as forty years of war with Spain had come to an end. They left but a few months before war broke out again. So by a happy chance—or as they would have said by the guidance of divine Providence—their twelve years were spent at the very time when they could profit most from contact with this intelligent, thrifty, orderly and freedom-loving people.

The story of the Dutch resistance to Spain is one of the noblest chapters in history of a people fighting for their freedom. The capacity for suffering, the stubborn devotion to a cause are almost beyond belief. They make the American Revolution with all its

* *Caritas,* love

misery seem almost like a tea party. Yet the essential quality, the spirit, was strikingly the same.

What was the origin of this Dutch passion for liberty, so important to our own?

The Netherlands arose out of feudalism by way of chartered towns which, as early as the twelfth century, had begun to function as small self-governing republics. By the thirteenth century such towns as Ghent, Bruges and Ypres had grown to one or two hundred thousand in population. Vigorous weaving industries brought the majority of the inhabitants into trade guilds which were powerful enough to oppose the patricians who had formerly controlled the government. When the patricians prevailed on France to help destroy these upstart laborers, the popular party proved itself as strong on the field of battle as in the marts of trade; the chivalry of France was utterly defeated. A similar though less striking manifestation of democratic government occurred throughout the Netherlands.

But ultimately, by treachery or force, the Netherlands came under the rule of the house of Burgundy, and then by intermarriage fell to the Hapsburgs and at last to Spain. Spain brought the Inquisition and in 1566 the Netherlanders began their long resistance against crushing odds—a resistance which scarcely has any parallel in history. To break down this unexpected stubbornness an army of Spaniards, Italians and Germans marched into the Low Countries. Almost without a hearing men were condemned in batches and sent out to be burned, hanged, or beheaded. Whole cities were sacked and put to the sword. The result was only to strengthen the resistance of the people, and to drive more of them out of the Roman church and into the Calvinist.

In 1574 the Spaniards laid siege to Leyden, home of the Pilgrims from 1609 to 1620. There were no regular soldiers within the town to defend it, yet the Spaniards though they had eight thousand troops made no effort to attack. Having learned what Dutch citizens were capable of, they preferred to starve them out.

William of Orange sent word that if the citizens would hold out for three months, he would relieve them. Though they lacked provisions, they agreed to wait. But his attempt to flood the Spaniards out by cutting dikes did not at first succeed. The three months stretched to four. After the first two months there was no food. Every weed, every blade of grass was consumed. Babies starved at their mother's milkless breasts. Plague was piled upon starvation, taking away eight thousand victims. The Spaniards demanded that the city surrender.

"Ye call us rat-eaters and dog-eaters," the Leyden folk said to their besiegers, "and it is true. So long, then, as ye hear dog bark or cat mew within the walls, ye may know that the city holds out. And when all has perished but ourselves, be sure that we will devour our left arms, retaining our right to defend our women, our liberty, and our religion, against the foreign tyrant . . . When the last hour has come, with our own hands we will set fire to the city, and perish, men, women and children, together in the flames rather than suffer our homes to be polluted and our liberties to be crushed."

Finally the wind shifted, the Spaniards had to fly before the rising waters, and a relieving fleet sailed up to the walls.

At once the sick and starving inhabitants formed in solemn procession and marched to church where they thanked God for their deliverance. But when they tried to close the service with a hymn of thanks, the strain was too much. As the organ swelled and the music rose, echoing against the high walls, the voices broke and the multitude wept with unashamed relief.

This was the people with whom the Pilgrims were to spend eleven years.

Nor was Leyden an isolated instance of Dutch resistance. Town after town withstood assault in the same spirit. At the siege of Ostend in 1604 every scrap of earth that could be spared from the job of keeping out the water was piled for defense. When earth gave out, the very bodies of the dead were raised into ramparts. When finally abandoned to overwhelming odds Ostend was but a heap of rubbish. For this the Spaniards had spent a hundred thousand of their men.

In 1579 the northern provinces joined together as the Netherlands Republic. Still the fighting went on for almost thirty years. Despite the bitterness of the struggle, and the fact that the sickening slaughter of the Dutch had been carried out in the name of the Catholic religion, the Declaration of Independence in 1581 directed that no "inquiries should be made into any man's belief or conscience, or that any injury or hindrance should be offered to any man on account of his religion."

Deceived and double-crossed by King James of England and Henry of France, both of whom feared the Dutch love of freedom and hoped to scoop the rich provinces into their own pockets, the Netherlands went on fighting Spain single-handed. In 1600 the army of the States-General, led by Prince Maurice of Nassau, decisively defeated Albert of Austria. In 1607 a fleet of little Dutch ships sailed to Gibraltar, then a Spanish stronghold, and destroyed the great Spanish navy in its own harbor. The victory was followed by a horrible slaughter of the survivors who were shot and stabbed by hundreds as they struggled in the water. For by now the Dutch had acquired a bitter thirst for revenge.

While engaging the world's mightiest power in battle by land and sea, the Dutch were also defying its alleged right to three fourths of the world including America. By sheer bravery and good management they captured the rich trade with the East Indies. While Spain was running headlong into bankruptcy despite its wide dominions, the Netherlands with no land except what it had captured from the sea was becoming rich through frugal industry and skillful management of its commerce. Without resources it had grown rich while Spain with resources almost beyond reckoning had grown poor. By intellectual power alone the Dutch people had raised themselves to a position of wealth and culture which no other people at that time could equal. And this in spite of the fact that they stood for the unpopular ideal of freedom—freedom of trade, religion, speech and government.

Worn out in the struggle to make such a people knuckle under, Spain finally agreed to an armistice in 1607. But for Spain it was already too late. She had lost her position of world dominance, never to regain it. When Spain sent her envoys to the Netherlands to negotiate, the whole world looked in wonder. When had anointed monarchs ever so humbled themselves to a people who had dared rebel against them? When had rebels ever been permitted to dictate a peace? Yet this was what happened, for the Dutch would not move an inch from the demand that their freedom be recognized. The negotiations dragged on for a year and a half, broke down and were resumed again. All the

great political issues of the day were involved in these parleys
—the right of a people to govern themselves as against the divine
right of kings; religious liberty, freedom of commerce, supremacy
of the seas. Unable to bring themselves to grant all this in a
permanent peace, Spain compromised on a twelve-year truce
which was signed in April 1609—just when the Pilgrims were
moving from Amsterdam to Leyden. The victory against the old
order was celebrated throughout the Netherlands with ringing
of bells, shooting of cannon, illuminations, and Te Deums in
the churches.

"It was inevitable," says Motley, "that a race, thus invigorated
by the ocean, cradled to freedom by their conflicts with its power,
and hardened almost to invincibility by their struggle against
human despotism, should be foremost among the nations in the
development of political, religious, and commercial freedom."

It was into this atmosphere of freedom that the Pilgrims came
from persecution in their own land, and even at the hands of
their own neighbors. The effect of this environment upon their
thinking and upon the history of the United States is incalcula-
ble. Yet even today the emphasis popularly given to the influence
of Plymouth is upon what it presumably brought from England
rather than upon what it indubitably picked up in Holland.

We have learned a great deal from mother England—enough
so that we need not credit her with virtues she did not possess.
Not, at least, in the seventeenth century. The Pilgrims found no
universal schooling, no freedom of religion, no representative
government in England. Nor a good many other things which
will be described in their place. The libertarian tradition at Plymouth, with its profound influence on American life, is not primarily English. It is Dutch. Simple justice demands that we
acknowledge this.

This, then, was the land to which the Pilgrims had come—a
land, as Bradford remarks, of "many goodly & fortified cities,
strongly walled and garded with troopes of armed men." Everything here was strange to them—the language, the manners and
customs, the mode of dressing, "all so farre differing from that of
their plaine countrie villages (wherein they were bred, & had so
longe lived) as it seemed they were come into a new world."

Amsterdam, the city they had first chosen to make their homes in, was one of the great commercial centers of Europe. Founded on a peat bog, its great churches and even its smallest houses were built on piles. From the arm of the Zuider Zee on which it was built, the great parallel canals and the smaller ones which crossed them divided the city into islands like a northern Venice, each of the main canals marking the line of the city walls at different periods. From streets often narrow and irregular the buildings rose up to create a fantastic skyline of gables, roofs and towers.

The reason for the Pilgrim's choice of Amsterdam was simple. Already there were Englishmen settled there, and not only Englishmen but friends—the congregation from Gainsborough which had arrived several months before under the pastoral care of John Smyth. This was the group from which the Scrooby congregation had split off, and this was the pastor to whom they had listened.

Yet they did not join this congregation of which they had once been a part. Instead, they worshiped with, but did not formally join, another group, the "Ancient Brethren" who had come over from England in 1595, and who were the congregation established in 1587 in London by the martyrs Barrow and Greenwood —the first Separatist congregation of importance.

Why did the Pilgrims fail to rejoin their old church?

Pretty certainly the answer is to be found in the character of John Smyth. The Pilgrim leaders, Clyfton and Robinson, must already have been aware of a certain instability in Smyth's religious principles. Not long after settling in Amsterdam their fears were confirmed by his explosive announcement that the Bible they used was not the word of God. Smyth went on to argue that only the original Greek and Hebrew Scriptures could possibly be directly from God, since the English version was but the work of men. His congregation had scarcely accustomed themselves to this discovery—and apparently to the necessity of learning two ancient languages—when Smyth uncovered the horrible possibility that the original Scriptures might also be man-made. From this position, too radical even for him, he drew back, but with the conclusion that it would be better not to use the Bible in his services, relying instead on pastor, teacher and congregation to speak and pray and sing as the spirit moved them.

Testimony as to the musical results has not been handed down.

Smyth's next discovery was that neither he, nor his flock, nor any other living man was a true Christian: that baptism being an act of faith, infants could not possibly be capable of such an act and therefore could not be made Christians by baptism. Since infant baptism had been the habit of the Christian world for centuries, there were no true Christians left! Out of this idea came the Baptist church of today, but it led to the breaking up of Smyth's congregation. For after making this discovery, dissolving his church and rebaptizing himself and his flock, Smyth then decided that the whole thing had been a "damnable error." This was too much. As Henry Ainsworth said of Smyth, "There was little need of another man's sword to pierce the bowels of his error, when his own hand fighteth against himself." The larger part of his group returned to England under Thomas Helwys where in London they established one of the first Baptist churches.

Steering clear of Smyth's congregation, then, Clyfton and Robinson led their group into a partial alliance with the Ancient Brethren. Yet here too trouble was brewing. In fact it had begun to brew years before in London when in 1594 Francis Johnson, the pastor, took to himself a buxom, well-to-do widow whose Elizabethan love of finery had irritated most of the congregation but most of all Johnson's brother George. This family linen, washed very much in public, remained a cross to the whole Separatist movement. Then, in 1597 the Johnson brothers and their elder, Daniel Studley, had been taken out of jail and deported to America with a group of settlers headed for Newfoundland. The colony was a failure. After many hardships the three Separatists managed to rejoin their congregation at Amsterdam in the same year. But soon it appeared that Elder Studley was lying with women to whom he was not legally attached; and not only grown women but girls. When he brought a suit for slander against his accusers, a Dutch court decided that the charges were true.

This was the group with whom the Scrooby folk had allied themselves. Clearly there was trouble ahead. Meanwhile they had trouble enough trying to make a living.

They were not a large group. Only the Robinson, Brewster and Clyfton families have been certainly identified. Bradford, now eighteen, was a member of the Brewster household. One of Clyfton's sons was about his age, and the boys must have been good companions, though Bradford has left no record of this.

Apprenticing himself to a French silk maker, William like all the rest began a way of life that was new to him. As newcomers, they had to take what they could get. What they got did not pay very well, for as Bradford remarked, "though they saw faire & bewtifull cities, flowing with abundance of all sorts of welth & riches, yet it was not longe before they saw the grime & grisly face of povertie coming upon them like an armed man, with whom they must bukle & incounter, and from whom they could not flye."

This spectacle of urban poverty was something new to a simple country people who, however primitive their mode of life, had been accustomed to plenty in the barn and in the larder. But now the means of subsistence were no longer in their hands. With unskilled fingers they had to weave an equivalent for the fields and flocks they had abandoned.

During the few months he spent in Amsterdam (probably from August 1608 to April 1609) William met Dorothy May. Henry May, her father, was elder of the Ancient Brethren who were then in the midst of the difficulties described above, so their first contact must have been by way of the church. Dorothy must have been a surpassingly attractive child, for at this time she was only eleven. Yet Bradford after knowing her but a few months was content to wait five years until she was old enough to marry. It was not for lack of other young women that Bradford chose her, for her older sister Jacqueline was married to Elder Jean de l'Ecluse in 1610.

Leaving her to grow up in Amsterdam while he went on to Leyden, he must have had some qualms about her safety. For the May family was in close contact with Studley, both men being elders of the church. And Studley had proven himself a pursuer of little girls. When accused of attempting to lie with the young daughter of Henry Ainsworth and confronted with the testimony of four of the brethren, his only defense was that he was interested in discovering the child's sex. No one else seems to have been in doubt about it.

The storms brewing in both English churches at Amsterdam soon determined Robinson and Brewster that if the Scrooby folk wanted to enjoy their religious freedom in a spirit of love and harmony, they would have to go somewhere else to do it.

So in February 1609, Robinson went to Leyden. After looking around, he asked the burgomasters if his small flock might settle there. Since Robinson stated the size of his group at one hundred, there must have been a number of Separatists from the other churches who were eager to join the Scrooby folk and remove themselves from Smyth's sudden upsetting revelations and the squabbles and fornications of the Ancient Brethren.

Just as arrangements seemed amicably settled, the long arm of tyranny reached out once more toward this much harried people, who having been persecuted in their own homes were now being pursued into their land of refuge. King James, through his ambassador, took the good burghers of Leyden to task for dealing with "certain Brownists" and attempted to prevent their being received in Leyden. Unwilling either to let them live unharassed or let them leave his own dominions, he now attempted to make life untenable for them anywhere else.

But the Dutch were by this time somewhat disillusioned by English promises and English political maneuvering, remembering the day when James had abandoned them to Spanish tyranny. So the Leyden city fathers, with characteristic courage and disregard of monarchs, informed the Pilgrims that they were welcome. When Clyfton decided to remain in Amsterdam with the Ancient Brethren, Robinson became the Pilgrim pastor.

Though Amsterdam had been but a brief stopover, important to Bradford largely because he met his future child-wife there, Leyden became a home. Here Bradford spent the important years of his young manhood, from nineteen to thirty. They were the years when he first came to grips with earning a living and when in the clutch of poverty he must have asked himself whether he had sacrificed too much for freedom. They were the years of falling in love, marrying, establishing a home of his own. They

were important years because what he learned in them he carried to the new world to lay the foundation of a nation yet to
be born.

Leyden in 1609 was one of the most beautiful cities of the
world. Shaped like a parallelogram, the city was built at the
mouth of the Rhine upon some thirty islands formed by the
river mouth and the canals. In ancient times a huge mound had
been raised at the junction of the two branches of the Rhine so
as to command both waterways. This citadel or burg still lay at
the heart of the city, surmounted by a circular tower whose
origin was so ancient as to be unknown. Fourteen projections
shaped like arrowheads stuck out from the city walls to form
bastions for defense.

As the Pilgrims approached the city by water they passed
through some of the richest meadows in the world. Before them
and inside the walls rose the spires of the guildhalls whose com-
manding position bespoke the controlling importance of workers rather than idle aristocrats in the thriving city. For Leyden
in the seventeenth century was a city of some hundred thousand,
far larger than it is today, and its manufactures of cloth were
known throughout Europe. Men then thought of Leyden in connection with cloth as they now think of Pittsburgh for steel.
Since weaving was done by hand, moreover, there was no grit or
dirt connected with the industry. Leyden could be both indus-
trial and beautiful, and was. Many of Leyden's most impressive
buildings, such as the gemeenlandshuis and the gymnasium were
then quite new. But others, like the church of St. Peter, were
of medieval origin, for Leyden had had a long history.

Polyander, one of the famous professors then teaching at the
university of Leyden, had written with a playful humor which
nevertheless expressed a real conviction:

"Of the four quarters of the world, Europe is the noblest and
nicest. The Low Countries are the best part of Europe. Of the
seventeen provinces of the Low Countries, Holland is the richest, the most flourishing and the finest. The most beautiful and
altogether charming city of Holland is Leyden. While the hand-
somest canal and the loveliest street in Leyden is the Rapenburg.
Wherefore, I am lodged in the most beautiful spot in the world."

After first housing themselves as best they could, the Pilgrims

settled down in 1611 in a street just off the Rapenburg. In the
Kloksteeg (Bell Alley) near St. Peter's church and the university
they bought a substantial house to serve as their meeting place
and the home of their pastor. In time twenty-one small houses
were built on the same lot for other members of the congregation.
It was a good location. The outlay must have been considerable,
suggesting that the group intended to make Leyden their permanent home.

Beautiful as Leyden was, and widely known for her cloth
manufactures and as a printing center, the greatest single source
of her fame was the university. It had been established by William the Silent as a tribute to the bravery of the people of Leyden in withstanding the Spanish siege. Though only thirty-five
years old, it had already attracted enough of Europe's finest
scholars to be an outstanding institution. Arminius, whose arguments against strict Calvinism were soon to explode in the Synod
of Dort, was there. And the brilliant young Grotius who at nine
was able to make Latin verses, at twelve had entered the university and at fifteen edited an encyclopaedic work in Latin.
Though not a professor, Grotius was a factor in the intellectual
life of Leyden. A few months before the Pilgrims came had died
the greatest scholar of modern times, J. J. Scaliger.

The presence of this institution next door to the Pilgrims
had its effect on Bradford. Under the tutelage of Brewster his
inquiring mind had already reached out into several fields of
learning, though chiefly religion and philosophy. Eleven years in
an academic neighborhood further confirmed him in his love of
books and his search for knowledge. We know that Robinson
was invited to dispute at the university. Bradford's proud reference to this distinction—for he fully valued the standing of the
institution—suggests that he was there to see his pastor's triumph. There must have been other lectures and debates such as
are always available to those who live in an academic neighborhood. Too, he overheard a deal of student talk. He watched the
professors on their way to and fro—followed them perhaps to
catch a bit of their conversation. He saw Polyander walking to
that most delightful spot in the world which he claimed as his
home. He knew the library where students stood at desks to read
the precious chained books. He was surrounded with an at-

mosphere of respect for learning and interest in ideas. It was in this way that he soaked up his knowledge. No one gave him an education, but he got one.

That he managed to do this without formal instruction is remarkable enough, but more so in view of the strenuousness with which at nineteen he had to devote himself to earning a living. The Pilgrims were immigrants in Holland, and generous as the Dutch were in receiving strangers they were no more likely than ourselves to surrender the easy jobs. The Pilgrims came with little capital. They came with no experience suited to the kind of lives they would have to live in a commercial city and in competition with those who were wise in city ways. So they took what work they could get.

Bradford who in Amsterdam had "served a Frenchman in working of silks," became a fustian worker. Fustian, a twilled cloth made of cotton and linen, was one of the many fabrics for which the Dutch had a reputation. Most of the congregation found similar work—as wool combers, silk workers, masons, brewers, carpenters and metal workers. In order to prosper in these trades, one had to become a member of one of the all powerful guilds. To become a guild member one had to be a citizen. So on March 30, 1612 when he was twenty-two, Bradford became a citizen of Leyden. About the time of his arrival in Leyden word must have come to him of the death of his Uncle Robert, that well-meaning man who had done his best to keep William from his appointment with destiny. In 1611, on his coming of age, Bradford had inherited and sold the property in Bentley-cum-Arksey which had come down to him from Peter. It consisted of a house, cottage, garden and orchard—nine and a half acres altogether. Now the last tangible tie with home was severed. Peter, that good yeoman, must have turned in his grave. Part of the money probably went to the purchase of the church building, for this was bought in May 1611—just two months after Bradford came of age. Part of it apparently went into establishing his own business, for according to Cotton Mather he now set up for himself—which probably meant the purchase of a loom. Finally, a part went to the purchase of a small house on the Achtergracht which was also close to the university. In the little house he no doubt set up his loom and went to work. Until now he had lived with the Brewsters, which had the advantage of continuing his education. In Bradford the thirst for knowledge never grew old, and one of the most touching facts of his life was the way he began to study the ancient Hebrew toward the end of his life.

But the move to the Achtergracht had another purpose. All his life long, as far back as he could remember, William Bradford had lived in other people's houses—in his uncle's, in the Brewsters'. He had never had a home of his own. Now he had one.

Citizen and householder, young William Bradford had suddenly become a man. Yet the change was not really sudden. For in his teens, as we know, he had already shown—even in a day when childhood was not romanticized and stretched out as in ours—a capacity for independent thought and action. In his quest for something firm to tie to, a father substitute possibly, he had been willing to face the displeasure of his uncles and the jibes of neighbors and companions. In the flight to Holland he had endured public shame and physical hardship. He had been marched through the streets of Boston with his companions, yelled at and prodded, regarded as an outcast, a dissenter, a red. He had reached Holland only to be seized as a criminal, and cleared of that charge had found himself an immigrant in a land whose language he could not understand and whose ways and works were strange. Like any boy coming up from the country he had been confused by the vastness, the noise, the grandeur and the complexity of city living. He had been both attracted and repelled by it—attracted by its great buildings, its power and productiveness, repelled by its impersonality and the loneliness one feels when set down in the midst of an unknown people.

All this was behind him now. Now he spoke Dutch with ease —a language not so very different from English once you got the hang of it. He was among a people whose religious convictions in the main were much like his own. He had acquired the sobering experience of day-long toil.

More than all this, his ambitions, his young man's dreams had been channeled into a straight course. For he was in love, and Dorothy May was going to be his wife. For her was the house in the Achtergracht, for her the citizenship which would lead to a better income and more comfortable living, and with thoughts of her the long day's work was sped.

It had been a long wait, since first he had seen her in Amsterdam. But now in 1613, she was sixteen and ripe for marriage though still, God knows, young. What it was that had drawn him so strongly toward her, no one now can say. The only word Bradford left about her concerns her death, and this notice is abrupt in the extreme, framing another mystery of his life for which no answer can now be found. Did she awaken some distant echo of memory for the mother who had died in his early childhood? Or of his sister? What makes a young man of twenty-three choose a maid of sixteen?

On November 9, William Bradford appeared in Amsterdam with Dorothy and her father to signify his intention of marriage. A week later he appeared alone at Leyden to arrange for the publication of the banns. The wedding took place in Amsterdam on December 10, after which William took his bride home to the little house on the Achtergracht. There was no religious service. The Separatists could find no authority in the Bible for it, and the use of a ring smacked of popery. So Dorothy —or Dority as she charmingly signed herself in a round, warm hand—was married without any of the ceremony women love.

The community into which Bradford brought his young bride was a small one, but it contained a number of interesting people. It was an emigré community, set down in the midst of a tolerant population and intent on preserving its English ways as well as its religious faith.

On its arrival in Leyden, the group had apparently been about a hundred strong. But within a short time the number had grown to three hundred, many of these coming from the Ancient Brethren at Amsterdam where dissension in the ranks arising from Thomasine Johnson's fineries and Elder Studley's fornications had led the more peaceable members to seek stiller waters.

The youthfulness of the group is indicated by the fact that forty-six English marriages took place while they were living in Leyden. Thirty-three men became citizens in order to join the influential guilds. Like Bradford, a few of the more prosperous bought houses. This much the excellent public records of Ley-

den divulge. What they do not disclose is the spirit of harmony
and brotherhood which held the group together, as Bradford
says, "in a comfortable condition, injoying much sweete & delightefull societie & spirituall comforte togeather in the wayes of
God." This was the beloved community, the mothering warmth
of which he later tried to reproduce in a new world.

Much of the credit for this harmonious community, as Bradford remarks, belongs to Robinson and Brewster. Robinson, now
a man of thirty-four, was more than pastor and preacher. He was
a wise leader of men, firm in principles but gentle in persuasion.
His personality shines clearly in every tribute Bradford pays
him. In disputation, when Separatist principles were questioned
or ridiculed, he could be sharp and scornful, but none of this
polemic spirit, common to the times, clung to his person. It is
a tribute both to his sweet reasonableness and to the tolerant
attitude of the Dutch that Robinson became more and more
liberal in his views the longer he lived in Holland. If the Pilgrims
had been able to continue his progressively liberal attitude in
the new world, they would have avoided the accusation of religious bigotry which is often cast at them today. After Bradford's death gave rein to the reactionaries at Plymouth it was
Robinson's son who stood steadfastly against laws discriminating
against Baptists and Quakers, and was disfranchised for his adherence to the principles of his father.

Robinson, in short, let his religion grow instead of penning
it up within stone walls. Once in a while he got himself into a
tight corner, as when he drew an elaborate and learned parallel
to show that Christian baptism was a substitute for circumcision.
The erection of this beautiful theory was easily pricked and un-
dermined, however, by the simple question, "Yes, but what
about the girls?"

After Pastor Robinson and Elder Brewster, the next church
officer was Deacon Samuel Fuller, leader of the group which
came over from the Ancient Brethren. Fuller, five years older
than Bradford, worked as a maker of serge. At Plymouth he
served as physician and surgeon though his particular qualifica-
tions for medicine have never come to light. Yet his people
trusted him—which is perhaps the most important condition for
successful medical treatment.

Though it is impossible to say who, outside of the Brewster family, would have been most intimate with the newly wed Bradfords, we can make a few logical guesses.

First came the marrying Whites. John Robinson's wife Bridget was a White from Sturton le Steeple near Scrooby. Three of her sisters became Pilgrim wives—Catherine of John Carver, Jane of Ralph Tickens and Frances of Francis Jessop who was considered a dangerous enough dissenter to have had a warrant issued for his arrest shortly before he left for Holland. Roger White, their brother, was in the Leyden congregation too, while William White, possibly of the same family, had in 1612 married Sam Fuller's sister Susanna who was but two or three years older than Dorothy. She and Dorothy bore their first children at about the same time.

Another wife-providing family was that of Alexander Carpenter who had come over first with the Ancient Brethren. Alice, who was later to marry Bradford, had become Mrs. Edward Southworth, and Agnes had married Sam Fuller the same year Bradford married Dorothy. Julia Ann (or Juliana) had married George Morton the year before. Priscilla was to marry William Wright in 1619, while Mary remained a spinster and ultimately became a member of Bradford's household in Plymouth.

A few weeks after his own marriage, Bradford attended Moses Fletcher when he was joined to Sarah Dingby.

These, together with the men who like himself worked in fustian, were most probably the members of Bradford's circle with whom he and Dorothy enjoyed "much sweete & delightefull societie." Not that there was much time for frivolity. Work and worship filled most of the waking hours of these earnest folk. They never quite got accustomed to what they considered the frivolous manner of spending the Sabbath which they found among the Dutch as among their own people in England.

It was in the meeting room of the building they had bought for their pastor's home and their church that they experienced to the fullest their oneness as a people united in faith. On Thursday evenings and for the greater part of Sunday they were together, the men sitting to one side of the hall, the women on the other and the children gathered into a place where they could be watched, prodded or punished. No one in those days thought

of providing more digestible religious fare for children than
the services lasting four hours or more which their parents attended. No one thought to make allowances for youth and im-
maturity. Though we would consider such treatment cruelly
inappropriate nowadays, there is no evidence that the young
were permanently harmed by it, or that Pilgrim children grew
up to be maladjusted half as often as our own offspring. Under
such a pastor as Robinson they were put in touch with a wide
range of information, speculation, and logical argument. Though
much of what he said would have been incomprehensible to the
youngest, they could not have failed to be impressed by the respect and attention their parents paid to his words. Curiosity
would thus be followed by the effort to understand, so that in
time every Pilgrim child must have become a precocious storehouse of adult ideas about man, God and the universe. As a
method of education it may have been, though somewhat rigor-
ous, far more effective than anything we have today. It directed
their minds toward conduct rather than toward the acquisition
of skills or facts. It was aimed at the making of moral men rather
than economic men—an aim therefore far higher than that of
the schools in a primarily acquisitive society. For whatever criticism our time may cast at the Pilgrims, we cannot measure up to
them in the purposeful shaping of our institutions toward moral
goals.

What was a Pilgrim service like? By eight o'clock on a Sunday
morning the worshipers were in their places. The opening prayer,
which might last an hour or more, was received by a standing
congregation, for kneeling like bowing, genuflecting, and the
use of an altar or musical instruments was associated with the
hated ceremony of Anglican and Roman churches. After prayer,
the pastor read two or three chapters out of the Geneva Bible,
explaining and paraphrasing as he read, for reading without com-
ment was also regarded as ritualistic. Then a psalm was sung in
unison and without accompaniment. After 1612 the psalms were
taken from the metrical versions provided by Henry Ainsworth,
pastor of the anti-Johnson congregation at Amsterdam. Though
a learned scholar, Ainsworth was a wretched poet. In a tortured
effort to put the psalms into meter he managed to rob them of
most of their meaning. Yet the Pilgrims doggedly went on using

them, together with the thirty-nine tunes the book supplied, for many years. Meanwhile scholars all over Europe who knew Ainsworth as a leading student of Hebrew charitably assumed that some other Ainsworth must have botched the psalms. Despite this handicap Edward Winslow, a young man of some culture, noted that many of the congregation were very expert in music. Perhaps he meant that they had to be, to surmount Ainsworth.

After the psalm came a sermon. Robinson's sermons were meaty, human, full of interest for his hearers—and long. Ordinarily he talked for two hours or more. While much of his matter—so far as it can be judged from his published works— is a kind of technical theology which does not attract us today, there is also much that is undated in its practical wisdom. Robinson ridicules those who hold that the pleasures of the marital bed are any more evil than the pleasure of good food and good wine. These natural joys are to be received as a part of God's bounty, says Robinson—thus cutting the ground from under those who like to think of the Pilgrims as stern men incapable of pleasure.

After the sermon came another psalm, then on occasion the sacraments of the Lord's Supper or baptism. Then the collection was taken and the service ended at mid-day with a final prayer.

After little more than time to eat, the congregation assembled again, this time for "prophesying." This, one of the most interesting aspects of Pilgrim worship, demonstrates the essentially democratic quality of their faith. For prophesying afforded every man in the congregation an opportunity to utter the religion that was in him. After Robinson or Brewster had read a brief text from the Bible and spoken on it briefly, the meeting was open for all. All the men, that is. The Pilgrims were strict believers in the double standard—because they found it in the Bible. It was not for them to lift women from the place where St. Paul had put them.

What sounds like an insufferable regimen to us was apparently a pleasurable experience to the Pilgrims. From the hard toil of the week it was sweet relief to sit even upon the hard church benches. The services provided their music and their drama, their school and their lyceum. When we marvel at the fortitude with which this people pursued their religion we assume that it was with them as with us a Sunday affair. We fail to value properly the central place of religion in their lives and the effect it had of drawing all experience together. We live in a secular age; non-religious institutions dominate our lives. These men and women formed a religious community. They experienced the satisfaction, rare in our time and culture, of fulfillment at the group level. Their lives were not oriented, as ours too often are, to the satisfaction of individual or family goals. They had a vision of a life to be lived in the manner (as they conceived it) of the first Christians in which burdens would be shared so that all might devote themselves to the knowledge and love of God. The earthly life was not an end in itself, but a preparation. The most important achievement of life was to understand the ways of God and to serve Him.

Efforts are constantly being made to debunk the Pilgrims. They had their faults, but whatever faults they had came from a failure to measure up, not from a failure (as in our own times) to have standards, to know what is important, to have a goal. The Pilgrims were perfectly sure of their goal, which is one reason for the power they have over us today. For we would like to possess such certainty as theirs if we could.

"Such was the true pietie, the humble zeale, & fervent love, of this people (whilst they thus lived together) towards God and his waies," says Bradford, "and the single hartednes & sinceir affection one towards another, that they came as near the primative patterne of the first churches, as any other church of these later times have done."

That was their goal. It was simple; it was difficult. It was a challenge and a comfort. It offered to the individual personality such scope and promise as was sufficient for men like Brewster and Bradford. It was a way of life. It was a vision. It was a partnership with God.

The Pilgrims were not the only English congregation in Leyden. As in Amsterdam, another group had preceded them which adhered to Calvinist beliefs and Presbyterian church government and was therefore popularly called the Scottish church though its members were English. Really an English-speaking congregation of the Dutch Reformed church, it had received from the state a free place of worship not far from that of the Pilgrims.

Through contact with this congregation and with the Protestant Dutch, the Pilgrims gradually became more liberal in their practices. In the early years at Leyden Robinson had maintained that there ought to be no communion—not even in a private meeting for prayer—between the members of a true church and those of a "false" church, however holy the members of that church might be in their persons. But by 1614 Robinson was willing to admit that one might pray or read Scripture even with Anglicans, while with their English neighbors it was permissible even to join in the Lord's Supper. The influence of liberal, tolerant Holland had begun its work.

Thus, during the Leyden years, were the Pilgrims perfecting themselves for the undreamed of work of founding a new nation. In religion, they grew milder and more tolerant. In business and craftsmanship they learned a great deal from the thrifty, ambitious and highly capable Hollanders. Too, the Dutch flair for efficient government and record keeping, the spirit of republicanism and civic responsibility were to bear unsuspected fruit in a distant land.

As for William Bradford and his young bride, we find but few traces of them in the official records—of Dorothy none at all after the betrothal and the marriage. Perhaps because of her youth Dorothy did not become pregnant until sometime in the second year of her marriage. But even the womanly triumph of bringing a man child into the world finds no place in the public record. They called him John, perhaps out of respect for their pastor since there were no Johns in the Bradford family. As it turned out, the little fellow was never to see much of his parents, and like his father before him was to have scarcely a memory of his mother. Yet we may imagine that for the first five years his mother, herself still a child in our eyes, loved him with the fierce and tender yearning of the young. For the house in the Achtergracht which had been lonely until now was full of his presence. No longer had she to talk to herself to fill out its empty silences, or to make ready with nervous hands for the homecoming of a husband she adored but feared, a little, for his energy, his efficiency, and his devilish way of spotting anything that had gone amiss. The child was her companion, marvelously sprung from her own body; he was the reason for her existence—he justified her; and his presence was sufficient excuse for any little disorder in the household caught by William's quick eye. She had learned all this in the first days after his birth. And that was why, sometimes, when she could be sure no one would hear her, she would snatch him from his cradle and clasping him close in her arms would dance with him about the room, dancing the song that was in her heart and humming a music never heard with Mr. Ainsworth's psalms. She supposed it was a sin, so to sing and dance; yet some instinct within her said that it would be a worse sin for such a little thing never to have known the music that was in her heart.

These were the happy years for Dorothy. William's intense and purposeful spirit no longer overwhelmed her, for had she not done a miracle he could never do? And had she not raised her stature somewhat nearer to his? Women were inferior creatures —that she knew, for surely she had heard it often enough. But the miracle of John told her that if this was so, it was an inferiority with which she could be well content.

If we had but a scrap of writing from William to tell us what he felt for Dorothy it would be precious. Lacking the word, we must read from the fact: for five years, with that sureness of knowing his own mind, that unrelaxed determination which were his mark, William had waited for the child Dorothy to ripen into the first bloom of maturity. He married; he spent his patrimony on a house for her. Old Peter's ewe lamb and all other substance that remained to his great-great-grandchild were converted into that house in the Achtergracht and into the tools of his trade; and of that investment young John was the dividend.

Such devotion merited the surplus of wedded happiness which William and his girl-wife must have found. To one who had lost his parents so young and who so long had been without a household of his own, the Leyden home must have seemed like some rare and dreamed-of haven.

Yet in the seven years between her marriage and the departure for America Dorothy bore but one child. If there were others they died in infancy, for there is no record of them. In a day of sizeable families this is remarkable. It remains as much a mystery as the manner of Dorothy's death.

A few scraps of evidence remain to show us what William was doing between his marriage in 1613 and the departure from Leyden in 1620.

On June 12, 1617, he borrowed four hundred guilders from Jan van Griecken, goldsmith, at 6¼ per cent, offering his house as security. Why had Bradford sudden need of cash at this time? One possibility is that he was helping his old friend and virtual foster father, Brewster, who at about this time had begun a new venture as publisher of the Choir Alley or Pilgrim Press, as it has come to be known in recent years. Brewster had spent most of his substance while helping his friends to leave England and establish themselves in Holland. For a while he had earned a living, probably a poor one, as a teacher of English. In his new venture he had as a backer a man of means named Thomas Brewer. But as three books are known to have been issued in 1617, and more may have been, it is possible that Bradford either invested in the venture or made a loan.

There is, however, a less attractive possibility—that Bradford had failed as a business man. For this we have as evidence only a rather unsatisfactory reference in Cotton Mather's account. "Setting up for himself," says Mather, "he found some of his designs by the providence of God frowned upon, which he judged a correction bestowed by God . . . the consumption of his estate he thought came to prevent a consumption in his virtue." Since he needed a sum as large as four hundred guilders, he must have been engaged in a commercial activity more extensive than that of selling the work of his own loom. In any case, the loss would have struck him hard. Yet it also helped to open the way toward the great decision soon to be made. A man who has suffered in business is far more ready to jump to something new. With Bradford, as with all strong men, failure proved to be one of the strongest rungs in his ladder.

On June 7, 1619, he appeared with Alexander Price to vouch for William Ring, a say weaver, when he was sworn in as a citizen. He had done the same for Samuel Lee in 1615. As one of the first Pilgrims to take that step himself, the wonder is that Bradford had not appeared for more of the men who had followed his lead.

On April 19 he sells his house to Jan des Obrys for 1,120 guilders, thus leading toward the opening of the next act in the Pilgrim drama.

Events in Holland were now taking a course that pushed the Separatists toward a critical decision they had long been considering. The victory over Spain had scarcely been assured by the twelve-year truce when a theological argument began in the University of Leyden which soon became the spearhead of a dispute involving all the important latent conflicts in the political and social structure of the Netherlands.

It all began when Arminius advanced a theory which attacked the traditional Calvinist doctrine of predestination. He was answered by a colleague, Gomarus. Today the whole argument seems futile and inane. It then seemed, to those involved in it, as important as the present struggle between democracy and communism. Around the two men formed parties that were soon fighting the issue hammer and tongs. Arminius died but the fight went on. John Robinson, the Pilgrim pastor, was invited by Polyander to jump into the fray. According to Bradford he completely non-plussed the Arminians and covered himself with glory. Not only once, but two or three times he disputed with the Arminian Episcopius. "The Lord did so help him to defend the truth & foyle this adversarie, as he put him to an apparent nonplus, in this great & publike audience."

As it spread, Arminianism became identified with what we would call the issue of states' rights versus centralization. The Netherlands were united under a federal principle. Barneveld (John of Olden-Barneveldt), the great political leader who had steered the states through the contest with Spain, favored states' rights and Arminianism, having shifted his ground when the end of the war diminished his power in all the states but his home province of Holland. Prince Maurice, the great military leader, was for orthodox Calvinism and central control.

By 1617 the dispute had grown so hot that the waard-gelders or militia were called out to maintain order, and one morning Bradford and the rest found the beautiful old town hall enclosed by a solid palisade of oak strengthened with iron bars, armed with cannon, and manned by a solid line of militia. This defiance on the part of the individual states was met by an order to Prince

Maurice from the States-General to disband the militia wherever they had formed. Behind Maurice was the power of the army which had been victorious over Spain. The resistance collapsed, Barneveld himself being executed in May 1619.

Meanwhile the theological side of the quarrel was being debated by the famous Synod of Dort which, two weeks after Barneveld's death, denounced Arminianism and proclaimed Calvinism as the creed of the reformed churches throughout Europe.

Barneveld and his supporters had represented the aristocratic element. They had backed Arminianism because of its insistence on the supremacy of the state in appointing ministers and in regulating discipline and dogma. The opposition to Barneveld had therefore stood for greater liberty both political and religious, and there is no doubt that the more liberal side won. The former easygoing alliance between church and state was continued, the state providing support for the church but making no attempt to interfere with its doctrine. The clergy were elected by their congregations. Neither church nor state interfered with the concerns of the other, yet the importance of religion in the state was recognized.

The model was to have an unsuspected influence upon the other side of the broad Atlantic.

Meanwhile the end of the twelve-year truce was approaching. A war which was to last thirty years had already broken out in Germany over a struggle between Protestants and Catholics as to who should be king of Bohemia. The struggle between Protestantism and Catholicism threatened to destroy Europe as the battle between communism and democracy now seems to threaten the foundations of our world. From the East Turkey, whose influence stretched all the way to Hungary, was making war on Poland. If Catholic and Protestant destroyed each other, it looked as if Moslem Turkey would overrun Europe.

To get away from the old world with its constant warfare the Pilgrims began to think of moving on once more. They had been twelve years in Holland, which, as Bradford observed, "is the more observable being the whole time of that famose truce between that state & the Spaniards." With war threatening again they had to face the possibility that Holland would be overrun and religious liberty stamped out. In the face of such a possibility the new world beckoned with an alluring promise. There they would have no laws or religions but of their own making. There if anywhere they could practice the "holy discipline" in its purity.

But there were other reasons.

Despite the respect they had gained for themselves, Holland had proven a hard place for them to earn a living. Not only had the grownups worked to the injury of their own health, but "many of their children, that were of best dispositions and gracious inclinations, haveing lernde to bear the yoake in their youth, and willing to bear parte of their parents burden, were, often times, so oppressed with their hevie labours, that though their minds were free and willing, yet their bodies bowed under the weight of the same, and became decreped in their early youth; the vigor of nature being consumed in the very budd as it were."

Moreover, their children spoke Dutch and probably went to Dutch schools. Some of them went into soldiering or sailing and were thus lost to the community. Others, says Bradford, "were drawne away by evill examples into extravagante & dangerous courses."

But on the positive side was a desire, entirely consistent with the sense the Pilgrims had of being a community, an organism whose motivating force was God, to "lay some good foundation . . . for the propagating & advancing the gospell of the kingdom of Christ in those remote parts of the world; yea, though they should be but even as stepping-stones unto others for the performing of so great a work."

Bradford, now nearing thirty, was ready to do his share. Better off than many of the company, with the money from the sale of his house available for investment in the new world, he was already looked up to as a young man of great promise. His signing of an important letter, with Fuller and others, bearing on the affairs of the group shows that his leadership was already taken for granted.

The William Bradford who prepared to leave Holland in 1620 was a very different person from the youngster who had come there at the age of eighteen. The sturdy virtues of his yeoman background were still with him, and the faults too. But to these basic and unsophisticated qualities of a simple country life had

been added the subtler qualities of a city culture. Bradford had
come to Holland knowing the seasons, the problems of foaling
and shearing, the simple crafts of barn and field. He left it knowing an intricate finger craft, knowing too something of trade and
commerce, of municipal records and the methods of republican
government. He had brought with him an education based on
the Bible and its picturing of a pastoral world much like his own
at Austerfield. He took away the knowledge of a civilization
which basing its prosperity on an industriousness and enterprise
outdistancing the rest of the world, still placed in high regard
learning, education and the creative arts. Coming from a nation
which forced all men to conform to the official religion, he had
found a land where even at the height of a doctrinal controversy
all manner of non-conformists had been allowed to worship
as they pleased.

For many of the things that Holland offered he had no time
—its enjoyment of the arts, its feasting and its fun. Because religion was a central thing in his life he not only did not miss them
but did not desire them. But the learning Holland offered he
snatched as he could. His own writing is full of surprising allu-
sions to books both classic and religious which he must have
read at this period. Did he read aloud sometimes to Dorothy in
the brief evening hours before he led her to bed? Did he enjoy
filling her young mind with the ideas that were so arousing to
him?

No one knows. But it is clear enough that these were years of
preparation, years of unsuspected value, not only for Bradford
but for a nation yet to be. Only toward the close, as the little
group began to plan its great venture and had need of leaders,
did Bradford begin to exercise his talents for leadership. They
were not to be fully tested until the new world was reached. Nor
was Dorothy to see his triumph. But the stirrings had begun.
He had begun to feel the capacity for leadership that was in him.
It was an exciting, a liberating thing. Talents that are pent up
are bound to gnaw at a man.

Across the wide water there would be room and enough for
them to expand.

"A Great & Honorable Action"

AS early as 1617 the Leyden congregation were thumbing
Smith's *A Map of Virginia*, Hakluyt's *Voyages* and Raleigh's
Discovery of Guiana as they began to look for a place in the new
world which would suit their desires and conditions. As they
searched, that old instinct began to take hold of them which had
caused the dispersion of the race throughout the world. The
Leyden group had reasons enough for wanting to move—reasons which could be pinned down with words and which would
have a respectable sound. But underneath logic lay the emotion
which sometime or other seizes all men of vigor and imagination—the urge to be somewhere else, to cross an ocean, to conquer the horizon, to follow the sun, to sleep under the "strange-
eyed constellations" of Hardy's phrase. The urge was particularly
strong in Elizabethan and Jacobean times, as in our own.

Part of this urge to move on was the desire to own land.
Though Bradford nowhere speaks of it, perhaps because it was
too much a part of his nature to be picked out and analyzed, it
was land hunger that lay behind the decision to leave Holland.
Raised in a well-to-do yeoman family, William had from childhood known that without land a man's life was not complete. As
far back as the Bradfords can be traced, there is to be found that
yeoman's love of the land and of the husbandry by which it is
made to yield its increase. Ownership of a house in Leyden had
been but a poor substitute for the ancestral lands at Bentley

which had purchased it. Moreover, to sit all day in a room making cloth was lacking in manliness. To a yeoman this was woman's work, and Bradford had never grown accustomed to it. Such work gave no feeling of security. You could not eat the thing you made, and without fields and pasturage, without chickens, sheep, and a cow to provide cheese and butter, how could a man ever be secure? This was the real explanation for the grinding poverty in which most of the Leyden congregation were forced to live. For all about him Bradford could see signs of comfortable living. The Dutch indeed excelled at it. Their beautifully clean, well-lighted homes, their well-provided tables, their clothing and porcelainware showed the benefits of industry —if one owned the land.

There was yet another reason, usually overlooked, why the Leyden folk wanted to move.

They were steeped in the lore of the Old Testament. Indeed they studied the Old more than the New. Because of the intensity of their desire to communicate directly with God, even Jesus was to them an impediment, an intermediary not unlike the priesthood and the ritual they abhorred. So to Bradford the pastoral life came to have a double meaning. It meant a return to the life of the patriarchs, but a return also to the ways of his youth. Now any man is entranced with the dream of returning to his youth. To William the idea had an extra attraction since he had probably never overcome the sense of guilt brought on by the sale of his ancestral lands.

Holland, beautiful and civilized though it was, had in it the same seed of corruption for which Sodom and Gomorrah had been punished. As a yeoman, William Bradford shared with the biblical patriarchs a suspicion of cities as dens of iniquity.

Similarly, America became the promised land, the land God had granted to Abraham and his seed forever. To get away from the temptations and corruptions of the city and the alarums of war, to carry the word of God to a new world and by careful husbandry to make the land yield its increase—this was what America promised. For this they were Pilgrims, and this was what William Bradford meant when he gave them the name.

Thus America and the Old Testament were joined before ever the Pilgrims set foot on Cape Cod.

The more they read about America, the more they saw in it
a land blessed with milk and honey. Particularly so when they
read Sir Walter Raleigh's account of Guiana.

> To conclude, Guiana is a Countrey that hath yet her Mayden-
> head, never sackt, turned, nor wrought, the face of the earth
> hath not bene torne, nor the vertue and salt of the soyle spent
> by manurance, the graves have not been opened for gold, the
> mines not broken with sledges, nor their Images puld down out
> of their temples. It hath never been entred by anie army of
> strength and never conquered or possesed by any Christian
> Prince.

Though not reluctant to force the "maydenhead" of so entic-
ing a piece, the Leyden folk regretfully abandoned this paradise
when they considered the danger they would be in from the
Spaniard—hatred of whom Bradford had drunk in with his
mother's milk only a few years after the destruction of the
Armada, a hatred well fortified by the stories Leyden could tell
of Spanish cruelty. So they turned from the land of perpetual
summer to a more northward clime.

For Virginia, they had the testimony of none other than Captain John Smith, whose *A Map of Virginia* described that piece
of English territory in such a way as to make them feel that the
dangers from savages and starvation, while great, had been overcome to such an extent that they could safely settle there. Yet
if they settled near the others already established, they would
be as much persecuted for religion's sake as they had been in
England. "And if they lived too farr of, they should neither have
succour, nor defence from them."

So they decided to live "as a distincte body by themselves, under the generall government of Virginia."

After they had made this decision, a piece of news came back
from Virginia which would have discouraged any but a strong
and stubborn people. In 1618 the remnants of Francis Johnson's
contentious Amsterdam congregation had set sail for Virginia
under the leadership of Francis Blackwell, who had become their
leader after Johnson's death. After betraying some other Separatists in order to save himself and after openly denying his Sepa-

ratist principles, Blackwell departed from England with one hundred and eighty of his people, speeded by the Archbishop of Canterbury's blessing. The ship was driven far out of her course by storms, sickness broke out amongst the close-packed passengers, the water gave out, and after the death of the captain and six other seamen it was only by luck that they found the Chesapeake and Jamestown. Only fifty of the one hundred and eighty lived to see the new world.

"If such events follow the bishop's blessing," Bradford drily remarked, "happie are they that misse the same."

As negotiators and agents the Leyden group now sent over to England two of its trusted members, both deacons. Robert Cushman, though a wool comber, was better off than most. He owned a house in Nun's Alley close by St. Peter's in the area where many of the congregation lived. A widower, he had recently remarried. With Cushman went John Carver, a prosperous merchant not long since turned fifty. Married to a sister of Pastor Robinson's wife, Carver was from the same part of England as William Bradford.

The two representatives were cordially received. As a matter of fact the Virginia Company, then in the midst of financial troubles, welcomed the prospect of a hardy and determined group of colonists. Taken under the wing of Sir Edwin Sandys, son of the Archbishop of York for whom Brewster had managed the manor at Scrooby, the two agents were encouraged to think that the king would allow them liberty in religion in the new world. Although Sandys had proposed laws against Brownists and Barrowists as a member of Parliament many years before (1592–1593) he had become a spokesman for the popular party as opposed to king and court. James the First indeed paid him the compliment of calling Sandys his greatest enemy. "Choose the devil if you will, but not Sir Edwin Sandys," he shouted when Sandys was up for re-election as treasurer of the Virginia Company. Active in the Virginia Company from its beginning in 1606, Sandys was the prime mover of the first representative assembly in America which met at Jamestown in 1619. He warmly supported the Leyden group, approved the seven articles they had drawn up in the hope of persuading the king that they

were orthodox enough to be harmless, and introduced them to
other influential members of the Virginia Company.

No less a person than Sir Robert Naunton, secretary of state
and a staunch Protestant, tried to get the king to grant freedom
of religion to the group as a reward for their willingness to face
the wilderness and strengthen British power in America. But he
was unable to bring it about. Ironically enough, this same Sir
Robert was before long to order the manhunt for the publisher
of the "subversive" *Perth Assembly* *—who was none other than
William Brewster, leader of this same group which had so humbly petitioned the king's majesty.

Cushman and Carver returned to Holland without accomplishing much, but bringing a friendly though cautious letter
from Sandys. Robinson and Brewster now drew up two further
declarations about their beliefs and again messengers went over.
But the more the Leydeners explained their religious principles,
the more questions they raised in the minds of the Privy Council. Thus matters went on for several years. "These things being in long agitation," says Bradford, "and messengers passing
too and againe aboute them, after all their hopes they were long
delayed by many rubs that fell in the way."

Two of these "rubs" were the internal war that broke out
within the Virginia Company, and the discovery that Brewster
was the publisher of *Perth Assembly.*

Trouble in the Virginia Company came to a head when Sir
Thomas Smith, its governor and treasurer, asked to be eased
of these offices. Yet when Sir Edwin Sandys was chosen treasurer
in his place, he raised a faction against him. The Virginia Company, in addition to financial troubles, was split between the
king's men and the people's party, and the king's objection to
Sandys was well known. Sandys had strong supporters on his side,
including the Earl of Southampton whose memory has been kept
green by Shakespeare's praise. Caught up in this struggle, the
Pilgrims became its victims.

As if this were not enough, a hue and cry was now raised
against the printer of *Perth Assembly,* and at the very time when

---

* *Perth Assembly* was a bold attack on James the First and his bishops for trying to force episcopacy upon Presbyterian Scotland. It was written by David
Calderwood, leader of the stubborn Scotch opposition.

Brewster was in London to help with the negotiations. By the time the king's people had identified the printer as Brewster, he was not to be found, nor was he ever located by the king's officers. His friends somehow managed to keep him hidden, to get him aboard the *Mayflower* under an assumed name, and to carry him to America beyond the king's reach and the king's memory. But for Brewster it had been a narrow squeak.

Before the responsibility for *Perth Assembly* had been traced to Brewster and Leyden, however, Cushman had at last got a patent for settling in Virginia. To avoid difficulty the patent was taken out in the name of John Wincob and sealed on June 9, 1619. Wincob, "a religious gentleman then belonging to the Countess of Lincoline" (Lincoln), was to have gone with them to America. But he never went, nor was any use ever made of the patent which had cost them such effort.

The next problem was to raise capital for transportation and supplies. In this matter the Virginia Company was apparently unable to do much. A way out next appeared when the Dutch New Netherlands Company offered free transportation and cattle if the group would settle in Dutch America. Naturally they would enjoy there the same freedom of worship which Holland had given them these past twelve years.

By this time it was 1620. Three years of wearying negotiations had passed. The Leyden congregation was about to jump at the Dutch offer when a London merchant named Thomas Weston appeared. He was well known to some of the group and had helped with the lengthy negotiations in London. Never mind the Virginia Company or the Dutch, he advised them. He and his friends would attend to all their needs. All that was necessary was to draw up articles of agreement—"not so much for him selfe as for the satisfiing of such frends as he should procure to adventure in this bussines"—and everything would be attended to. There must have been something very convincing about Thomas Weston, for he impressed a people wearied with three years of negotiation as a man who meant what he said and would perform what he promised. How well he lived up to this measure will soon appear.

Now that something definite seemed to have been accomplished, the Leyden folk began to liquidate their estates and to put their money into the common stock. Bradford, as we have seen, sold his house for 1,120 guilders. Something seems to have gone wrong, however, for he was unable to collect a payment of one hundred guilders due him in May, 1620, and had to leave a power of attorney to collect it. In the preparations for departure William Bradford was soon deeply engaged. With that modesty which graces his character but which makes him hard to follow, he fails to say who were those chosen to take such business in hand at the Leyden end. But Brewster was in hiding, Carver and Cushman in London, so it is pretty clear that much of the management fell upon him. It has even been argued that he went to London in March 1619/20, the name of William Bradford having been found on a subsidy roll of Aldergate ward and with a residence in the Duke's Place where Edward Southworth was living. As Bradford later married Southworth's widow, it is tempting to weave Dorothy's mysterious death and Alice Southworth's sudden arrival in Plymouth after her husband's death into a romantic and not too pretty tale. Yet when all the evidence is weighed it seems more likely that Bradford had his hands full of affairs at Leyden.

In any case the business which now occupied him must have come as a relief, after all the delays and parleys, to one of his active temperament. But the relief did not last long.

Back in London, Weston managed to form a joint stock company of seventy "adventurers" who put up seven thousand pounds, a sum equivalent to perhaps four hundred thousand dollars in 1950. Weston claimed that the adventurers would realize half the profit and the settlers half, as if they were two partners in business.

Meanwhile the second or Plymouth Virginia Company had been reorganizing its affairs, had renamed its territory New England (as Captain John Smith had already persuaded the Prince of Wales to name it), and expected to receive a royal patent which would give it clear title to the lands it claimed. Prime mover behind the development of New England was Sir Ferdinando Gorges, whose path was to cross that of the Pilgrims many times in the future. Known to his contemporaries as the friend who betrayed the Earl of Essex and thus brought it about that the noble gentleman lost his head, Gorges had been interested in New England since 1605. In that year, while serving as captain and keeper of the castle and fort at Plymouth (England), he met a sea captain named George Weymouth who had just returned from what we now call the New England coast bringing five Indians with him. Like all the adventurous spirits of his time, Gorges was fascinated by dreams of the wealth and feudal domains to be had in the new world. He therefore "seized upon" three of the five Indians and kept them by him for three years. Through them he learned all about New England. And one of the three was an Indian known to every American schoolchild—Tisquantum or Squanto, the friend who was later to save the Pilgrims from starvation.

Obsessed with the idea of "planting" in New England, Gorges was instrumental in organizing the Popham colony which settled at the mouth of the Kennebec in 1607 but was abandoned the next year. He continued to send ships for trading and fishing, and he continued to dream of a permanent colony. He was instrumental in having Captain John Smith explore the coast in 1614. In 1616 Smith published his *Description of New England* which the Pilgrims read with eager interest, poring over the excellent map with which it was furnished. Sometime in 1619 Smith made contact with their agents in England, offering himself as guide, to which they replied that his books and maps were "much better cheap to teach them" than himself. Whether by this time they had contracted with Standish we do not know. Certainly Smith's record in Virginia proves that he would have been a wonderful help to them.

"Worthy is that person to starve that here cannot live," Smith wrote of New England, "if he have sense, strength and health." The Pilgrims would have cause to remember those words in the months to come, and perhaps to regret that they had not taken Smith with them. "Their humorous ignorances," he later wrote, "caused them for more than a year to endure a wonderful deal of misery with infinite patience . . . thinking to find things better than I advised them."

In 1619 while the Pilgrims were negotiating with the London Virginia Company, Gorges had sent Captain Thomas Dermer on another exploration of the New England coast. With him was Squanto, who had been returned once to America by one of

Captain John Smith's ships, captured and sold into slavery in Spain, but finally had found his way to England again. While the Pilgrims were still negotiating in London, Dermer in 1620 was visiting the very beach and harbor where they would settle.

On June 30 he wrote to Gorges, describing the harbor at new Plymouth and urging that a plantation be made there. It is possible that Gorges received this letter at old Plymouth and showed it to the Pilgrims before their departure from that port on September sixth. Sir Ferdinando, who for fifteen years had been looking for colonists to settle New England, and who as captain of the port would have known all about the Pilgrims, was not the sort of man to let such an opportunity escape him, even though his wife had just died.

The energy and enthusiasm of Gorges was of course well known to Weston. So to New England "Mr. Weston, and the cheefe of them, begane to incline it was best for them to goe, as for other reasons, so cheefly for the hope of present profite to be made by the fishing that was found in that countrie."

The suggestion broke open an old sore at Leyden. Again the arguments for going to Guiana, to Virginia, were heard until those who had sold their estates and laid out their money "were brought into a greate streight, fearing what issue these things would come too." But at length all agreed on New England.

That is what Bradford clearly says, though historians and scholars to this day have insisted that the Pilgrims intended to settle in Virginia—the Virginia of the London Company. "Those that were most relied on," he says, "fell in utter dislike with Virginia, and would doe nothing if they wente thither." Then in the next sentence, which begins with describing the fear of the Leydeners as to what "these things would come too," he concludes, "but at length the generalitie was swaid to this latter opinion"—that is, the opinion of those that were most relied on. Later on, when the voyage was ended and they were off Cape Cod, "the which being made and certainly knowne to be it, they were not a little joyfull," they headed south. According to *Mourt's Relation*,* their plan was to go to a river ten leagues

---

* An account of the first year, written by Bradford and Edward Winslow but published in London 1622 as a *Relation . . . of the Beginnings . . . at Plimouth in New England*, by G. Mourt.

to the south of the Cape. This would be either the Sakonnet River or Narragansett Bay. But shoals forced them back around the Cape, and ultimately to settle at Plymouth.

From the London Company they had received fair promises but little else. Yet they did have their patent and time was slipping by. Although Sir Ferdinando's new patent for New England was assured, it had not yet passed under the great seal. A royal charter had been granted on July twenty-third, but until the patent was issued the Leydeners could hope for no formal permission from him to settle in New England, nor could he afford to steal these colonists from the London Company, much as he desired it and much as he had labored for fifteen years to build a New England colony. Both Bradford and Gorges in their writings are careful not to implicate him at this point, but as soon as the Pilgrims had settled in New England they sent back to him for a charter. If any further link is needed, Gorges' eldest son John had married the daughter of that same Countess of Lincoln whose "religious man" Wincob had received the patent from the London Company. Also there is the interesting fact that the London Company later tried to get his charter for New England revoked. Was this partly in revenge because they believed he had stolen their colonists?

The elaborate theories which have been erected to account for the Pilgrim's settling in New England—that the ship's captain was bribed to land them there, that Dermer was to meet and lure them in, that Gorges was plotting against them behind the scenes or the Dutch attempting to lure them to the trading post at New Netherlands—or to keep them away, seem as unnecessary as they are ridiculous. The Leyden folk planned to settle in New England before ever they left Holland. They had originally settled on some place south of Cape Cod, but may have been persuaded by Dermer's letter to go farther north. They had a gentleman's agreement with Gorges or someone who could speak for him by which their settlement was confirmed to them as soon as they asked for it, and under a patent finally sealed at about the time they reached the new world.

But the decision to head for New England was far from ending the difficulties of this much-tested group of the Lord's chosen people. Trouble now broke out in London over the agreement with the merchant adventurers. Weston, while in Holland, had seen and agreed to a set of conditions which were to govern relations between settlers and capitalists. But when he returned to London he either changed his mind or was persuaded by his partners to make two significant changes. These changes Robert Cushman agreed to, thereby exceeding the authority granted him by the Leyden group. The letters which now passed between Leyden and London grew full of accusations and recriminations, forsaking the spirit of love and brotherhood in which the brethren had been wont to deal. Even the gentle pastor Robinson cast his barb at Cushman, calling him "most unfitt to deale for other men, by reason of his singularitie, and too great indifferancie for any conditions, and for (to speak truly) we have had nothing from him but termes and presumptions."

Stung by his critics, Cushman jumped vigorously to his own defense. "If I doe such things as I cannot give reasons for," he wrote to Bradford, Fuller, Winslow and Allerton who now appear as spokesmen for the Leyden group, "it is like you have sett a foole about your bussines, and so turne the reproofe to your selves, & send an other." The irony of the ambiguous "another" was no doubt unintended, yet there was something to be said for Cushman. One investor had already drawn out his money. The whole enterprise was threatened unless Cushman bowed to the new terms.

What were the conditions that raised such a storm in Leyden?

First, the settlers were to retain no ownership of the land they improved or the homes they built, but all was to be equally divided between settlers and merchants at the end of seven years. Second, the settlers were refused two days a week to labor for their own needs, and were rather required to work unremittingly for the common interest.

To understand the furor these conditions aroused it is only necessary to recall the class distinctions which existed in seventeenth century England and to remember that Bradford and the Scrooby folk who formed the nucleus of the group were yeomen. A yeoman, as we have seen, had a good deal of pride and independence. He owned his land with as clear a title as English law then permitted. Though unlike the squire he got his living by the work of his own hands, yet he might have bond servants working for him—people bound in a kind of temporary serf-dom whose labor for a term of years was entirely at the command of their master.

And Cushman's terms, Bradford immediately saw, would make bond servants of them all. For seven years—the length of the contract—no man could earn a penny for himself. Each share in the joint stock company was rated at ten pounds. Each settler was equally rated. So the London investor who simply put in his ten pounds stood to gain exactly as much after seven years as the man who risked his life on a perilous ocean voyage and then labored unremittingly in the wilderness for the same length of time. The two points on which Cushman had yielded were thus the only avenues of escape from bondage and the only source of incentive to an able and enterprising man to improve land and property. Giving in on these two points was nearly to result in wiping out the colony.

As a matter of fact, the Leyden group never did acquiesce and when they finally left England for America they were on very poor terms with the merchants on that account. Yet once they reached Plymouth they honored the agreement Cushman had involved them in, with consequences that nearly altered the whole course of American history.

The result of all these difficulties was a rapid falling off in the number of those willing to make the voyage—so much so that other volunteers had to be found. Overtures were therefore made to Ainsworth's church at Amsterdam. No one knows by whom this was done, but as Bradford had now come to the fore as a leader and as his father-in-law was an elder of the Amsterdam congregation, it is more than likely that he was the negotiator. His own account is generally so careful to give credit to others while at the same time so reticent regarding his own activities, that the absence of credit given to another is pretty certain evidence that he himself was the active agent.

And with the departure to America imminent, it is not too much to assume that to Amsterdam with William went Dorothy and their son John, now a lad of five. For even a scrap of a letter or a line from a journal that would let us see this family group we would be grateful. But there is nothing. The story of William Bradford often has to be reconstructed from what is seen by

reflection and at a distance in time, as the astronomer sees only
reflected light, and that already old, in forming his picture of the
universe.

With some confidence then, if only by inference, we may imagine the three of them making the leisurely twenty-five-mile
voyage by canal boat—the cheapest means of travel. Young John
runs joyfully up and down the deck, fascinated by the motion
of the fields and buildings as they pass by, run after by his young
mother as he leans out over the gunwales and reaches for the
water, forgetting to eat the food that is handed him from a
basket at noon because of the wonder of things about him, finally
falling asleep in his father's arms, unconscious of his pretty
mother's warm eyes resting on him and on the man who holds
him.

We may hope that Dorothy May's visit with her parents was
a pleasant one, but as for William, the agreement reached with
some of the Amsterdam congregation was in a short time broken
off and Robert Cushman was celebrating the event in these none
too charitable words: "As for them of Amsterdam I had thought
they would as soone have gone to Rome as with us; for our
libertie is to them as ratts bane, and their riggour as bad to us
as the Spanish Inquision."

The Pilgrim love of liberty was as "ratts bane" to a good many
of those they had to deal with; but as it is the foundation of
ours, it will bear watching. Cushman's phrase, incidentally, provides interesting evidence that the Pilgrims thought of themselves as freedom-loving.

Desperate now for enough colonists to make up a group able
to cope with the dangers and uncertainties of the wilderness,
the London merchants began to recruit anyone who was willing
to accept the terms and who looked capable of the kind of labor
that would return a profit. So now the colony would not be a
homogeneous group of like-minded men sharing the same religious beliefs. It would be made up as much of strangers as
"saints." This too was a hazard that had not originally been foreseen, spelling trouble for the future.

And not entirely for the future. For already one of this group,
a Christopher Martin of Billerica in Essex, had been chosen to
represent the "strangers" and to act with Carver and Cushman

as an agent in the purchase of supplies and in making other arrangements for the voyage. It was an honest gesture on the part of the Leyden group. But, as Bradford remarked, it "turned to great inconvenience unto them, as in the sequell will apeare; but however it shewed their equall & honest minds."

As might have been expected, the three agents were soon at loggerheads. Carver was at Southampton, the port from which the Pilgrims planned to depart, buying supplies against the wishes of Cushman and Weston in London. Martin took himself into Kent where he bought whatever caught his eye. With some truth Robert Cushman complained, "We will, with going up & downe, and wrangling & expostulating, pass over the summer before we will goe. And to speake the trueth, ther is fallen already amongst us a flatt schisme; and we are redier to goe to dispute, then to sett forwarde a voiage."

This was the state of things in June 1620. By this time the Pilgrims, to have a safe winter ahead of them, should have reached the new world and planted their crops. Yet they had never seen themselves as a self-sufficient plantation once they reached America. It was their plan to raise some food but to rely upon fishing and trading with the Indians for their principle source of income. King James himself had been informed that fishing was to be their principal calling. "So God have my soul," he had exclaimed, " 'tis an honest trade; 'twas the Apostles' own calling."

Both for coasting voyages and for fishing the Pilgrims would have to have a seaworthy ship. And for this purpose the *Speedwell*, a small craft of sixty tons, was bought. She had to be overhauled and provided with a new suit of sail and larger masts. Perhaps this fell to Bradford too, though he was cumbered now with much business looking toward the departure; for the work was done in Holland. Whoever had the management of it was soon to regret that he had had any part in it.

The summer slipped away, but at last they were ready. A day of "solleme humiliation" was held, the most part of which Pastor Robinson filled "very profitably" with a sermon on the text: "And ther at the river, by Ahava, I proclaimed a fast, that we might humble ourselves before our God, and seeke of him a right way for us, and for our children, and for all our substance."

There followed a feast at the pastor's house, given to the departing by those who had chosen to remain behind. Winslow, by no means an uncultured man, remarked that the psalm singing which followed "was the sweetest melody that ever mine ears heard."

Apparently on the next day the Pilgrims set out for Delft Haven, accompanied by most of the congregation who were to remain behind as well as by some of their friends from Amsterdam, amongst whom must certainly have been Dorothy's parents. "So," says Bradford, "they lefte that goodly & pleasante citie, which had been their resting place near 12 years; but they knew they were pilgrimes, & looked not much on those things, but lift up their eyes to the heavens, their dearest cuntrie, and quieted their spirits." Here in this sentence Bradford came as near as any of the congregation ever did to giving themselves a name, though not until about 1840 did the Pilgrims come to be commonly known as such.

The journey from Leyden to Delft Haven was only a matter of some twenty miles, most easily accomplished by canal boat since they had all their household goods to carry with them. No spot in Leyden is very far from a canal, and the Pilgrims lived close to the Rapenburg which Polyander had so highly praised. At the Nun's Bridge, then, they no doubt embarked, with many last-minute comings and goings to get all their goods aboard.

Down the quiet waters of the Vliet and past the water gate they went, and so out into the country through the rich Holland fields. Turning away from The Hague toward Delft at the Hoorn Bridge they sailed parallel with the highway for five miles, on through Delft with its gates and then on a straight course to Delft Haven, carried all the while on a water course high above the surrounding pastures. Passing through one set of sluice gates after another they were finally lifted to the harbor level and so to the waiting *Speedwell*.

There once again were prayers said and a feast spread. That the occasion was a tearful one both Bradford and Winslow have testified. Almost embarrassing to the modern reader is the openness with which tears flowed. Arriving too late to set out on the same day, both Pilgrims and friends sat up through the night, so precious were these last hours together.

"The next day," says Bradford, "the wind being faire, they wente aborde, and their freinds with them, where truly dolfull was the sight of that sade and mournfull parting; to see what sighs and sobbs and praires did sound amongst them, what tears did gush from every eye, & pithy speeches peirst each harte; that sundry of the Dutch strangers that stood on the key as spectators, could not refraine from tears. Yet comfortable & sweete it was to see shuch lively and true expressions of dear & unfained love."

Fashions change, in habits as well as hats. It caused no embarrassment to these sincere people to let the tears stream down their faces, and who can say that this honest outpouring of the emotions is not the better way?

If any excuse were needed for the unrestrained grief of these partings, it may be found in the severance of the families involved. Mistress Brewster left behind her eldest son Jonathan who had but recently lost his wife and child, and with him her two daughters Fear and Patience, the former in her early teens. Francis Cooke took along his son John, parting from his wife and three small daughters. Thomas Rogers, John Crackston, John Turner, Degory Priest, Deacon Samuel Fuller, Moses Fletcher—even John Goodman who had been married but a few months—left their wives behind and in some cases children too. Many, dying in that cruel first winter, were seeing their own flesh and blood for the last time.

And here too Dorothy left her little five-year-old son John, possibly with her parents. His scared cries, his pleadings, his struggles as he realized that he was being separated from her must have rung in her ears for the rest of her short life.

Other children as young as John or younger made the voyage— Remember and Mary Allerton, Wrestling Brewster, Resolved White. Why had the Bradfords decided to leave him behind? But one reason seems likely—the fear that conditions at first might prove too hard for him. They may have thought him a delicate child. In any case they fully expected their pastor and many of the others to follow as soon as they were established, and of course to bring John with them. In seven years of marriage Dorothy had borne but one child who lived. The instinct of motherhood, it seems, would have led her to take John with her. Was she overruled? And was this a reason for the tragedy soon

to befall her? Little is known about "Dority." But of one thing
we may be sure—that of the tears that flowed on that memorable
day, a share were hers. It is a small thing to be rescued from the
obliterating wash of over three hundred years, but it brings her
close to us. Here, on one foreign shore and bound for another,
a young mother wept for her son.

"In Perils of Waters"

AS the high chalk cliffs of Dover came in sight, William Bradford had a view of his homeland for the first time in twelve years. The *Speedwell* coasted past neat English landscape where towns stood forth from the rich summer foliage with a kind of precise clarity in the warm flood of sunshine. So bright was the glare on the water that he had to squint to see the shore. There was plenty to see, for Dover was but halfway between Delft Haven and Southampton where they were to meet the *Mayflower*. Past Folkestone and Hastings, past Brighton and Portsmouth the little ship made her way and, with the Isle of Wight on her port side, up into Southampton water.

With its walls, towers and castle, Southampton had from the water a military aspect not at all resembling the rural village Bradford had left twelve years before. Yet when the *Speedwell* tied up to the calls of English dockhands, Bradford felt that peculiar stirring of the heart known only to a man who has lived for years in the insulating atmosphere of a foreign language and has at last come home.

Though Southampton was almost as far from Austerfield as Leyden had been, there was at least an English look and an English sound to it that summoned up the remembrance of things past. Yet even if he had been able to make the trip, there would have been little to attract William Bradford to Austerfield now. His sister Alice had died in 1607 just before he left for Holland,

his Uncle Robert in 1609. Though Austerfield and the neighborhood were full of cousins of all degrees, none of his immediate family remained. As for the lands that had once been his,
what remained of them traveled with him in the ship, transformed into supplies that would be useful in the new world.

Looking at the loiterers on the dock, William Bradford's mind
came to focus on a more immediate problem, and he looked
eagerly for a familiar face. The fact was that the Leydeners
were greatly concerned over their elder, William Brewster, who
had found it the better part of wisdom to keep himself hidden
ever since the hue and cry over the printer of *Perth Assembly*.
For printing works no less offensive men had been hanged in
England. Yet it was in England rather than in Holland that
Brewster had apparently chosen to hide, and now came the
ticklish business of getting him out of the country before he
could be identified and stopped. Since Brewster was to be the
spiritual leader of the group in the new world, and since the
whole motive of the hazardous voyage was religious, the anxiety
Bradford felt for the safety of his virtual foster father was
acute.

Yet stronger than anxiety was the feeling that his talents were
soon to be tried in the balance, and in a cause to which he had
dedicated his life. During the months just past a new experience had come to him—the recognition of his ability as a leader
of men and as an efficient agent for their interests. You could not
yet call this a talent for government, although the Leyden congregation was so self-contained, so self-sufficient that it was almost
that. We would call it today administrative ability. The discovery
of it within himself had come to William Bradford with something of the same impact on the spirit as his first religious awakening. To know that one could manage affairs and men—this,
after the rural life of Austerfield and the long hours of drudgery
as a weaver, disclosed new prospects of living of which he had
scarcely been aware. Nor was it simply that he would be exercis-
ing these new-found talents for his own good. The planting of a
colony in the new world was to him and his companions a work
shared with God. The Pilgrims saw in their venture a close
parallel with the entry of the Jews into the promised land.

The *Mayflower* with its load of "strangers" was already waiting at Southampton. Hurrying aboard at the first opportunity, Bradford found his beloved foster father Brewster somewhat ignominiously hiding below deck and protected with the alias of Mr. Williamson. (Brewster's father had also been William.) It was imperative that they set sail as soon as possible, before Brewster could be identified and apprehended. But the *Speedwell* had proven to be a wet ship, even on the Channel crossing. Before she could sail, changes had to be made.

Bradford found the delays and disagreements which greeted them in England both inappropriate and vexatious. The squabble with the London merchants had now come to a head, the Pilgrims refusing to sign the articles Cushman had agreed to while Weston cursed them for an ungrateful crew and refused to advance the large sum, nearly a hundred pounds, which they needed to clear the port. Christopher Martin was acting high-handedly about the management of his share of their affairs, flying into a rage when asked to account for his expenditures. To settle their debts, the colonists had to sell sixty or eighty firkins of butter, thus leaving themselves with only a small supply of that commodity and without oil, or soles to mend their shoes.

At last on August fifth, with some of the passengers transferred to the *Mayflower* of which Martin was chosen governor, the *Speedwell* with Cushman as governor put out to sea at the stern of the *Mayflower*. As two or three assistants to the governor were also chosen for each ship it is likely that Bradford was one of these and that he remained on the *Speedwell*. "The cheef of them that came from Leyden wente in this ship to give the master contente," he says.

The *Speedwell,* however, soon belied her name. She sped so ill that the two ship's captains decided after a conference to put in at Dartmouth where she could be searched and mended, at an expense which the colonists could ill afford. After these repairs everyone was sure the ship was seaworthy, yet within a hundred leagues of Land's End she was leaking so badly that Captain Reynolds said he must take her back to port. Back they went to Plymouth where careful searching discovered no leaks at all. It was therefore concluded that the ship must have some general weakness which no repairing could overcome. As a matter of fact, she had probably been overmasted in the re-

fitting in Holland and was crowded with too much canvas, for
after returning to London and being put into her old trim "she
made many viages & performed her service very sufficiently, to
the great profite of her owners."

If Bradford had been congratulating himself for the efficiency
with which things had been done in Holland while the agents
in England were at loggerheads, the experience with the *Speedwell* must have been very chastening. He would have taken it as
a direct mark of God's displeasure with him for having thought
himself a better manager than the others. Perhaps this was the
beginning of that willingness to defer judgment which we shall
see in him later on. For although he was thorough in condemn-
ing a man once he had made up his mind, he always showed
himself willing to listen to the other side. Yet in assigning causes
for the failure of the *Speedwell* he laid a good share at the door
of Reynolds who, having contracted to remain a year in the new
world, had apparently got cold feet.

Abandoning the *Speedwell* was a bitter blow to the colonists,
who had counted on it as the cornerstone of their economy. Fishing and trading for fur, as Captain John Smith had pointed out,
were the most likely sources of income. The Pilgrims never
planned to be self-sufficient. They counted on making enough
profit from their principal occupations to buy what they needed.
Sailing without the *Speedwell* would necessitate a fundamental
change in their plans.

Abandoning the *Speedwell* meant turning back some of the
passengers. By this time more than a few were glad of an excuse
to put back, among them being poor Robert Cushman who to
all his other crosses had added that of being woefully seasick. His
letters show him to have been a pessimist, never too strong in
body, inclined to peevishness and complaining. Yet the job he
had taken on was a thankless one, which might have driven any
man into a frenzy. Bradford makes perhaps the most charitable
judgment when, after remarking that his heart and courage had
gone from him, he says that "after this he continued to be a
spetiall instrumente for their good, and to doe the offices of a
loving freind & faithfull brother unto them." Still it is clear
that Bradford, with his new-found strength in dealing with men,

and with his strength of body and spirit, had perhaps too little patience with a man of Cushman's sort.

Seven weeks after leaving London the *Mayflower* * finally set sail from Plymouth—probably after some contact with Sir Ferdinando Gorges who was "governor of the forts and island of Plymouth." It was now September sixth (the sixteenth in present style)—close to the equinox and almost certain storms on the Atlantic. The colonists had been reduced to one hundred and two—a large number for a ship of one hundred and eighty tons, though the *Mayflower* was not a small ship for her day. She was, in fact, a high-pooped, deep-bellied vessel measuring one hundred and thirteen feet from the taffrail aft to the end of her beak under the bowsprit. Her greatest beam was twenty-six feet, with a stern twenty-seven feet above the water when loaded—a point to be remembered in view of the fate in store for Dorothy Bradford. She carried three masts (the mizzen mast being fore-and-aft rigged) and was double decked. On her main deck she carried a forecastle where the crew of thirty were housed, with a poop house and cabin aft. Below this were three levels for cargo, stowage, water casks, spirit stores, sail lockers. The cook's galley was all the way forward and beneath the forecastle.

With the captain in the poop house and the crew in the forecastle, where did a hundred and two passengers sleep? They had the cabin, of course—a space perhaps some twenty feet square. The single men were probably accommodated in the tween decks under the main hatch. But as this would still scarcely allow enough room for so many people to lie down in, it is probable that the captain shared his quarters with them.

When the *Mayflower* finally set sail from Plymouth most of her passengers had already been aboard her for seven weeks, with another two months ahead before they would sight Cape Cod. How did they live?

To us the conditions would have been intolerable. There were no sanitary conveniences—no toilets, no washbowls, no provisions of any kind for bathing. Water in any case was a precious commodity aboard ship, not to be wasted on washing. For bodily necessities only a slop bucket was provided. It must necessarily have been used practically in public—perhaps in a crowded

* *Mayflower* details are based on Nickerson's reconstruction. See p. 329.

corner with a bit of curtain to screen it. To these discomforts was added, of course, the curse of seasickness. As that misfortune always seems to be induced sympathetically, conditions in the crowded quarters must have been offensive in the highest degree.

Food for the most part was eaten cold by the passengers, though the crew was served hot meals from the cook stove in the galley. When the passengers could no longer swallow the hard biscuit, cheese and salted beef or fish which made up their diet, they could have hot food only by cooking over an open charcoal fire laid in a box of sand. Having no coffee, tea or chocolate, their drink three times a day was beer—and lucky they were to have it, as the sequel will show.

Even more upsetting, especially to the young married couples like the Bradfords, must have been the arrangements for sleeping. As the available space made it impossible to set up beds, most of the passengers must have slept in hammocks or on the decks with whatever pallets, mattresses and blankets they could come by. There were some built-in bunks, and the married couples would have had first claim on these. In all likelihood the passengers never removed all their clothes from one end of the voyage to the other—or for some time afterward, since they had little privacy for months after going ashore.

Separated from her little son and her parents, Dorothy needed to be alone with her husband. She needed more than ever the peace which had settled between them when he had read to her from his Bible, or when he had talked to her with shining eyes about the future, or when he had led her to bed with manly impatience. They had no life of their own now—nothing but a few hurried, shame-filled moments when need growing heavier than modesty brought them together in the bunk of the pitch-dark, crowded cabin where perhaps they had been able to pin up a curtain but could do nothing to shut sound in or out. This degradation of what had been sacred between them—for even their pastor had spoken of the sanctity of married love—was a hard thing for Dorothy to endure. Home and family were her life, and both had been snatched away from her.

William had other interests, other drives to sustain him. After his "soon and long sickness" he had developed a sturdy physique, as events were soon to prove. His energy, his curiosity, his responsiveness to new scenes and new situations carried him where Dorothy could not follow and made her, almost in self-defense, draw back as if such spending of energy would infect her and prove beyond her strength. Yet at the same time she could admire what she could not be. For it was soon apparent that Bradford was the most popular of passengers. Dignity and a sober sense of mission he had. Yet there ran out ahead of him an eager interest in his fellowmen which drew others to him. He had that quality of intellectual curiosity which always marks a leader among a roomful of men—a quality of testing as if with invisible antennae the attributes of each environment he enters.

He watched the motions of the sailors as they ran up the ratlines to reef sail. He marked the devices by which the ship was made to sail her course despite a contrary wind. He asked questions of the captain when with sextant and compass he took his bearings. He made it his concern—not as a duty but because he was interested in people—to know the strangers who had joined the company from homes in England.

Who among the passengers would have interested him most? Brewster, of course, his teacher and the man he regarded as a father, was after Dorothy the nearest of all. After more than a year's separation while Brewster was hiding in England, Bradford would have made the most of his opportunity to talk with this well-informed, much experienced man. They had news to exchange—Brewster of his trials in England, Bradford of the congregation at Leyden and of the things that had been done in preparation for departure. They discussed the strangers on board, speculating upon the effect their number (sixty percent) would have upon the colony and no doubt thinking of ways by which they might be kept in hand. For the Leyden group considered the colony theirs; they had no intention of abdicating in favor of the newcomers. Discussion of the form this colony would take since, as their pastor had pointed out, they would "become a body politik," must have used up many an hour, perhaps with John Carver, Isaac Allerton (later to prove their Judas) and their physician and surgeon Sam Fuller (like Bradford once a say maker) taking part. Edward Winslow too, though only twenty-five, was already showing an ability to deal with men. He may have joined in.

There were also a few men among the strangers whose opinions were sought. But John Billington, the only man aboard
who was exactly Bradford's age, was not one of them. It is clear
Bradford never cared for him—which perhaps is just as well in
view of the fact that ten years later he would have to condemn
him to death by hanging. Nor would Christopher Martin have
been included. Martin throughout the voyage was the chief
thorn in the flesh of the much-suffering passengers. He may have
served his purpose as a counter-irritant, keeping their minds off
the well-nigh insufferable stench and crowding, but it is doubtful whether anyone aboard could command philosophy enough
to accept him on this basis. "He so insulteth over our poore people, with shuch scorne & contempte," said Cushman, "as if they
were not good enough to wipe his shoes."

But Master William Mullins, a man of some substance, would
have been welcomed in counsel. Richard Warren, also dignified
with the title "Master," was soon found to be "a usefull instrumente," while Master Stephen Hopkins was deferred to as the
only man among the passengers who had hitherto visited the
new world.

Amongst all these strangers, however, was one whom the Pilgrims had persuaded to accompany them and who from the very
beginning was a member of the small, innermost council though
not a member of the Pilgrim church. This of course was Captain
Miles Standish whose very name (*miles* is Latin for soldier) bespoke his profession. Short, stocky, with red hair and beard and
a ruddy face which quickly took fire when he lost his temper,
Standish was dubbed "Captain Shrimp" by his enemies. "A little
chimney is soon fired" was the way they pinned his character to
paper. But the men who worked with him found him a stalwart
and dependable leader. As a young man he had, like many other
Englishmen, gone to fight the Spanish in Holland. It is likely
that he met Robinson and perhaps some of the other Leydeners
before the English troops were withdrawn in 1609. What happened to him in the intervening eleven years no one knows.

One of the most unfortunate errors popularly made about the
Mayflower company is that they were elderly people. Such paintings as the fanciful representation of the signing of the compact
or the landing at Plymouth tend to confirm this mistake. As a

matter of fact of all the one hundred and four passengers on the *Mayflower* (counting Oceanus Hopkins who was born at sea and Peregrine White who was born on the *Mayflower* after the new world had been reached) only four had reached their fifties. They included Brewster and Carver, each fifty-four, and Mrs. Brewster who was fifty-two. James Chilton, a stranger and a tailor from Canterbury, was the oldest of the whole lot, and he was fifty-seven. Two more, Francis Cooke and Christopher Martin, had passed forty while two, Degory Priest and William Mullins, had just reached it. Of the other married men Bradford, Fuller, Standish and Hopkins were in their thirties; Goodman, White, Winslow and Eaton in the twenties. Ages of most of the wives are unknown, but where known they run from two to fourteen years younger than their husbands.

Then comes a group of men, mostly in their twenties, who came alone. Eleven of these were bond servants, but among them were men like George Soule, Edward Dotey and John Howland who worked out their time and became valuable citizens. Four were sailors, hired to stay and help the little colony with its intended maritime ventures. The rest, all but one, were from the London group. All of these but Peter Browne and Gilbert Winslow, a brother of Edward, died within a few months of their arrival, so we know almost nothing about them. The last of this bachelor group was, of course, John Alden who, far from being the scholar Longfellow has depicted was tall, muscular, and blond—a cooper, a maker of barrels. The colonists had engaged him at Southampton because of a law requiring that when barrels were taken out of the country, a compensating number of barrels or new staves must be brought back. To tend the numerous barrels of water, beer and wine during the voyage and to cut new staves for shipment back home, the Pilgrims had hired Alden though "left to his owne liking to go or stay when he came here." He chose to stay, and as all the world knows, the cause thereof was Priscilla Mullins. Just twenty-one, his practical knowledge of carpentry was an important asset to colonists who must build everything they needed.

As against the twenty-three unattached men there were but three girls—Priscilla, who was eighteen, Desire Minter, twenty, and a maid servant of the Carvers' whose name has been lost,

and who married soon after the arrival at Plymouth but died a
year or two later. There must have been something wrong with
poor Desire, whose name suggests a hankering never to be satisfied, for despite the lack of eligible girls she did not marry. In
1625 she returned to England and died there, apparently with
desire still unfulfilled.

There still remains the noisiest, most active group of all—the
children. Ranging in age from fifteen down to a "sucking child,"
thirty-three of them—nearly a third of the passenger list—
swarmed over the ship, pestering the sailors with questions, following them about at their tasks, learning no doubt some stiff
sea language their parents would have to beat out of them, rac-
ing each other up and down the gangways, popping into the galley to beg a biscuit or a cup of soup from the cook, raising such
a clatter as had never before been heard by English sailors en
route to the new world. Since twenty-five of the thirty-three were
boys, we may be sure that the racket was impressive. They also
no doubt raised the tempers of crew and passengers alike. But
they saved the colony. It was their presence which made Plymouth a permanent settlement instead of an expensive failure like
the many attempts which had preceded it. By bringing their
families, these colonists had committed themselves. They could
not turn back. And through the youngsters another generation,
and beyond that still others, were assured.

It happens that the Leyden and the English family groups were
of almost exactly equal size, each having seventeen men and ten
women (if Priscilla is reckoned as an adult), with fourteen Leyden children and thirteen from England (plus six servant children). In addition there were five hired men and eighteen servants. Bradford, incidentally, brought no servant—which may
mean that he had lost money in Leyden and could not afford
one, or that he preferred to invest it otherwise. Chief advantage of a servant would be that you could shift to him the heavy,
back-breaking labor of building a settlement in the wilderness.

If we include the two children born after the *Mayflower* set
sail, and the man servant who died during the voyage, there is
a total of a hundred and four passengers, seventy-five of whom
were males. On this slender human thread hung the destiny of
half a continent.

Another false notion about the Pilgrims for which admiring descendants are responsible is that they were noblemen, or at least gentry entitled to coats of arms. This is especially ironic in view of the fact that the chief distinction of the Pilgrims and their claim to our continued veneration is that they established a caste-free government of free men, making no attempt to duplicate the system of degree and station which existed in England and by which the leaders, if they had been smaller men, might well have hoped to advance themselves in the new world.

Not one of the *Mayflower* passengers was entitled to a coat of arms. Not one had completed a university course. Brewster came perhaps as close to distinction as any, and he had spent but a couple of years at Cambridge and had been postmaster in a small northern town. Standish at his death declared himself to be the rightful heir to the estates of the Standishes of Standish, a wealthy family. Why he waited until making his will to stake such a claim can only be guessed at, but his pretensions have been disproved.

Mrs. Carver's father, Alexander White, was the nephew of a poor lad who became Sir Thomas White and lord mayor of London in the time of Edward the Sixth. It has been claimed that William White, also a *Mayflower* passenger, was the son of another nephew who became chaplain to King James, and that Thomas Rogers was the grandson of John Rogers the martyr who went to the stake in 1555, a few months before John Bradford with whom he had been thrown in prison. Francis Cooke * was the grandson of Sir Anthony Cooke, a stout Protestant who had fled England in bloody Mary's time.

Efforts have been made to prove that Edward Winslow came from a higher step in the English stairway of classes. There is nothing to sustain this. As the eldest son in a family of eight children it seems unlikely that he would have been a printer's assistant if there had been a family estate to which he would succeed. The fact that he finally brought all four of his brothers to Plymouth throws further doubt on the story.

Unlike the soldiers of fortune who settled Jamestown or the well-to-do merchants, gentry and university graduates who settled Boston, the Plymouth group were humble folk. Though some, like Bradford, could claim the rather indeterminate title

---

* Banks in his *English Ancestry* (see Bibliography) contests this.

of "Master," not one signed himself "Gent." They were all working men—tailors, merchants, wool combers, weavers, sawyers, hatters, carpenters. They did something much more important for American history and legend than to bring doubtful distinctions of class from the old world. They were of the rising middle class, and they established in America the inspiration, the habits, the pattern of the "self-made man."

The *Mayflower* ploughed steadily westward across the Atlantic before a good wind and under clear skies. But she was, even for those days, a slow ship. It took her sixty-five days to cross from Plymouth to Cape Cod, at an average speed of less than two miles an hour. Remembering the fate that had overtaken the Amsterdam congregation, Bradford and his friends had good reason to fear the effects of a late season voyage.

Their fears were confirmed when the equinoctial storms came on, tossing and shaking the ship in a fearful manner. Weakened by long voyaging, foul air, lack of exercise, bad food and seasickness, the poor passengers were in no condition to endure the frightening toss and roll of the vessel, nor the showers of cold sea water that fell upon them through boards loosened by the working of the ship. No landsman could go through such an experience without being sure that the end was near. Yet there was worse to come.

In the midst of the storm one of the main beams amidships cracked with a sound which to these close students of the Bible must have seemed the crack of doomsday. But the provident Leydeners had brought along a "great iron scrue" which they contributed to raise the beam in place, after which it was made fast with posts and braces.

Still there was a question whether they should take the risk of going forward, or whether they must turn back if they wanted to save their lives. Even among the sailors there was great difference of opinion, but in the end Captain Jones decided that for all her leakiness in the upper works the ship was sound. So on they went.

Instead of abating, the storm grew worse, so that "they could not beare a knote of saile," as Bradford wrote, "but were forced to hull, for diverce days togither." In the midst of the storm while the ship tossed and rolled at the mercy of the wind, young

John Howland made his way up on deck from the intolerably crowded, stinking cabin for a breath of air and was immediately swept overboard into mountainous seas. He had the presence of mind to grab at the topsail halyards which were hanging over the sides. They let him fall astern and under several fathoms of water. Half-drowned, he was hauled up to the surface and caught with a boat hook, and lived to the ripe age of eighty—doubtless to repeat the tale to many an admiring audience.

The storms continued, and with them the misery of the passengers who by now were unable to keep dry or warm. John Howland's experience had taught them to stay below decks, yet here it was so crowded that a man could scarcely move without disturbing a neighbor or irritating his flesh by contact with sodden clothing. Nor would the tossing of the ship let him hunch himself against the cold and the wet, withdrawing himself inward to a small, untouched core of being. Forever the ship was throwing him out of the precarious balance he had established, forever stirring him to a consciousness he would rather avoid.

There was one passenger aboard who had still one more misery to add to the rest. Elizabeth Hopkins, in the midst of that harrowing voyage, labored and brought forth a son who was named Oceanus but did not live long enough to grow into such a name, dying at the age of seven. The death of William Butten, a young man who was servant to Samuel Fuller, left the number of passengers unchanged.

To a man of Bradford's energy the enforced idleness must have been almost beyond endurance, to be suffered only because whatever came to a man was from God. Yet champing and fretting there must have been, since he was both young and very human. The brunt of this would have fallen upon Dorothy who was apparently in no condition to receive added burdens. Those she had were to be borne silently, and she bore them. But the voyage had been hard on her. The very length and desperateness of it made a gulf between her and her son vaster than any she had dreamed of, and what she dreamed had been painful enough. One consolation was the presence of Elizabeth, Edward Winslow's wife—just Dorothy's age, married but two years and as yet childless. (She was never to know motherhood, dying within a few months of her arrival in the new world.) Of the nine wives who accompanied their husbands from Leyden three were of middle age and three were of age unknown. One other beside Dorothy and Elizabeth Winslow was in her twenties— Susanna White, sister of Deacon Samuel Fuller, the Pilgrim doctor. Both Elizabeth and Susanna, having been married at Leyden and having been of the select congregation there, would be well known to Dorothy. Toward Susanna she now felt espe-cially drawn because of little Resolved White who was just her own son John's age and because Susanna was great with child. It gave her both pain and comfort to tend the little fellow for his mother, who found it almost impossible to move herself safely about the rolling ship. The Whites had been able to bring Re-solved—why not they John? She found herself resenting her husband's decision, then feeling guilty that she should harbor such an unchristian feeling, then hugging little Resolved in a sudden wind of passion which he found puzzling and uncom-fortable, or perhaps merely attributed to the strange motions the world had of late acquired. She found too that when she thought of John, which was almost continuously, it was in the past tense as if he were dead. And dead he might be, without her ever knowing it for months. Half in resentment and half in love she would hug Resolved closer, seeking both atonement and solace in a flush of mingled emotions she did not understand.

And William Bradford, seeing her way with the child and knowing what it meant, wondered whether out of an equal love for his only son he had made the wrong decision in leaving him behind. When the storm had quieted he found it solacing to walk to the bow of the ship, there with the wind rushing by his ears to imagine what kind of world lay before him. The talents of leadership which he now felt within him were impa-tient to be set in motion. With the exhilaration of the young he had cast off what was past, raising his head toward the future and finding in the clean, astringent smell of the sea wind a promise that was good. The worlds of Austerfield and of Leyden were far behind, though what he had gained from them would serve him well for the rest of his life—a love of the land, a knowledge of growing things, a way with animals, all part of his sturdy yeoman heritage. And from Leyden the atmosphere of courageous independence, both in politics and religion, a love of cleanliness and good order, a capacity for good business and good government. Everything in the past had been a preparation for what lay ahead, even back to those ewe lambs of his great-great-grandfather which he had probably never heard of. That he was to be one of the most important (perhaps the most important) links between the best of old England and the qualities of a nation yet to be formed he had, of course, no notion. But he knew, and in his own fine words set it down, that what was now undertaken came from "a great hope & inward zeall they had of laying some good foundation . . . though they should be but even as stepping-stones unto others for the performing of so great a work."

The ship pointed her prow toward free land and free worship, ideals whose twinship was firmly established in the holy book. What better foundation could there be for a young man with zeal and ambition burning in his veins?

"After longe beating at sea," wrote Bradford with the memory of the experience still warm within him, "they fell with that land which is called Cape Cod; the which being made & certainly knowne to be it, they were not a litle joyfull."

The Pilgrims' first sight of land was the bold clay bluffs of Truro where Cape Cod Light stands today. Darkness, apparently, was coming on by the time they had made certain of their landfall, so they stood off shore until morning. The next day, November 10, was a harrowing one for Captain Jones, who had to deal with the meanest stretch of water on the American coast. For when he headed south along the shore according to the desire of the passengers, he was soon in a tight box. No navigator could get far in these waters without knowing the tides. After a morning's sail they suddenly found themselves off present-day Chatham and in the midst of such bars and breakers as threatened to destroy the ship—just where Champlain had nearly foundered fifteen years before. It took Captain Jones the rest of the day to get his ship out of danger, and he was doing well to extricate himself at all, according to competent nautical opinion.

During the night of the tenth the *Mayflower* was off the head of the Cape, jogging off and on until daylight. Then instead of

putting out to sea and running to the south she headed for
Provincetown Harbor, anchoring inside Long Point at mid-
morning of Saturday the eleventh. Apparently the Pilgrims had
made up their minds to settle in this area, for they made no
further effort to explore southward.

The long voyage was over. The hiss of the main cable as the
anchor was let down must have seemed to the passengers like a
sigh of relief and thanksgiving for that safe deliverance which
they had many times despaired of. The deck was crowded with
passengers too grateful for the sight of land even to mind the
curses of sailors who found their working space monopolized.
Youngsters were lifted up so that they could see over the gunwales—see the graceful curve of sandy shore shining golden
yellow in the morning sun.

But while William Bradford stood with Dorothy at his side
thinking of what lay ahead, she—perhaps with a sidelong glance
at young Resolved in his father's arms—looked back toward the
sun, the east, and the past.

Before anyone could go ashore there was a piece of business
to be attended to. Pastor Robinson in his farewell letter had
reminded the Leyden congregation that they were to constitute
themselves a "body politik." Just what form this act should
take, or how it should be approached, must have been a subject for long debate and meditation during the voyage.

There was no precedent for what must be done. To a man
of the seventeenth century the notion of complete independence
in government was unthinkable. When shaking off the Spaniard, even the stout Hollanders with their great love of liberty
had begged foreign potentates, including Elizabeth, to be their
sovereign, so ingrained was the concept of government from
above, so thoroughly implanted in European minds the notion
of fealty, of feudal allegiance and dependence. This feudal habit
of mind extended, as we have seen, to such vital things as ownership of land, there being at this date in England no such thing
as land held absolutely free.

The Pilgrims, then, thought in terms of this feudal background. Yet they surmounted it. Behind the remarkable docu-
ment which they made the foundation of their colony lay the

yeoman yearning for a sound land title, the Dutch adherence to the theory that the sovereign is accountable to his people, and the Congregational way in religion which was then the nearest thing to a democratic institution in the world and the fructifying source of American democracy. But there was also a special need for a government to which all would be subject.

During the voyage a good deal of bragging had come to the surface on the part of men who expected a holiday from all laws in the new world. Inevitably the decision of the Leyden group to settle in New England rather than Virginia had come up for discussion, and some of the strangers aboard had let it be known that since no patent was held from the Plymouth Company, they would feel free to "use their owne libertie" once they had reached land. It was partly to head off such action by "the discontented and mutinous" that a compact—"a combination" as Bradford calls it—was prepared.

In his claim of mutiny Bradford names no names. It might be expected that Stephen Hopkins would have been the leader of the discontented and mutinous, for on a previous trip to America he had been court-martialed for mutiny and rebellion, sentenced to death, and had only got off by pleading his wife's certain ruination. But Stephen Hopkins—if this was the same man—had come up in the world since that voyage eleven years ago. He now had two servants of his own and would scarcely encourage independence of all law, the first effect of which would be to rob him of his servants. Yet if we are to judge by the men who most often ran afoul of the law after the colony was established, we would guess that Billington and Hopkins were leaders. Perhaps Hopkins hoped to establish a settlement independent of the Leyden folk and had managed to attract Billington and some others into his conspiracy.

Whoever they were, the mutineers were prevented from carrying out their threats by a document unique in world history. As John Quincy Adams said, having rescued it in 1802 from nearly two hundred years of neglect, it is "the first example in modern times of a social compact or system of government instituted by voluntary agreement, conformably to the laws of nature, by men of equal rights, and about to establish their community in a new country." After acknowledging allegiance to King James, it obligates the signers to combine themselves into "a civill body poli-tick" by virtue of which they are to have the power to "enacte, constitute, and frame such just & equall lawes, ordinances, acts, constitutions, & offices, from time to time, as shall be thought most meete & convenient for the generall good of the Colonie, unto which we promise all due submission and obedience." By contrast with this specific and sweeping assumption of power and obligation, the formal statement of allegiance to James seems of little importance—rather like the "one red rose" or "five pep-per corns" due to a feudal lord from a yeoman whose land was otherwise his own.

Every male passenger known to be of age signed the compact, except the two sailors Ellis and Trevore who were not perma-nent settlers and were otherwise bound by seamen's contracts. Four of the ten menservants signed—Soule, Howland, Dotey and Leister. The other six did not—whether because they had not yet reached the age of twenty-one or because of the indentures under which they were bound is not known. But the fact that hired hands and servants did sign the compact indicates that there was no attempt to set up a closed corporation; rather the effort was made to include and bind all who were legally able to bind themselves. No attempts to depreciate the importance of the Mayflower Compact can wipe out the fact that it established government by consent, that it set up no hierarchies or privi-leged groups, and that it laid a sound foundation, probably even beyond the intent of its makers, for democratic govern-ment.

No trace of the original compact has ever been found, nor is there any certain reference to the existence of the original docu-ment after April 1621. The text, but not the signatures, was printed in London in *Mourt's Relation*, 1622. Bradford copied it—again without signatures—into his manuscript history, writ-ten between 1630 and 1650. Not until the publication of Na-thaniel Morton's *New Englands Memoriall* in 1669 were the names of the signers recorded, and this is the only way in which the list has been preserved. Morton must have copied from the original compact or from an official copy, but whatever he copied from is lost. If it existed, it would be beyond price.

Morton puts Carver's name first, following it with Bradford's and then with all the other prominent men. Whether this was the order of signing, or whether it is a re-arrangement of Morton's is now impossible to tell, useful as it would be to know whether this mark of favor was shown to William Bradford at so early a stage. Since Howland and Alden, then only servant and hired hand though they later rose to prominence, have been placed well up on the list while the other hired men and servants are at the bottom, it rather looks as if Morton were trying to create an order of precedence where none existed.

If this is what he was doing, there was good reason for him to put Carver first. For Carver was clearly the most affluent of the passengers. Of the nine men who brought servants, most brought only one though Winslow had three. But Carver had five. His wife had the only maidservant aboard. In addition they had as one of their household Desire Minter whose father was a member of the Leyden congregation. Deacon of the church, successful merchant, experienced negotiator with the London adventurers, John Carver at fifty-four was as clearly marked for leadership in the colony's secular affairs as was Brewster for religious leadership.

So when the compact had been signed and it was necessary to elect an officer whose powers would give it life, Carver was chosen—"or rather confirmed," as Bradford says. He does not tell us where Carver was first chosen, but the most obvious inference is that while the Leyden folk had picked him as their leader before leaving Holland, the new election was a confirmation of this earlier choice by all the tiny electorate. In any case, Carver's election was a further step toward dominance by the Leyden group even though, when hired hands and servants are counted, they made up about forty percent of the electorate.

The first response of the Pilgrims, upon finding themselves in a safe harbor, was to fall upon their knees and thank God for a safe deliverance. The making of the compact and the choice of governor was second. For with these men the first compact, entered into while they were still a secret congregation at Scrooby, was with God. It is perhaps impossible for most men of the twentieth century to understand or to experience the personal nature of this relationship. But we cannot understand William

Bradford without attempting to enter into his feeling of a close walk with God.

With these essentials attended to, all were eager "againe to set their feete on the firme and stable earth, their proper elemente."

But by the time they had finished their business it must have been well toward noon, and as the day was Saturday no lengthy exploration could be undertaken, since that would interfere with the Sabbath. Desperate as the Pilgrims were for water, firewood, laundering, and a place for the young ones to let out their pent-up energy, they made no exception to their observance of Sunday as a day of rest and worship.

A brief exploratory trip ashore on Saturday discovered nothing, but on Monday the women were rowed to the beach to wash the heaps of dirty clothes accumulated on the long voyage, thus establishing the New England tradition of Monday wash which lives on today. The men, meanwhile, those who were not guarding the women, brought the shallop ashore and began to repair the damage done by the storm and by "the people's lying in her." Others found shellfish—clams, mussels and oysters—enough for a feast so rich to their unaccustomed stomachs that many could not keep it down.

By the fifteenth it was clear that the shallop would need a good deal of work before she would be seaworthy. Instead of waiting any longer, therefore, sixteen well-armed men were authorized to go exploring under the command of Captain Standish. All were volunteers, and one of them was Bradford who, together with Stephen Hopkins and Edward Tilley, was named as a council of advisers to Standish.

From the fact that they had to insist on going before the majority would sanction it, it is clear that danger was expected. There lay before them, as Bradford said, "a hidious & desolate wildernes, full of wild beasts & willd men." For guidance they had Captain John Smith's map and his description of the country, which to the Pilgrims on a gray November day must have seemed altogether too optimistic. And Smith had been especially optimistic about this very section of the New England coast, which reminded him of Devonshire.

Though the Pilgrims did not know it, they were landing on a unique piece of the earth's surface. Nowhere else is there an annex to a continent like Cape Cod. Other peninsulas are rocky and rugged but this one is frail and sandy, a shifting heap of glacial remains where no bedrock has ever been found. Perhaps, with their trust in the Bible, it is as well they did not know they would be building on sand. In climate, soil and vegetation the area they were to claim is different from all the rest of New England, for geologically Plymouth is one with the Cape.

Well armed, then, and with Standish at their head, the sixteen explorers set out in search of wood and water. Doubtless the face of Dorothy, small with fright, was the last thing Bradford saw as he went over the side. After walking a mile up the beach the party was electrified by the sight of five or six men and a dog coming toward them. The Indians immediately turned and fled while the English pursued. Easily outdistanced by the swift-running savages, Bradford and the rest made camp for the night. The next morning they tried to follow again, but "soone lost both them & them selves, falling into shuch thickets as were ready to tear their cloaths & armore to peeces."

Though they failed to catch the Indians, the Indians managed to catch Bradford in a manner which provided the company with a laugh and a story that must have been told and retold until Bradford was heartily sick of it.

"We came to a tree," *Mourt's Relation* tells us, "where a young Spritt was bowed downe over a bow, and some Acornes strewed under-neath; Stephen Hopkins sayd, it had beene to catch some Deere, so, as we were looking at it, William Bradford being in the Reare, when he came looked also upon it, and as he went about, it gave a sudaine jerk up, and he was immediately caught by the leg; It was a very pretie devise, made with a Rope of their owne making, and having a noose as artificially made, as any Roper in England can make."

It is likely that Bradford thereafter kept his eyes open for such "pretie devises."

At length they stumbled upon a spring of fresh water, "being the first New-England water they drunke of, and was now in thir great thirste as pleasante unto them as wine or bear had been in for-times." To their teetotaling descendants, the Pilgrim love of wine and beer has always been an embarrassment, but to the Pilgrims these liquids were as necessary as meat.

Crossing the neck of the Cape, the exploring party now came out on the ocean side, then back in search of the river whose mouth they had seen from the ship, passing a pond of clear water on the way—one of the many glacial ponds on the Cape formed by the burying of huge blocks of ice. Next they came upon Indian cornfields and graves, and then the remains of a house including planks and a great kettle. In near-by mounds of sand the explorers found Indian baskets filled with corn, "some in eares, faire and good, of diverce collours, which seemed to them a very goodly sight, (haveing never seen any shuch before)." It is hard for one accustomed to Indian corn to imagine how exotic, how beautiful it must have appeared to these travelers, though they could not have known that life itself was held for them in the ears they now looked at. What they carried away was their seed corn in the spring. And the harvest it provided kept them from starving the following winter. To a farm-raised man like Bradford the exuberant growth of these ears when compared with the small grains of England must have given promise of abundant harvests and well-filled stomachs.

They were now on Corn Hill in Truro, and back near the mouth of the Pamet River which they had first set out to investigate. Actually the Pamet (as Bradford truly observed) is tidal water, running up into one of the largest of the dozen little valleys which extend east and west across the Cape. Having decided that it would be good harborage for the shallop, the adventurers headed back for the ship, Bradford with the image of Dorothy's fear in his mind knowing that she would not have an easy hour until he returned.

The shallop was still unfinished, though they had a capable ship's carpenter as well as John Alden and plenty of sailors to put her in shape. Meanwhile the *Mayflower* crew were grumbling about the delay, fearful of exhausting their food supplies and running into winter storms on the way home. As for the passengers, inactivity had been bad enough when voyaging had made it unavoidable, but with the land in view and with winter coming on, it seemed criminal. And as usual, idleness bred discontent, short tempers, and low spirits.

But at last after more than a week of waiting, the boat was ready and an expedition of thirty-three men, including Bradford and nine of the *Mayflower* crew, set out, steering again for Truro. This time Captain Jones was chief of the party. When bad weather forced the crew to take the shallop back to the ship, the Pilgrims went ashore. As the ground was now covered with snow, which blew about them all that day and night, and as they had waded ashore through icy water, they had a miserable time of it. When the shallop returned the next day, more corn was loaded aboard her from the supply at Corn Hill. Then, with a lack of regard for Indian property which has all too often been the white man's way of introducing himself to a native race, they opened several graves, adding a number of bowls and trinkets to the already purloined corn. One of the graves turned out to be that of a blond-haired man, apparently a European sailor, which the so-called savages had left undesecrated. After picking up a few more objects from Indian houses, the Pilgrims sailed back to the *Mayflower*.

By now the end of November had come (actually the tenth of December by modern reckoning), and still no satisfactory location had been found. The weather had turned cold, snow covered the ground, exploration in an open boat and sleeping overnight exposed to the weather had already begun to attack the health of the men. The ground was frozen so that building would be difficult and the seamen were openly hostile as a result of the long delay. Yet the Pilgrims had seen nothing that satisfied them as a place to "plant." Some were for settling at Corn Hill, but others—who apparently included Bradford—felt that it would be too inconvenient to haul their supplies up the slope, especially since every drop of water they used would have to be carried up.

Once again, on December sixth (our December sixteenth) an expedition set out, and again Bradford went with it as one of the ten "principall men" who took a few seamen with them. Again Dorothy feared his going. Her very fear now gave him confidence. From much tramping up and down in the country he had begun to lose his own fear as the unknown became the known and as the expected wild beasts and wild men failed to materialize, except to run away. Vast, fertile, and unploughed land excited him, for with his yeoman's love of land he could imagine what crops waited to be raised there, what merry fires could be made from the endless forests, what flocks and herds would some day grow fat and increase after their kind. Land—free land! There could be no safer, surer wealth than this. Perhaps he tried to tell her this. Certainly like all husbands he pooh-poohed her fears, thus bolstering his own resolution and fulfill-ing the pattern expected of a man.

And because he was young, and because after years pent up in a Dutch city, however beautiful, he had now been able to stretch his legs on open land again, and because he had an imag-ination capable of seeing beyond present discomforts to what with God's grace might lie ahead, he left the ship on this third discovery with a feeling of guilt because he was glad to go in spite of Dorothy's fears. Perhaps she read this in his face as he turned toward her before dropping down into the shallop. And possibly a sense of the gulf between them—of his readiness to do battle with the wilderness and her feeling of horror for it—perhaps this had something to do with the tragedy that lay ahead.

The shallop had not gone far before its occupants were literally frozen stiff, the sea spray having clung to their clothes as it blew against them in the bitter cold. Toward night they saw a dozen Indians busy on a near-by beach, but when the shallop headed in the Indians ran away. After making a barricade of logs and boughs the explorers slept—or at least spent the night. The place was Nauset, near the inner crook of the Cape's elbow. Exploring down shore in the morning, they found that the Indians had been cutting up a grampus. "So they ranged up and doune all that day, but found no people, nor any place they liked."

Again at nightfall they made a barricade and after supper lay down around a fire to take what rest they could. About midnight they were all awakened by a hideous cry and by the shouting of their sentry. All stood to their arms, but after a couple of shots the sound ceased. By five o'clock they were up again to catch the tide. After prayers, and while breakfast was making, some of the men started carrying things down to the boat. Some, in spite of Standish's warning, left their muskets there when they returned for breakfast. Then suddenly came a strange cry. "Woach! Woach! Ha! Hach! Woach!"

"Men, Indians, Indians!" yelled one of their company, and came running into the barricade pursued by a flight of arrows.

Standish and one other who had flintlocks fired immediately. The rest had to light the clumsy matches (fuses) which fired their muskets. When the men ran for the shallop to recover the arms they had foolishly left, the Indians wheeled out of the woods as if to cut them off, but were scared away by brandished cutlasses. Once the muskets were "let flye," the Indians calmed down a good deal—all but one lusty fellow who stood shooting arrows from behind a tree within half a musket shot until Standish made the tree fly in splinters about his ears, whereupon "he gave an extraordinary shrike, and away they wente all of them."

Bradford apparently never connected this attack with the rifling of the Indian stores, homes and graves which had been going on. Man of God though he was, he could not think of these savages as men entitled to the same respect or subject to the same love of their own property as Englishmen.

After chasing the Indians into the woods a way the explorers came back impressed with the fact that though their coats hanging in the barricade were shot through with arrows, no one had been scratched.

When further coasting in the shallop brought no likely place for a settlement into view, they decided to follow the advice of their pilot, Robert Coppin (or Coffin), who had been in the country before and who told them of a good harbor not far away. As they had brought Captain Smith's map with them in the *Mayflower*, it is strange they had not gone to this harbor before. Apparently they were determined to explore the whole coast for themselves and draw their own conclusions. Making what headway they could in foul weather, for it had begun to snow and rain, they soon lost their rudder in a rough sea and had to fight their way toward shore while two men struggled to steer the boat with oars. As night came on they raised more sail, whereupon the mast broke into three pieces and had to be cut away. They were now in a very dangerous situation—without sail or rudder, half frozen, and "in a very grown sea." When at last they had worked the ship into what they thought was Coppin's harbor he suddenly cried out:

"Lord be merciful unto us; mine eyes never saw this place before."

Coppin and the mate were now for running the shallop straight into the breakers. But a lusty seaman who was at one of the steering oars yelled, "If you are men, about with her, or else we are all cast away!" This they did with speed. "Be of good cheer and row lustily," he called after a while, peering through half-frozen eyelids at the shore ahead. "There's a fair sound before us, and I doubt not we'll find a place to ride in safety." Finally they got under the lee of a small island. Though exhausted and frozen, they felt themselves lucky to be alive. Some, who could no longer endure the stinging cold of the open boat, waded ashore through icy waves, taking their chance with Indians, and somehow or other managed to kindle a fire with their awkward flint and steel in the midst of the downpour, the wind, and the sodden condition of their tinder.

Having got through the night they were greeted by a beautiful, sunny day and with the discovery that they were on what seemed to be a small island uninhabited by Indians. They named it Clark's Island, in honor of the ship's mate who had risked his life to go ashore. The day was spent in thawing out and drying out, for the condition of their clothes must have been horrible. Even the stoutest were exhausted from what they had been through, and for once the profane seamen were no doubt glad of the Sabbath holiday which followed.

"On Munday," Bradford writes, "they sounded the harbor, and founde it fitt for shipping; and marched into the land, & found diverse cornfeilds, & litle runing brooks, a place (as they supposed) fitt for situation; at least it was the best they could find, and the season, & their presente necessitie, made them glad to accepte of it." This was Plymouth—so named by Captain John Smith long before the Pilgrims had set sail from old Plymouth.

So they sailed quickly back to the *Mayflower* where Bradford mounted eagerly to the deck and eagerly sought out Dorothy to tell her that her suffering was over and they would soon have a home of their own again.

But Dorothy's sufferings were already over; for Dorothy was lying, drowned, somewhere in the cold, clear, gently lapping waters beneath the ship.

"Hard & Difficulte Beginings"

AS the *Mayflower* headed for Plymouth from her anchorage near the tip of Cape Cod, William Bradford stood at the stern, his eyes trying to fix the place where the ship had rested. For this anonymous patch of water was the only monument there would ever be to Dorothy May, lying somewhere beneath its surface.

She had been drowned on December seventh, the day after he had left the *Mayflower* on the final voyage of exploration. For five days she had been dead and he had not known it. He had come back full of plans for settling their home in the wilderness, full of eagerness to tell her what he had seen, full of that tremor of excitement all wanderers since Odysseus have felt as they return to the one who waits. Could he have saved her if, instead of volunteering to explore, he had remained on the ship?

How was it no one had been able to save her, the ship lying at anchor in a quiet harbor? John Howland had fallen overboard in mid-passage, yet they had managed to save him. Could she have drowned without a cry being heard, close to the crowded ship? With the strength of her youth, could she not have kept afloat if she had wanted to live?

The mystery of Dorothy Bradford's drowning has never been solved. Bradford himself, careful to record many things of far less importance, merely says: "William Bradford his wife died soon after their arrival." Does this hide a suicide as some have guessed? Suicide was of course regarded with horror and if the rigors of the new world had led Dorothy to this way of releasing herself from it, Bradford might have hoped to bury the event in silence. Yet there was no evidence for suicide. Dorothy was young—still only twenty-three, and so far as we know as healthy as any of the group.

It is equally possible that Bradford's silence covered a feeling on his part that those aboard ship had been grossly negligent in failing to save her. Most of the crew and all the women and children were aboard. Even if Dorothy had wanted to commit suicide it is hard to see how she could have accomplished it if any determined efforts had been made to save her. The fact that swimming was at this time practically an unknown art, even among sailors, may have had something to do with it. But then why could a rope not have been thrown to her? It is a pity that Bradford's letter to her parents has not survived. Several years later he was still writing to them.

Poor Dority's death will always remain a mystery. Yet in a curious way it helped complete the making of a leader out of William Bradford. Once recovered from the initial shock, he threw himself so wholly into the work of settling that everyone soon recognized in him the man best fitted, in spite of his youth, to lead the struggling little colony.

Despite everything that lay behind the settlers—the irksome negotiations with the merchant adventurers, the faulty *Speedwell,* the perilous voyage, the conflict with Indians, the miserable weather that had met their exploring parties—despite all this, the worst of their trials were still before them.

The choice of Plymouth was one of the few fortunate things that had happened to the Pilgrims. There was no other place along the coast where they could have settled without arousing Indian enmities, no other place where they would have found open fields waiting to be planted. It is easy enough by hindsight to criticize them for not settling in Massachusetts Bay—a criticism they were applying to themselves within a few months. But it is also doubtful whether they could have survived there. The Massachusetts Indians, once learning of their weakness during the early months of 1621, might easily have wiped them out.

Plymouth had less to offer, either as a harbor or as farmland. But Plymouth kept them alive.

Wiped out by smallpox, the Patuxet Indians who once inhabited Plymouth had left an untenanted area into which other Indians feared to move because of the disease. Captain Dermer, after carefully exploring the New England coast a few months before the Pilgrims reached America, had reported that no other location in New England was as favorable.

On Monday, December 18, a landing party went ashore in the shallop to make a final selection of the spot where they would build. They looked at the trees, the berry bushes and herbs, the character of the soil. Still they were not satisfied. The next day they sailed to the present site of Kingston up a stream which they named after the *Mayflower*'s captain the Jones River.

Bradford pressed for a settlement on Clark's Island, the piece of land jutting out from a narrow neck into Plymouth Harbor. Here, he argued, they would be safe from Indian attack. But closer inspection proved the place unsuitable. Finally on December 20 they chose the Plymouth site.

Twenty men went ashore to begin building. Before they could put up anything to shelter them, they were drenched with a driving cold rain. The storm rose to a gale and the shallop had to be beached for two days, leaving the men with as little food as shelter. Out in the bay the *Mayflower* tossed and pulled at her anchor, making those within almost as miserable as those ashore. Amidst all this misery, Mary Allerton gave birth to a stillborn son, and within a few days was dead. Just as the storm abated, Sunday came round again.

So it was Christmas Day (a Monday) before the Pilgrims could begin to build their village. Believing that Christmas was a man-made institution nowhere decreed in the Scriptures, they held no holiday but made a start on temporary huts of turf, thatch and branches while others began to fell timber for permanent buildings. Those who stayed ashore that night were visited with another storm of driving wind and rain which came through their flimsy shelters and left them drenched, miserable and cold. This was the first Pilgrim Christmas. Weather continued to plague the Pilgrims for the next few months, yet the winter of 1620 was as a matter of fact unusually mild.

Gradually the buildings began to rise. From the harbor a road was marked out to the foot of "The Mount," known today as Burial Hill. Narrow lots were laid out along this street (now Leyden) and cottages built. Only nineteen cottages were planned at first, men without wives being assigned to families. But after the general sickness had done its work, not even nineteen were needed or built.

More important even than the cottages was a storehouse to which their goods could be removed from the *Mayflower*. Captain Jones and his men were impatient at the long delay—it was more than six weeks after the first landing before the Pilgrims began to build their town—and were anxious to head for England. A building of wattle and daub twenty feet square was put up, its roof thatched. It was not, as generations of schoolchildren were taught to believe, a log cabin, nor were any of the other buildings. Construction at Plymouth was after the fashion the Pilgrims had been acquainted with in their English homes— of wattle and daub, then when time permitted of frame and boards.

All the supplies were now carried a mile and a half by boat from the *Mayflower* to the storehouse, often in foul weather.

In the midst of all this activity, Bradford fell sick. Ever since the frightful cold and exposure of the third discovery which had ended in the selection of Plymouth, he had been complaining about his ankles. On January 11 while he was at work in the clearing he was so "vehemently taken with a grief and pain, and so shot to his huckle-bone [hip-bone] it was doubted that he would instantly have died." Moved to the common house which had now become a hospital, he recovered somewhat toward night.

But on the night of January 14 the common house, as full of the sick as it was possible to crowd them, caught fire. A spark had touched off the thatch roof which soon burst into flame. A spray of fire began to fall upon the defenseless sick beneath. Open barrels of gunpowder and charged muskets lay in the same room. Only a miracle—or quick action on the part of these hardy people—prevented the complete destruction of the building and possible severe injury or death by fragmentation from the ignited gunpowder. Those aboard the *Mayflower*, mindful of the several Indian alarms and the disappearance of a couple of the company in the woods, were certain that Indians must have attacked and left the little village in flames.

Although the fire was put out before it had seriously damaged the building, it gave the sick another setback and destroyed clothing and other items beyond price in this wilderness. Carver and Bradford had the greatest loss.

The sickness was soon raging throughout the small company. Combining the worst features of pneumonia, tuberculosis and scurvy, it killed as many as two or three a day. In January and February when the disease was at its worst there were often but six or seven sound persons to tend all the rest—to fetch them wood and make their fires, to cook and feed them and make their beds, to dress and undress them, to wash their loathsome clothes, bury the dead, and, as Bradford said, to do "all the homly & necessarie offices for them which dainty and quesie stomacks cannot endure to hear named." Among the stalwarts who went thus untouched through the sickness were William Brewster and Miles Standish.

At the height of his illness, Bradford begged a seaman for a small can of beer—on the theory then held by all the Pilgrims that drinking water was a dangerous business and one of the chief causes of their disease. The seaman replied that if it were his own father asking for beer he should have none. For the sailors were equally alarmed at the prospect of having to drink water on the voyage home.

Now, says Bradford, seeing a cause and effect in which Providence was immediately concerned, "the disease begane to fall amongst them also, so as allmost halfe of their company dyed before they went away, and many of their officers and lustyest men." Captain Jones, also impressed by this outcome, sent word to Carver that as many as needed beer should have it.

This is the way Bradford sees the story and reports it. For divine Providence was a thing immediate and present to him, not too remote or too busy even to see to it that the faithful had beer.

Finally on March twenty-first the last of the passengers came ashore from the *Mayflower*. By this time whole families had been wiped out, only three married couples remained unbroken, yet among the few families to come through without loss—Bradford does not say how Providence made this error—were the profane and contentious Billingtons. Rose Standish, Miles' loved wife, was dead, and Edward Winslow's Elizabeth. John Goodman, who had brought Plymouth's only dogs, a mastiff and a spaniel, would never see the young bride he had left in Leyden. William White left Susanna, Dorothy's friend, to tend her newborn babe and her five year old alone. Priscilla Mullins lost her whole family—father, mother and brother. Christopher Martin departed, leaving the plantation accounts in a woeful state. Of the four orphaned More children who had come as indentured servants, only seven-year-old Richard remained. "The greater halfe dyed in the generall mortality," Bradford wrote, "and most of them in 2 or three monthes time."

Thus weakened and with only a handful of well men, the Pilgrims had to build permanent houses, find sources of food supply, and prepare themselves against possible Indian attack.

The very lack of contact with the Indians scared them. Aside from the brief encounters during their exploring trips, the Indians had given them no trouble. Yet they had seen and heard enough to be frightened. Indians frequently "came skulking about them," sometimes appearing at the edge of the woods but fleeing if anyone tried to approach them. Pilgrims who had wandered afield had seen plenty of signs of Indian activity near by. One day toward the middle of February a Pilgrim had seen a dozen warriors marching toward Plymouth and had heard others he could not see. When he reached Plymouth and gave the alarm, those working in the woods dropped their tools and retreated to the buildings. When Standish and Cooke went back to pick them up, the tools had disappeared.

The next day two brilliantly painted Indians, appearing on the hill across the brook, made signs to the Pilgrims to come over. But when Standish and Stephen Hopkins approached they fled. The settlers hurried to add two large cannon to the two smaller ones already installed on the platform at the top of The Mount. The largest of these, a saker, weighed nearly a ton though its greatest range was three hundred and sixty yards.

Finally, about the sixteenth of March, a tall and handsome

warrior with very little clothing stepped out of the woods and marched into the settlement at the very moment when a meeting on the subject of defense was being held by the dangerously weakened company. He carried a bow and arrows and his hair was cut short in front but hung down long behind.

After the suspiciously reticent behavior of the Indians up to this time, the boldness of this man came as a surprise. Still more surprising was his "Welcome," spoken in English "which they could well understand, but marvelled at."

It was immediately apparent that this warrior, who gave his name as Samoset, had dealt with Englishmen—his first request was for beer. They had to substitute "strong water." It was from Samoset, finally, that they learned why there were no Indian inhabitants where they had chosen to settle and why the cornfields had been abandoned. It was Samoset who told them of the neighboring Indians, including the big chief Massasoit. Having feared the enmity of the Indian, the Pilgrims had now found one whose friendliness began to prove embarrassing. He refused to leave when night came, which forced them to keep a watch over him since in their weakness they were still suspicious.

The next morning they sent Samoset off to fetch some of the Wampanoags he had told them about. The following day he was back with five warriors who after eating danced and sang for the Pilgrims under the mistaken impression that the white strangers would appreciate the entertainment. How could they know that these men thought dancing a sin, or that since the day was Sunday the frivolity seemed doubly offensive? The warriors, incidentally, brought back the tools which had disappeared; also a few skins for trading. But much as they wanted to trade, the Pilgrims would not do it on the Sabbath. So the Indians were sent off with an admonition to bring more skins when they returned.

Samoset, who had taken up residence at Plymouth, was dispatched again when after four days the Indians had not come back. This time he returned with the news that the great chief Massasoit himself was approaching. He also brought with him the Indian who was to spend the rest of his short life as a resident of Plymouth and a companion to Bradford on his voyages and dealings with the Indians.

Squanto, who spoke more English than Samoset, had lived a full and much traveled life. If he had not, he would in all likelihood have been dead along with the rest of his tribe. But when the smallpox wiped out the Patuxets, Squanto had been in Europe. Carried first to England in 1605 by the exploring party under Captain George Weymouth, he had returned with Captain John Smith, the man who gave New England its name to balance the New Albion which he knew Drake had marked off in the same latitude on the other side of the continent. After putting Squanto ashore, Captain Smith had left Captain Thomas Hunt behind, with instructions to load his ship with fish and fur before sailing for England. But Hunt decided that slaves would make an easier and more profitable cargo. He rounded up twenty of the Patuxets, including Squanto who had just been reunited with his family after a separation of years. Sold as a slave in Málaga, Squanto had the good fortune to fall into the hands of the local friars who busied themselves to convert him. Somehow or other he managed to get to England and finally in 1619 came home with the same Captain Thomas Dermer who had reported Plymouth as the best place in New England for a settlement.

Coming eagerly ashore in search of his family after six years' absence, Squanto was horrified to find the entire village wiped out by the white man's disease. Homeless, he had gone to live with the Wampanoag tribe, of which Massasoit was chief.

Perhaps his long years abroad had accustomed him to different tastes and standards. It may have been that he looked with a somewhat European eye upon the discomforts and shortages of Indian village life, some examples of which we are soon to see through the eyes of Edward Winslow. In any case he preferred to live at Plymouth. From the day of his first arrival there, Plymouth was his home and Bradford his closest friend. Without his services as translator, agriculturist and adviser, Plymouth and the Pilgrims would have been but a footnote in American history.

But now the great excitement was not over Squanto but Massasoit who was finally persuaded to cross Town Brook with twenty of his braves, Winslow staying with the rest of his warriors as hostage. Met at the brookside by Captain Standish and a squad of armed men, he was escorted down the street through a lane of onlookers to one of the new and not quite completed houses. A handsome man, Massasoit towered over squat little Miles Standish as did all the other braves. He was painted a "sad mulberry." A deerskin covered one shoulder, a large chain of bone beads hung around his neck with a large knife hanging down in front and a small tobacco pouch behind. His followers had painted their faces black or red, yellow or white—"some with crosses, and other antic works; some had skins on them and some naked; all strong, tall men in appearance."

The Pilgrims took great pains to impress Massasoit. They had furnished the reception house with a rug and cushions. Governor Carver was not waiting there to receive him, but was ushered in after Massasoit's arrival with a flourish of brass and drums —dressed no doubt in his most impressive magistrate's gown of purple or deep red. Then, with Squanto and Samoset serving as translators, a plainly written treaty of peace and mutual aid was drawn up which—unlike most treaties—was with one exception faithfully kept on both sides until after Massasoit's death in 1661.

Relations with the Wampanoags proved, if anything, too amiable. Massasoit had no sooner left with his braves than he sent his brother with a large group to sample the English hospitality. They liked what they found—including the liquor— so well that they were back the next morning for more. Hungry Indians kept dropping in, often with all their families, until it was necessary to do something to prevent a serious drain on the already inadequate food supplies.

So Edward Winslow, whose wife had died on March 24 only a few days after the appearance of Massasoit, was sent to see what he could accomplish. Already marked as the diplomat among the Pilgrims, he left with Stephen Hopkins and Squanto for Sowams (now Warren), the Wampanoag headquarters. Massasoit was away from home but was sent for, and on his arrival the next morning he was presented with a suit of clothes and a red horseman's coat which pleased him greatly. Winslow deftly came round to the point that while the big chief would always be welcome, and any of his men when they had beaver to trade, the unrestricted visits of all and sundry would have to stop. Massasoit assented with good grace, though at a length which Winslow found "very tedious."

The Pilgrims, having eaten nothing all day, hopefully waited for supper. The reason for the Indian visits to Plymouth soon became apparent: they had nothing to eat at home. As if to atone, Massasoit invited them to share his bed with himself and his squaw. This they did, finding it not only hard but lousy. Their discomfort was further heightened when two more lusty braves came in and flopped down on the same couch, and also by the fact that the Indians had the disconcerting habit of singing themselves to sleep. These may have been some of the reasons why Squanto preferred Plymouth to Sowams.

The next day Massasoit bestirred himself and caught a couple of fish—two bass for a whole village! Winslow and Hopkins had had enough. Weak from lack of sleep and food, they made their excuses and headed for home.

With the beginning of a new year (March 25) Carver was re-elected governor. As events turned out, he had but a little time to serve. Shortly after the much-delayed departure of the *Mayflower* on April fifth, he was hoeing in a field when he grew suddenly very sick and staggered back to the village, complaining of a pain in his head. A few hours after lying down, his senses failed him so that he never spoke again, and within a few days was dead. He was buried, says Bradford, "in the best manner they could, with some volleys of shot by all that bore arms." It was many years, incidentally, before anything like a burial service was read at a Plymouth funeral. Such ceremony was thought too much like the church they had separated from. As for Mrs. Carver, she died soon after "of a broken heart." Two of the Carver servants had died before, the maidservant not long after. John Howland apparently had the good fortune to inherit his master's estate, and purchasing his freedom married Elizabeth Tilley.

With the death of Carver, Bradford's importance in Plymouth really begins. He was elected to succeed Carver, and continued to be re-elected until his death, except for five years when he insisted on being relieved. The selection of Bradford, not yet fully recovered from his illness, also marked a new deal in Plymouth's affairs. Standish was thirty-six, Winslow twenty-six, Alden twenty-one, and Allerton—Bradford's assistant—about thirty-four. None of these men were officers of the church. Plymouth never made the mistake which led to the theocracy of Massachusetts. Boston was dictated to by its pastors, but not Plymouth. It may in fact be significant that Plymouth had no regular pastor at all for many years and never within Bradford's lifetime had one it was entirely pleased with. Plymouth chose and controlled its pastors. Boston allowed itself to be controlled by them. The pattern of American democracy was formed in the Old Colony far more than at Massachusetts Bay. Perhaps that is why Americans have instinctively elevated the fact and myth of Plymouth above that of Jamestown or Boston.

The young men who now came to the fore were vigorous, determined, hard muscled, full of the optimism and driving energy of youth. A change came over Plymouth in the spring of 1621 which was not entirely a result of the weather. Decisions were more quickly made, plans more sharply drawn, projects more quickly accomplished. Bradford, Winslow, Allerton and Standish were all young widowers, and it is possible to see in the new spurt of energy a determination on the part of these young men to overcome their grief and to sublimate desires which now had no natural outlet. Since Cooke and Fuller had left their wives in Holland, all the civic leaders were in their prime and without women—a circumstance which has never been noted and which gives a picture very different than that popularly conjured up by the term "Pilgrim fathers."

For a colony so haphazardly formed, in the sense that none except Standish had been picked for proven qualities needed in the wilderness, the combination of abilities worked out remarkably well. Standish had bravery, military knowledge and the personality which is supposed to go with them. He was impetuous, often with a chip on his shoulder, and on more than one occasion he killed Indians without necessity. For him two and two always made four, even if the counting had to be done in the dark. He believed that the best defense is a strong offense, and he trained the inexperienced colonists into a fairly efficient fighting force.

Winslow was a natural diplomat with the open, friendly qual-

ity that immediately inspired liking and confidence. His wide
mouth, capable of a winning smile, did not disguise the quick
intelligence in his eyes or the sensitivity suggested by his small,
rather delicate hands. Soft of speech, patient, persuasive, he was
a perfect counterpart to Standish.* From the time when Bradford first sent him to treat with Massasoit, Winslow was Plymouth's ambassador—not only to the near-by Indians but on
several voyages to England and to open trade along the Kennebec. Greatly to Plymouth's regret he did not return from
England after 1646. His remaining nine years were spent in the
service of Oliver Cromwell, his last mission being as head of a
commission to conquer the Spanish West Indies. Dying on the
flagship of William Penn's father, he was buried at sea off Ja-
maica. Before this happened, however, he had managed to bring
four other brothers to Plymouth—Gilbert who came on the
Mayflower, John on the *Fortune* in 1621, Kenelm on a different
Mayflower in 1629, and Josiah who was sent over to straighten
out the Pilgrim accounts and succeeded only in making them
worse. Kenelm, official coffin maker to the colony, was Plymouth's only builder of fine furniture.

Winslow was also the first of the widowers to remarry. On
May 12, seven weeks after the death of his wife, he married
Dorothy Bradford's friend Susanna White and thus became the
stepfather of little Resolved whom Dorothy had cherished. This
was the first marriage at Plymouth and in keeping with Pilgrim
convictions it was a civil, not a religious ceremony, performed by
Bradford as governor in defiance of English canon law. This
"laudable custome" as Bradford calls it was picked up in the
Low Countries and is another evidence of the Pilgrim determination to keep church and state separate—and to ignore the
laws of England which ran counter to their religious convictions.

Marriage, Bradford explains, is "a civill thing, upon which
many questions aboute inheritances doe depende, with other
things most proper to their cognizans . . . and no wher found
in the gospell to be layed on the ministers as a part of their
office." This caution in handing over the reins to the church
is one of the remarkable things about Plymouth, considering the
religious motivation of the Pilgrims' removal to America and

* Of all the Pilgrims Winslow is the only one whose portrait has survived.

the tendency they might be supposed to have to thrust all responsibilities upon the church for which they had sacrificed so much. Is it not a fact too often overlooked that, while they spoke the language of the theological-minded seventeenth century, they were intent upon establishing a *commonwealth*, a way of life the full scope of which they dared not utter in a time when the divine right of kings still had a tenacious hold?

To complete the roster of the colony's leaders, Sam Fuller as deacon and physician combined healing with teaching in a manner that seemed perfectly appropriate to his Bible-reading friends. "A great help and comforte unto them," as Bradford testified, he owned a gentle and loving spirit. Healing was his vocation in the strong original sense of that word: he had been called to it. It was part of his nature; it was not a profession but a ministry, for Fuller understood that there is no health that is not of the spirit.

Isaac Allerton was a different sort. Elected the governor's assistant because Bradford was still weak from his illness, he soon made himself master of the colony's commercial affairs— with disastrous consequences that will be entered into later. Probably one of the Ancient Brethren at Amsterdam, admitted a citizen of Leyden two years after Bradford, he was regarded as a shrewd man of business and pitied for having lost his wife when he had three small children to look after.

That these young men should have been the ones to pick up the reins is perhaps not very remarkable. Most of the older men were dead. Brewster was the only man in the company over fifty who still lived. Whatever the elders had planned at Leyden, it is clear that Bradford and the younger generation wanted to create, under God and His guidance, a Christian commonwealth in which Scripture should be the guide but with civil and religious functions clearly separated. Their attitude is nowhere made clearer than in the matter of marriage. What Scripture does not specifically claim as a religious function remains a civil one. Powers not reserved by God for His church remain under civil authority. The distinction is, in a way, not unlike that of our Constitution which reserves to the states all powers not assigned to the federal government.

Surely one of the most remarkable things about the little government was the way a farmer (Bradford), a tailor (Allerton), a printer, an amateur physician and a soldier, all without experience or education in statecraft, successfully carried out an experiment in self-government which changed the course of world history. In the old world they would never have discovered what talents for governing they possessed. But the new world gave them that chance. And despite the fumblings, the setbacks and the errors, they proved their talents answerable to the difficulties and the opportunity.

To Bradford especially the challenge came with real impact. Still weakened with sickness, he fully realized the trust he had to fulfill. And as his strength returned he began to respond with that inner vibration felt by any capable man when a challenge is put before him. Bradford was devout, and his devotion taught him that God had assigned him to this great task. He had long since dedicated his life to establishing a Christian commonwealth. But never until this moment had his powers been fully tested. Never until this moment had it been at all certain that he possessed any considerable talents. As a youth, sickly and orphaned, he had retreated within himself. His religious awakening had begun in a retreat from the things of the world, in a search for certainty, for a vital relationship which could supplant his lost parents. In the community of the church he had found this substitute and also found himself—the larger self which is the individual become a part of a functioning group. But because of his youth, Bradford's part in the church community had not been conspicuous. The governing of the church was done by older men. But now there was a whole world to be built and governed —by young men. It is the youth of the Plymouth leadership that accounts for many of the differences between Plymouth and Massachusetts Bay.

As Bradford's administration started with the coming of spring, there was an auspicious beginning all the way round. Squanto, busily showing the settlers how to catch the alewives which would fertilize the corn hills and how the fields must be guarded until the fish had rotted beyond temptation to the wolves who liked to dig them up, helped give a hopeful cast to the reviving colony. Since everything else the Pilgrims planted came to nothing, it was Squanto's advice which made the difference between living and starving when the next winter came.

The relationship between Squanto and Bradford was vital to the life of the colony. Squanto attached himself to Bradford, probably lived in his household, was his adviser on Indian affairs, and his key to the strange and difficult new world. Making Plymouth his home, he set out to capitalize on his knowledge of England and English. He used his influence at Plymouth to lord it over the surrounding Indians and even made them think the Pilgrims kept the dreaded plague buried in casks and that he could get them to let it loose against any who neglected to win his friendship.

But Squanto was not to enjoy his influence uncontested. To Plymouth Massasoit sent one of his chief warriors, Hobomok, who also took up residence there, becoming the companion and adviser of Miles Standish. Between Hobomok and Squanto a rivalry soon developed which Bradford was keen enough to use to his own advantage.

Hobomok, says Bradford, was "a proper lusty man" who continued faithful and constant to his English friends until his death.

One summer's day Hobomok came running all of a sweat to Bradford with the tale that he and Squanto had been visiting an Indian chief named Corbitant (Cauntabant) who had begun a quarrel with them because they were friends to the English. Hobomok told how he had fought free of Corbitant, who had tried to stab him. But Squanto when last seen—it appeared that Hobomok had not stopped to inquire too particularly—had been in danger of losing his life and might even now be dead.

Bradford called together the handful of young men who made up his informal council. In short order they decided that such a challenge had to be met head on or they would soon be the prey of every Indian in New England. Captain Standish was to take fourteen men to Nemasket (Middleborough) and, if Squanto had been killed as they feared, to cut off Corbitant's head. Since there were no more than twenty grown men left, it is clear the Pilgrims were willing to commit the larger part of their strength in this contest. Whether Bradford himself went we do not know. Since he was never backward when danger threatened, it is likely that he did.

To gain the fullest possible advantage the attack was launched at night, the chief's hut surrounded. A few who tried to escape were wounded. They were later taken to Plymouth where their wounds were dressed and cured. Corbitant was not to be found, but Squanto turned up unhurt after all.

Many other sachems now came hustling into Plymouth to bind themselves in peace and friendship. Even Corbitant ultimately made his peace through the intercession of Massasoit but, as Bradford drily remarks, "was shie to come neare them a longe while after."

Pretty well occupied throughout the summer with farming and building, the Pilgrims turned as soon as possible to the trading on which they had originally planned to base their economy. On the eighteenth of September the shallop departed for Massachusetts Bay in search of beaver, with Standish in charge. The party made friends with the Massachusetts tribe and found plenty of beaver. As they were coming away some of the women ran after them to the shallop, removing the skins which were their only covering and offering them in trade. Needless to say, the Pilgrims accepted. But they were impressed by the shamefastness of the women, who tried to cover themselves with leaves and branches—an incident which must have put these avid Bible readers in mind of Mother Eve.

Bradford, though satisfied with the trade in skins, listened enviously to the report of Boston Harbor, wishing that his colony had been seated there. Yet it was too late to begin over again. Humble as Plymouth was, it represented an expenditure of too much precious effort to be abandoned. Even this early it was clear to Bradford that Plymouth was to be a very modest enterprise. Yet as he looked back to the perilous winter they had survived, it seemed as though they had come a long distance and that the Lord was with them in all their ways. Surely a part of the glow he felt came with the realization that he had proven himself capable. For the leadership, under God, was his. He found, sometimes, that it was necessary to humble himself for this surge of confidence that swept through him like a sudden wind. He had to keep reminding himself that it was

God's strength, not his own, which had kept the colony alive.

The wound made by Dorothy's death had healed considerably. In a day when deaths were so frequent and sudden a man had to learn to adjust himself. And Dorothy, if she had lived, might only have suffered a worse death in the general sickness. Given to searching the ways of God, he was willing to believe that her loss might have been a punishment for his loving her too well, and a means of directing all his energies to the saving and care of the colony. For now he, to whom the symbol of a father had meant so much, had become a father to the little community. They trusted his judgment, looked to him for guidance, depended upon him. The relationship was a fulfillment of a need that lay deep in his mind and far back in childhood. It healed the wound of Dorothy's loss, though still in the dark night he would turn restlessly in his lonely bed, needing and missing her.

Seven plank houses were built during the summer, probably under the general direction of John Alden and of Francis Eaton, a carpenter and shipwright. These were the only two men left alive who had followed woodworking trades.

On their first coming ashore the Pilgrims had thrown up temporary shelters of wattle and thatch. They had followed these with the common house which was probably of wattle and daub —a kind of primitive clay plaster laid upon wattles or rushes which were fixed to a rough framework. The haste with which this first semi-permanent building was completed makes it clear that it could not have been of plank construction. The ease with which the roof caught fire and was consumed while the sick lay beneath it confirms the fact that it was of thatch, as were the roofs of Plymouth for some time to come. This common house (which never shows on the popularized but inaccurate pictures of early Plymouth) continued to be used for meetings until the erection of the fort the next year.

The dwellings which went up during the summer were of more permanent fabrication. They were *not* log cabins; the Pilgrims knew nothing of such construction. First a sturdy frame was built. To this were fastened vertical boards. The roof was thatch, the chimneys first of wood covered with clay and later of stone. The small windows were covered with paper dipped in linseed oil. Tiny dwellings they were, of one room and a loft overhead where the youngsters could sleep, and with fireplaces proportionately huge.

Yet small as they were, these houses cost heavy effort. Every scrap of building material had to be wrested from nature—the trees cut down and sawed or hewn into planks, clay banks searched out and buckets full of clay brought to the site, stones gathered for the hearths and foundations. Great piles of rushes or marsh grass were needed to complete the thatching of one small roof. Plaster (which was probably not used in the earliest houses) had to be made by burning shells for lime.

By autumn there were eleven structures—seven little one-room houses and four other buildings including the old common house which served as a workshop when not in use for worship or meetings. The other public buildings were for storage. *Mourt's Relation* (by Bradford and Winslow) tells us that the first houses were assigned to Peter Browne, John Goodman, and Elder Brewster—these three on what is now Leyden Street below Main. Then continuing up the hill beyond Main Street and still on the south side of Leyden, Billington, Allerton, Francis Cooke and Winslow had their homes.

This is a curious assignment. When the first sickness was over only three married couples remained unbroken. Winslow soon added to the number of couples by marrying Susanna White. Thus we might expect that these four families—Brewster, Billington, Hopkins and Winslow—would have the first four houses. Yet Hopkins, who had the largest family group in the colony—four children and two servants—did not get a house.* The next group who might be expected to claim houses would be those with children. Allerton was left with three, while Eaton and Cooke had each one, Samuel Fuller probably taking charge of his dead brother Edward's youngster. Allerton and Cooke did get houses, but Eaton and Fuller did not. Neither, it will be noted, did Bradford and Standish. Yet houses were assigned to John Goodman who died during the first year, and to Peter Browne who was a bachelor until 1623.

These seven householders and such family members as they

---

* *Mourt's Relation* speaks of Stephen Hopkins' house as the place where Samoset was lodged in February. This must have been a temporary building of wattle and daub, and several of these may have been used until more frame houses were built. The Hopkins lot was east and across the road from Bradford's.

had (including servants) would account for only twenty-two of the fifty-one to be housed. Yet an average of more than seven inhabitants had to be accommodated in each of these tiny cabins. The two unattached young women, Priscilla and Desire, were probably divided to the Brewster and Winslow households —the only ones where Bradford would have considered them safe. Bradford no doubt went back to live with the Brewsters, as for many years he had been virtually a member of their family. Browne's house was probably bachelor quarters for Ellis and Trevore the sailors, Alden, Howland, Carver's servant boy Latham (who later was part of Bradford's household) and perhaps Standish. Gilbert Winslow would have joined up with his brother. Then there were three orphan girls—Elizabeth Tilley, fourteen, Humility Cooper, eight, and Mary Chilton, fifteen. Whether they would have been put in households without women in order to do the household chores, or placed under the protective wings of Mrs. Brewster and Mrs. Winslow cannot be determined. Knowing the Pilgrim concern for morality and their equal understanding of the weakness to which all flesh is heir—thanks in part to the lesson Elder Studley had taught them—it seems likely that the teen agers, at least, would have been so protected, though sent out to labor in the other households during the day. Perhaps Humility Cooper or the Carver maidservant was entrusted to Allerton to help care for his three young ones. Eaton with his son, "a sucking child," may have boarded with the Billingtons. Yet unless the baby had been weaned by this time, it would have fallen to Susanna White or possibly to Elizabeth Hopkins to nurse him. Perhaps Warren squeezed in with the Billingtons too.

This leaves only the Rogers and Crackston boys and little "Henery" Samson, a cousin of the deceased Tilleys and apparently an orphan, to go into the Cooke or Allerton homes, thus leaving each house with a population of between six and eight. Yet we must still tuck in somewhere Hobomok, his wife and Squanto.

Coming from the most beautiful spot in the world, as Polyander had shown Leyden to be, what must Bradford have thought as he surveyed the pitiful little row of houses that started not far from the joining of Town Brook with the ocean and marched

up to the shoulder of The Mount, later to be known as Fort
Hill? The contrast would no doubt have impressed him. Yet
having shared the labor of building them, the houses must have
given him a glow of pride too. Since the act of creation always
generates love as well as originating in it, Bradford must have
been in love with what he looked upon, remembering how all
this had been created against incredible odds, fabricated almost
entirely out of pure fortitude and faith.

Yes, they had gained their foothold on an inhospitable continent. But at what a price!

> They were alone as few we know are alone.
> They made a small bustling noise in an empty land.*

In addition to the neat little houses, they also had reason to
be thankful for a good harvest from their twenty acres of Indian
corn, for being "well recovered in health & strenght," for having
made their peace with the near-by Indians and for the continued
assistance of Squanto and Hobomok. Small as their number was,
for only twenty men were left, they had made some beginnings
in the beaver trade, while "others were excersised in fishing,
aboute codd, & bass, & other fish, of which they tooke good store,
of which every family had their portion." Also, as autumn came
on, great numbers of wild fowl flew in, settling on the many
little lakes and ponds where they were easily taken.

With all these things to be thankful for, Bradford remembered
the fine Dutch custom of an annual Thanksgiving Day on October third, the anniversary of Leyden's deliverance from the
Spaniard. As governor he declared a holiday, thus beginning as
every schoolchild knows the most distinctively American of all
our holidays. For several days food was gathered—wild fowl
including "great store of wild Turkies," shellfish from the widespread sandflats which appear before Plymouth at low tide, eels
trod out of the bottom of Town Brook, "Sallet Herbes," † and
wine made of wild grapes.

To strengthen the friendship with the Indians, an invitation
was sent to Massasoit who not only came himself but brought
ninety hungry braves. The astonished Pilgrims accepted this

---

* Stephen Vincent Benét: *Western Star*
† Salad or sallet originally meant something salted, which tells us how the
Pilgrims dressed their greens.

pledge of friendship with whatever grace they could muster and were somewhat eased when the Indians went out and killed five deer to add to the feast. Then for three days the whole party stuffed while the poor women—there were only ten of them even if you count the teen agers—wore themselves ragged trying to fill a hundred and forty-two demanding stomachs. No one has ever paid sufficient tribute to their part in the festivities.

While the women cooked, the men relaxed. Captain Standish put on a military review, so apparently he had taught his little company the manual of arms.

"Rest your musket!" The men fixed their pieces in the spike-like rest which supported the weapon from the ground during firing.

"Draw out your match!" The long and clumsy fuse or match was made ready.

"Try your match! . . . Guard your pan! . . . Present! . . . Give fire!"

Never easy at the sound of a musket, the Indians must have jumped at the noise of a volley. Then followed a series of commands for the disposal of musket, match and rest, ending with: "Bring up your musket! . . . Poise your musket and recover your rest! . . . Shoulder your musket!"

Then came games of strength and skill. The Indians were amazed to learn that the white man could play games not unlike their own. Nothing had made them feel as close to the English as this, nor had they ever suspected such humanity in men who seemed strangely addicted to labor. Flushed with food, exercise and the magic beverage these knowing strangers could press out of the grape, Massasoit and his braves headed home at last with a warmth of feeling which survived even the tests to which it was soon to be subjected.

A few weeks later while the colony was busily chinking its houses and otherwise making ready for winter, an Indian brave came running in with the news that a ship was off Cape Cod, headed for Plymouth. Fearing a possible raid from the French settlements in Canada, Bradford called his council together, ordered the cannon on the hill to be fired as an alarm to those who were out fishing or cutting wood, and turned over to Standish the business of making their defenses ready.

When the ship ran into the harbor every man and boy of the determined little army was ready. But the ship broke out an ensign bearing the red cross of England, and soon who should come ashore but their old agent Robert Cushman. Muskets were cast down as the men came crowding around him to ask news of their families. Five of them had left wives or children or both at home; Richard Warren had separated from a wife and five small daughters. Perhaps some of these were even now in the *Fortune* as she rode at anchor a mile or so from shore!

To the peppering of questions Deacon Cushman replied as best he could. The only family connections aboard were Brewster's twenty-eight-year-old son Jonathan and Winslow's brother John. Not Robinson, their pastor. Nor Brewster's two daughters, nor any of the other longed-for wives and children, though Cushman had brought his thirteen-year-old son Thomas. Phillipe De La Noye had come, but his fame was to wait several centuries until the time when he could become an ancestor of Franklin Delano Roosevelt. Altogether thirty-five passengers, mostly male. Two wives and a girl child were aboard, but for all the bachelors there and already ashore there was but one prospect—Martha Ford whose husband had died at sea and who celebrated her arrival by promptly giving birth to a son. (She married Peter Browne in 1623.)

The pleasures of reunion were soon spoiled for Bradford by the information that the group had been sent without as much as a "bisket-cake" in provisions. Nor had they bedding, household goods or any clothing to speak of but what was on their backs. This was a frightening situation. For while the harvest of Indian corn would be enough to see the *Mayflower* group through the winter, it would not take care of thirty-five extra stomachs. In place of provisions there came a letter from Weston, "full of complaints & expostulations," but promising that if they would send back a signed copy of the agreement they had previously refused to sign, a particular account of the moneys expended, and a well-laden ship, he would never forsake them.

To Weston's complaints Bradford replied in a letter whose dignity and restraint cannot hide the righteous anger he felt as he relived the frightful days when "it pleased God to visitte us then, with death dayly, and with so generall a disease, that the

living were scarce able to burie the dead," and when "we went
in so tedious a time to make provission to sheelter us and our
goods, aboute which labour, many of our armes & leggs can tell
us to this day we were not neclignet."

Nevertheless Weston got what he asked for—the signed agreement, the accounts, and a ship laden with clapboard (for barrel
staves), wainscoting, and beaver and otter pelts to a value almost
half that of their debt to the adventurers. As the clapboards had
to be cut by hand and carted pickaback to the ship's boat, the
cargo represented a vast amount of labor. Cushman, after delivering a sermon on "The Dangers of Self-Love" intended to
make the settlers content with the communal economy the adventurers had saddled them with, departed in the *Fortune*,
carrying with him the manuscript written by Bradford and
Winslow now known as *Mourt's Relation*, which was published
in London in 1622 and provided the first public account of the
settlement at Plymouth.

Alas, the *Fortune* never got to England with her cargo. She
was overtaken by a French privateer, her crew robbed and de-
tained for weeks on food fit only for animals, and allowed to
go only when everything of value had been stripped from her
and them. Cushman carried to the adventurers Bradford's warning that the coming of the *Fortune* people "would bring famine
upon them unavoydably, if they had not supply in time." Bradford says nothing of the housing situation. Yet thirty-four people
(after Cushman's departure) had to be jammed into quarters
already humiliatingly overcrowded. Perhaps the common house
was used as a dormitory, but even so the conditions went beyond
anything the worst of our city slums know today. Yet somehow
they managed to cook and eat, to sleep and beget and bear children. Sex education, which troubles many a modern parent,
would have been no problem in these intimate households:
rather the reverse!

One thing the *Fortune* had brought was a patent legalizing the
presence of the Pilgrims in New England. A request for the
patent had gone back on the *Mayflower*. As Sir Ferdinando
Gorges reports it, they had "hastened away their ship with an
order to their solicitor to deal with me" for a grant from the
Council for New England "which was accordingly performed

to their particular satisfaction." The patent was issued promptly, for it was dated June 1, 1621, less than two months after the *Mayflower's* departure from Plymouth. Like that granted by the Virginia Company, it was drawn up in the name of proxies— to John Peirce and his associates. The next year Peirce got himself another patent which came close to blowing little Plymouth clean off the map, as will be seen in its place. But for the time being it gave Bradford a feeling of relief to have a legal basis for his governorship. The patent authorized the establishing of such laws and ordinances for better government as might be agreed to by the greater part of the settlers, and permitted the allotting of a hundred acres to each man transported, with a rental of two shillings the hundred after seven years. As this provision was directly opposed to the communal economy enforced upon the Pilgrims by the adventurers, it seems to have been ignored.

Crowded into the little houses and aware that their provisions would hardly last six months at half rations, the Pilgrims faced the oncoming New England winter. To add to their troubles, the *Fortune* had scarcely departed when a Narragansett brave strode into the settlement and flung down a bundle of arrows tied with a snakeskin. Called by Bradford to interpret this omen, both Hobomok and Squanto agreed that it was an insulting challenge.

In miniature, Bradford was faced with a threat of aggression to which he must respond like Great Britain at Munich—or on the Nazi invasion of Poland. For the little colony the results were just as important, and perhaps for the settlement of all North America. With the advice of his informal council, Bradford stuffed the snakeskin with musket balls and sent it back to the Narragansetts with the message that "if they had rather have warre then peace, they might begine when they would; for they had done them no wrong, neither did they fear them, or should they find them unprovided."

The Narragansetts refused to touch the ominous snakeskin. But the men of Plymouth took the incident as a timely hint to strengthen their defenses, which they began to do without delay. The houses were surrounded with a stout palisade provided with gates which could be locked at night. All night long, throughout the winter, a guard made the rounds. The men were now divided into four squads, one of which was commanded by Bradford, with stations assigned them in case of alarm. Fearing possible treachery, Bradford and Standish perfected a plan by which some would quench any fire that might be started while others would act as a guard.

The work of building a mile-long palisade was a tremendous undertaking for the colony. When Bradford called the men out to work as usual "one the day called Chrismasday" most of the newcomers complained that it went against their consciences to work.

"If you make it a matter of conscience, I'll spare you till you're better informed," he told them, and marched off with the remainder of the company. But coming home at noon he found them playing in the street, "some pitching the barr, & some at stoole-ball, and shuch like sports." Boiling within, he strode up and took their implements away from them, remarking that it was against *his* conscience that they should play while others worked. There are few incidents in Bradford's life that show his character more clearly, or his notion of justice and square dealing.

The palisade was finished about the beginning of March. It was eleven feet high, enclosing not only the houses but garden plots for each, with a goodly portion of the Mount or Fort Hill. When this major work was finished, they began to get ready for a trading trip to the Massachusetts, having promised to return in the spring. Sometime before the boat's departure a meeting was called and William Bradford re-elected governor.

The boat had scarcely disappeared behind Gurnet's Nose carrying Squanto, Hobomok and ten of the most trusted men, when a member of Squanto's family came flying in from the south with news that the Narragansetts, their old enemy Corbitant, and he thought Massasoit as well were coming to destroy them. Bradford noticed that the Indian "would still be looking back, as if they were at his heels." Now Hobomok, before the departure, had brought news that the Massachusetts were in league with the Narragansetts against the colony and that Squanto was somehow mixed up in the business. For some time the two Indian advisers had been at loggerheads, each trying to gain the greater influence with the colony—a circumstance which Bradford had shrewdly made use of. It now appeared as if Squanto were trying a shrewd trick of his own, having sent one of his relatives to carry out his design, whatever it was. Or was Hobomok to be distrusted? It was another one of those moments carrying with it all the factors, but size, of an international crisis —as serious for the Pilgrims as for England would have been conflicting advice from Spanish and French ambassadors, with the likelihood of a foreign invasion.

Bradford handled it with a decisiveness that had begun to be a habit with him since he had assumed the governorship. For his character was growing in response to the demands made upon it—a fact confirmed by his handwriting. The man who signed the marriage register at Amsterdam was youthful, somewhat careless and impetuous, not too careful of appearances. But in Plymouth Bradford's hand became increasingly firm, smooth, regular, neat—almost as even as engraving and far more beautiful. It is one of the most distinguished hands of the century, and it reveals a man firm in judgment, knowing his own mind, a clear thinker who almost never has to cross out what he has written because he knows where he is going. Though firm, it is small with a becoming humility. There is no careless scrawl at the end of a word or sentence, the last stroke being as firm as the first. This is a man who finishes what he begins—deliberately, unhurried and unharried, with staying power and with love for the task. Even when there are long letters to be copied no signs of impatience with the tedious job appear. Yet there is in every line a strength and vitality the possession of which usually leads a man to impatience. With such a cluster of virtues clearly revealed, it is likely—and events prove it—that Bradford's chief fault and perhaps his only one was an expectation that all men should live up to the standard his qualities made possible for him.

Acting therefore on the news Squanto's man had brought, Bradford ordered his little army to stand to their arms and a few cannon shot to be fired to call the boat back. When it came, he told Hobomok to send his wife to Massasoit's village, "pretening other occasions," to see what was going on. She returned with the information that there was nothing stirring.

It was now clear to Bradford that Squanto "sought his owne

ends, and plaid his owne game, by putting the Indeans in fear, and drawing gifts from them to enrich him selfe; making them beleeve he could stur up warr against whom he would, & make peece for whom he would." His purpose was to make himself more important than Massasoit. To outwit the Indians at their own game Bradford lent his ear to Squanto while advising Standish to do the same with Hobomok, "by which they had better intelligence, and made them both more diligente."

Yet Bradford had acquired a fondness for this Indian who followed him around, chattering in his amiably atrocious English, asking questions, and giving sound advice on agriculture. Gratitude was always one of Bradford's strong points—it is soon to be seen in his dealings with Weston—and no matter what Squanto's offense, he had saved the colony from certain starvation. So Bradford tried now to protect him against Massasoit's perfectly justified anger. For by the time the trading expedition had returned after a safe and successful exchange at Massachusetts Bay, Massasoit was at Plymouth demanding that Squanto be turned over to him according to the terms of the treaty. Somehow Bradford, who must have had a way with the Indians, managed to satisfy him and send him home. But in a little while he boiled over again, sending a messenger and then a whole company of painted braves with his own knife, a large present of beaver skins, and the demand that his braves be allowed to bring Squanto's head and hands home to him.

Bradford was in a tight corner. The treaty of peace with Massasoit was an essential cornerstone of Plymouth diplomacy. It had established the pattern of their peaceful dealings with the Indians. If the Pilgrims failed to live up to its conditions the Indians might well feel justified in attacking and wiping them out. Yet Squanto because of his knowledge of English was indispensable to the Pilgrims, none of whom had yet learned enough of the native tongue to conduct affairs for themselves.

Scarcely knowing what course he could take with the impatient braves, Bradford with the instinct of the diplomat seized upon the one point where he would have the advantage by putting them in the wrong.

"It is not the manner of the English," he told them, "to sell men's lives at a price, but when they have deserved justly to die, to give them their reward." With a tone of righteous indignation he refused the gift of beaver.

Having thus skillfully gained a tactical advantage he sent for Squanto who accused Hobomok as the author of his difficulties, leaving it to the governor whether or not to hand him over to his executioners.

Had Bradford hoped that Squanto would run away, as he might have done, instead of coming when summoned? If so, the strategy had failed. He had held out against Massasoit as long as he could, had used every possible excuse. There was nothing left but to turn Squanto over to the braves who were ready to finish him off on the instant. The welfare of the colony demanded it.

In the silence that fell before Bradford would speak the fatal words, someone happened to glance out to the bay. A ship's boat was crossing before the town and as the party watched, it disappeared behind Manomet Point. It was not a very substantial straw, but Bradford seized it. He must know whether the ship was friend or enemy before delivering Squanto up, he told the braves. "Mad with rage, and impatient at delay, they departed in great heat."

The coming of the ship had saved Squanto, at least temporarily. But did it bring a new threat to the plantation and a new challenge to Bradford's fast developing diplomatic talents?

The Pilgrims Abandon Communism

THE ship's boat, a shallop, soon turned back and headed in toward the little settlement which it had missed before. The Pilgrims, armed in case it should prove a Frenchman, stood on the beach and waited.

It was not a Frenchman. Seven men jumped out of her and waded ashore. They had been sent out from England by Thomas Weston, they reported—the vanguard of a colony which was to establish itself near Plymouth. The shallop, after leaving them, was to return to its mother ship which was with the fishing fleet from England, some forty leagues to the northeast. Letters from Mr. Weston, which they now handed over to Bradford, would explain the rest.

Before opening the letters, Bradford tried to discover by a few discreet questions what supplies they had brought with them.

None at all, the men replied with amazing good cheer. Let him read the letters and he would see that Mr. Weston desired him to feed them until—well, the termination of this vague interval was not at all clear.

Striding up the hill from the beach with the hope that the heat of exertion would overcome the heat of anger, Bradford went into Brewster's house and opened the letters. They were still addressed to Carver and what they contained was worse than he had feared. Plymouth was to entertain the seven men, sent out on Weston's private account, with whatever they needed in-

cluding food, seed corn, salt. Within a month was to come another ship with an unspecified number of passengers, also on
Weston's private concerns, who were also to be entertained while
their ship sailed off to Virginia. And with the next ship sent out
to Plymouth he intended to send still others to join with the first
in setting up a new colony under a separate patent. After sad-
dling Plymouth with all this, Weston then had the effrontery to
criticize the other adventurers for failing to send relief to the
colony! He concluded by saying that any refusal to perform all
these requests would be "extreme barbarisme." And this after
dumping the thirty-five (including the Ford infant) from the
Fortune upon them had already nearly brought the colony to
the brink of starvation!

But this was still not all. Another letter from Weston announced, in terms confusingly vague, that the adventurers had
decided to dissolve the joint-stock company and desired a confirmation from Plymouth!

To Bradford a sinister pattern now began to be clear. The
wild young men from the *Fortune,* these arrivals by shallop,
and those still to come were a fifth column, a Weston majority
which would overrun the colony, depose him as governor, and
destroy the holy discipline which he and those of Leyden had so
often risked their lives to establish. Neither hunger nor Indian
hostility had been as dangerous as this. Never had the colony's
prospect seemed darker.

Calling together the few trusted leaders—Brewster, Standish,
Allerton and Winslow—Bradford passed the letters around. A
good deal of talk came to but this conclusion, that in Christian
charity they could do no less than feed the seven even though
they had arrived too late to share the burden of planting. The
letters from Weston were so disturbing that it was decided for
the present not to reveal their contents to the colony.

But with what were they to be fed? The Pilgrims, thinking a
supply long overdue from London, had hoped that the shallop
was bringing news of it. Instead, the letters it brought practically
told them to look for no more supply.

Among the letters brought ashore, however, was one from a
Captain Huddleston whose ship was fishing to the eastward. He
wished to inform the colonists, he said, that a massacre of four

hundred settlers had recently taken place in Virginia and that it might be well for Plymouth to look to its defenses.

The friendly tone of his letter led Bradford to suggest that Winslow, already a proven diplomat, should immediately set sail in their own shallop to thank Captain Huddleston for his timely warning and to see if he and other captains of the fishing fleet—an unusually large one this year—would trade provisions for furs.

Winslow found "kinde entertainment and good respect, with a willingnesse to supply our wants." Since Huddleston did not have as large a supply as Winslow wanted to purchase, he refused any payment though giving Winslow enough to see the colony through, if on short rations, till harvest time. On his return, Winslow found a marked change in the colonists. Some had gone alarmingly thin while others had become unhealthily swollen. Bradford received the supplies, locked them up, and doled out a daily ration of a quarter of a pound of bread to a person, knowing that otherwise the improvident would have glutted themselves and then starved to death.

Yet here is a strange thing; while the Pilgrims were hungering and looking toward England for a supply, the English were coming three thousand miles to get their provisions out of the sea in the Pilgrims' front yard. Winslow, moreover, had written home—and the letter at this moment was about to be published —boasting of the great store of fowl and fish to be had for the taking. Winslow himself in a later publication tried to explain the apparent inconsistency, his chief excuse being that the very abundance of fish had proved their undoing since they lacked seines strong enough to hold them, the few that they had breaking through and carrying all away. Then why had he failed to negotiate with the fishing fleet for even one such net? Surely the kindness of Captain Huddleston prompted by Winslow's persuasiveness would have extended that far.

The plain fact is that the art of fishing is not learned overnight. The Pilgrims, being farmers or artisans, had no background and no knack for it. Consequently they were starving in the midst of plenty.

It is even possible that they were starving because of the dogged, die-hard determination of the Englishman to stick to

familiar ways. For all winter there were mussels and clams practically at their doors, and lobsters big enough to feed four men.
Were they, steeped in Old Testament lore, prejudiced against
all creeping and crawling things as unfit for human diet? Their
plight was pitiful enough, yet it may be that a people who
thought themselves dying of thirst when they had to take water
instead of beer may also have thought themselves starving when
they had to eat shellfish instead of beef.

In any case they were hungry enough so that their plight was
known to the Indians, who now "began againe to cast forth
many insulting speeches, glorying in our weaknesse, and giving
out how easie it would be ere long to cut us off." Even Massasoit,
their staunch friend, was now against them because of the
Squanto affair, and neither came nor sent messengers as before.
So, in the midst of hunger and at the risk of scanting their attention to the crops on which another year's subsistence depended,
they began the heavy work of building a fort at the top of The
Mount, hereafter known as Fort Hill. This was no log house, but
a structure of square-hewn oak timbers laid solidly one on top
of the other with a simple kind of battlement atop a flat roof
where cannon were mounted on every side. When it was finished
it became their church and their meeting hall, and very proud
they were of it.

About the end of June the promised, but not eagerly looked-
for, ships of Thomas Weston dropped anchor in the harbor, setting ashore sixty men who were to plant a separate colony on
Weston's behalf. The larger ship sailed immediately for Virginia,
the smaller, a pinnace, soon setting out in search of a spot to
colonize.

With the men came letters, and very unsettling ones they were.
Weston blandly announced that he was quit of them, having sold
out his share of Plymouth. This was the man who but a short
time since had promised that he would never forsake them.
He also confessed that he had smoked out a letter to Bradford
from two other adventurers which had privately been gotten
aboard sewn into a shoe, and had opened and read it. This letter,
from Edward Pickering and William Greene, reported that they
were glad to have Mr. Weston bought out, that he refused to
carry letters or supplies for Plymouth in his ships, and that he

planned to rob the colony of its goods by pretending he was to pick them up for the adventurers. Also Bradford was warned that the men sent over were a rude lot who would only make trouble for Plymouth. Weston sent this letter on to Bradford with a rebuttal which appears as unconvincing today as it must have seemed to Bradford.

The governor's suspicions were further confirmed by a letter from Cushman, enclosed in a letter from a wife to one of the men in the colony in order to elude Weston's censorious hand. Weston's men must not be allowed to join the colony, Cushman warned, nor must anything be given them except upon immediate payment or "a good pawne." It should be made clear to the Indians that these men were a distinct body, for they were bound to make trouble.

That they had a talent for trouble-making soon appeared when they "would sometimes seeme to helpe us in our labour about our corne, yet spared not day and night to steale the same." Very happy the Pilgrims were when Weston's gang finally settled upon a place in Massachusetts Bay (now Weymouth) for their plantation, even though in departing they left their sick and lame to be tended—and fed—at Plymouth. Where the Pilgrims managed to stow sixty-seven of Weston's men they do not tell us.

The Indians soon began to complain that the Weymouth men were stealing their corn as they had robbed the Pilgrims. There was little the Pilgrims could do about it except "advising them to better walking" (i.e., "walking in the paths of righteousness"). They might as well have saved their breaths.

Once more harvest time came around, "in which all had their hungrie bellies filled." Yet that the harvest was disastrously small Bradford was well aware. Out of weakness and unfamiliarity with the ways of Indian corn they had failed to tend it as they should. And now there was not even the likelihood of being supplied from England. Their trading goods, moreover, were all used up so that they could not hope to buy corn from the Indians. This time there seemed to be no way out.

Yet, says Bradford, "behold now another providence of God; a ship comes into the harbor, one Captain Jons being cheefe therein . . . This ship had store of English-beads (which were then good trade) and some knives, but would sell none but at dear rates, and also a good quantie togeather. Yet they weere glad of the occasion, and faine to buy at any rate . . . By this means they were fitted againe to trade for beaver & other things, and intended to buy what corne they could."

After having entertained so many ruffians, Bradford was delighted to make the acquaintance of John Pory, formerly secretary to the Virginia colony, who was on his way home. Pory was a lover of books and religion, so that an evening's conversation with him was sweet relief from the vexing problems which now weighed upon the young governor. They became good friends at once, with the feeling of long acquaintance that sometimes will draw two strangers together, and Pory's praise of Plymouth when he got to England "did this poore-plantation much credite amongst those of no mean ranck."

The Plymouth folk had no sooner secured trading goods than Weston's men were upon them, suggesting a joint trading expedition—the Pilgrims of course to provide the trade goods, "and they would undertake to make paymente when Mr Weston, or their supply, should come." Bradford accepted the proposition—apparently because the *Swan*, the thirty-ton pinnace of the Weston colony, would make possible a longer voyage than they could have undertaken in their shallop. For Bradford had in mind a trip all the way around the Cape and then southward. Just as the ship was ready to set out, Weston's brother-in-law who had charge of his affairs died. Twice the ship was driven back by strong winds, and the second time Standish who represented the Plymouth contingent came back so sick that he had to be taken off. Bradford decided to go in his place, and the *Swan* at last set out in November with Squanto for pilot and interpreter, a shallop from Plymouth being towed behind.

But once again the Pilgrims were defeated by the shoals, in spite of Squanto's assurance that he could lead them through. So they headed into a narrow and crooked channel (at Chatham) and went ashore with Bradford as leader. The natives kept hidden until the sight of Squanto or the friendly manner of the English made them understand no harm was intended, whereupon they brought out venison and other food in great abundance. Still they seemed fearful, attempting at first to keep the English from entering their village, and then carrying away all their movables when Bradford declared his intention of staying overnight. When one of the English stumbled by chance upon the place where their goods were hidden, all were suddenly mysteriously carried off and hidden again. This happened several times.

At last, thanks to Squanto's efforts, eight hogsheads of corn and beans were purchased and the party prepared to head south again, still intent on finding a passage through the shoals. "Yet God had otherways disposed." For Squanto, who had been their tongue, their farming expert and their foreign relations adviser ever since their first coming, grew violently feverish. Bradford did his best for him, but there was little he could do, especially after Squanto began to bleed at the nose—a symptom which the Indians took as a sure sign of death. But when Squanto asked the Governor to pray for him that he might go to the Englishman's God in heaven, Bradford experienced one of the most moving moments of his life, like all great moments a mixture of joy and sorrow. For one reason which had led the Pilgrims into the wilderness was the hope of bringing the savage to the knowledge and love of God. So far, having fought a hard fight to keep alive, they had spent no time on the souls of the savages. Except Squanto, and perhaps Hobomok. Squanto went everywhere with Bradford, observed his ways, talked with him about many things including God and His heaven. The barriers of language and race had gradually dropped away. Bradford, troubled at the colony's failure to carry Christianity to the Indians, must have been all the more earnest in talking religion with Squanto in the hope that through him others too might be reached. And now, entering the valley of the shadow of death, Squanto with his hand in Bradford's begged for a Christian guide.

We know that tears were manly and legitimate expressions of great joy or great sorrow to these men of the seventeenth century, and we may be sure that Bradford shed some now as he promised to lead his guide and friend through prayer into the heavenly kingdom. We may be sure he spoke comfortably to the frightened man, and with a vision clarified by faith, of the joys that awaited him. For heaven to Bradford was as real as Austerfield, and much nearer.

For several days Bradford tended him and prayed at his side

until with a weakened voice Squanto bequeathed his few belongings to his English friends. According to Pilgrim custom he was
buried without prayer, but surely with a volley of shot to mark
his passing. Bradford would have seen to that. Yet the only eulogy
he cared to record were these few words: "They had a great loss."

Bradford had made up his mind to have one more try southward. But Squanto's death put an end to that possibility. So the
pinnace headed for Massachusetts Bay where the Plymouth men
had previously arranged to have the Indians plant corn for them.
But here they found many sick with what appeared to be the
plague—one of the numerous blessings conferred by civilization
upon men in a state of nature—and in addition very out of sorts
with the behavior of the Weymouth or Wessagusset men who
now came as partners with the Pilgrims though Plymouth had
formerly disclaimed any connection with them. Bradford did his
best to pacify them, though how he accounted for the sudden alliance between Plymouth and Weston's colony is not explained.
But when he began to trade, an ironic punishment awaited him.
For Weston's men had been paying so high for the food they
needed, giving as much for a quart of corn as the Pilgrims had
been used to give for a beaver skin, that they had quite ruined
the trade.

The pinnace next headed for Nauset at the bottom of Cape
Cod Bay. Here and at a near-by settlement they were able to get
both corn and beans. But the sea was so stormy that they lost
their shallop and with it the means of carrying their corn aboard
the pinnace. "Hereupon," Winslow tells us, "the Governour
caused the corne to be made in a round stack, and bought mats,
and cut sedge to cover it, and gave charge to the Indians not
to meddle with it, and promising him that dwelt next to it a reward, if he would keep vermine also from it." Bradford also
persuaded the Indians to hunt up his lost shallop. They found
it almost buried in sand at high water mark, somewhat battered
but still with many things remaining unharmed within. After
arranging with the Indians to watch out for it until it could be
sent for, Bradford led the Plymouth men home by land while
the Wessagusset men returned by sea, stopping to unload corn
at Plymouth. The marchers beat the ship by three days, arriving
safely but with sore and blistered feet. Altogether the voyage had

brought in about twenty-eight hogsheads of corn and beans, which however was far short of what Bradford had counted on from the projected voyage south of the Cape.

Though weary and footsore, he immediately assembled another party and set out westward to visit some of the inland villages, determined to avoid the previous year's experience of summer hunger. At Nemasket he not only got corn from the people of Corbitant whose head he had once threatened to borrow from his shoulders, but squaws to carry it back to Plymouth. Then to Manomet (now Bourne) where the purchase was left on the ground as at Nauset and Mattachiest (Cummaquid).

Now recovered from his fever, Standish went to bring back the damaged shallop and the corn stored on the Cape. He found both carefully preserved for him. But as he was leaving with the corn he discovered that some beads, scissors "and other trifles" had been stolen. So he marched an armed party up to the lodge of the sachem Aspinet, demanded a return of the missing articles by morning, and refusing all offers of entertainment marched back to the shallop. In the morning Aspinet came bowing and licking Standish's hand all the way up to the wrist, returned the beads, and assured the captain that the thief had been punished. A short time later a similar episode took place at Cummaquid where Iyanough was chief. But in this case the missing beads were found lying in plain sight in the shallop when Iyanough suggested that the captain send a man to look for them.

By February Weston's men were so desperate that their leader John Sanders sent a message to Bradford to inquire whether he might not take corn from the Indians by force since they refused to sell to him. Bradford replied that they should do nothing of the kind, that they had already endangered Plymouth as well as themselves by stealing from the Indians, and that they must learn like Plymouth to live on ground nuts, clams, and whatever else could be found. Incidentally, Winslow's boast of a year ago that there was plenty of fowl in the winter finds no repetition this year. Yet fowl there must have been. Were the Pilgrims as poor fowlers as they were fishermen, or were powder and shot running short?

Compared with Wessagusset, however, Plymouth was in good shape. For Weston's men had grown so needy that they were selling their clothes and bedding to the Indians, or even cutting wood and fetching water for them in return for a capful of corn.

News of Sanders' proposed treachery soon spread throughout the Indian tribes. Since Plymouth had joined with Wessagusset in trading, it was obvious to the Indians that whatever the Wessagusset men planned also had the connivance of Plymouth. The Indians began to plan counter-measures of their own. The first intimation came during a chance encounter between Standish and Wituwamat, a Massachusetts brave who came to Manomet while Standish was there to collect corn previously purchased by Bradford. Taking a dagger from about his neck, Wituwamat presented it to Canacum, the local sachem, following it with "a long speech in an audacious manner." Standish, who of the Pilgrims best understood Indian, could make nothing of it at the time, but according to Winslow it was later learned to have been a proposal for a war of extermination against both Wessagusset and Plymouth, since Plymouth would certainly attempt to avenge any action against Wessagusset.

While Standish was at Manomet and an Indian confederacy was apparently forming for the extinction of Plymouth, news came of the mortal sickness of Massasoit. This was bad news indeed, for Massasoit of all the Indian chiefs had been their staunchest friend. Bradford therefore hustled Winslow off to see what could be done, sending along some cordials—but not the colony's physician Samuel Fuller. Winslow found Massasoit lying in a house full of people, "making such a hellish noise, as it distempered us that were well, and therefore unlike to ease him that was sicke."

Massasoit had already lost his sight, but when he heard that the English had come he asked who it was.

"Winsnow," they told him, being unable to pronounce an *l.*

Winslow was then led up to the bed where Massasoit put forth a groping hand.

"*Keen Winsnow?*" he said. "Art thou Winslow?"

"*Ahhe,*" said Winslow. "Yes."

"*Matta neen wonckanet namen, Winsnow!* O Winslow, I shall never see thee again!"

Winslow then asked Hobomok to explain that while Bradford had been unable to come himself, he had sent some useful drugs which he hoped would restore his good friend to health. Forcing a bit of medicine between Massasoit's teeth on the point of a knife, Winslow managed to get him to swallow it—the first thing he had taken in two days. Next he scraped his bloated tongue, getting "abundance of corruption out of the same." After taking a good draft of the medicine Massasoit soon opened his eyes and was able to see again. Dr. Winslow next inquired when he had slept and when he "went to stoole," offered to supply chickens and other medicine if Massasoit would but send a messenger to Plymouth for them, and dispatched a letter to Fuller asking for such medicines as the symptoms seemed to call for.

Before the messenger could return from Plymouth Winslow had improvised a broth—much improved no doubt by being strained through his handkerchief—and then when the chief's appetite improved went out and shot a duck. This he accomplished at some six score paces, much to the admiration of the Indians. If Winslow could do this for Massasoit, we wonder, why were the Pilgrims going hungry?

By the time Winslow had made broth of the duck Massasoit was in a ravening hunger and would not listen when Winslow begged him to let the fat be drawn off before he took it. Within an hour the sachem was very sick again, losing the broth and bleeding at the nose, this time apparently destined for a journey to the happy hunting grounds. But when the nosebleed stopped he slept. When he awoke and Winslow began to bathe his face, he suddenly ducked in to the water, breathed it in and then snorted it out so violently that he started the bleeding again. Again the Indians gave up all hope, but Winslow realized it was a superficial thing which would soon stop, as it did.

The chickens were now come from Plymouth, but Massasoit found himself so well that he decided to keep them for breeding, while Winslow wisely concluded to use no more medicines. Meanwhile Indians from as much as a hundred miles away had come in to see Massasoit. To all he told the story of his marvelous recovery at the hands of his friends the English.

"Now I see the English are my friends and love me," said Massasoit. "And whilst I live, I will never forget this kindness they have showed me." The breach that Squanto's treachery had made was now healed. More than that, Massasoit now proceeded to reveal the plot against Wessagusset and Plymouth and to advise that the Pilgrims seize some of the chief conspirators. All this he ordered Hobomok to explain to Winslow on the way home so that the governor might be informed.

Stopping overnight with Corbitant, the man whose head the Pilgrims had once sought, Winslow found him a merry fellow after all, full of "jests and squibs." When the horseplay was over Winslow took the occasion to tell him of God's works and laws, especially of the Ten Commandments. Much impressed, Corbitant objected only to the seventh, observing that it was inconvenient that a man should be tied to one woman, "about which we reasoned a good time."

Returning to Plymouth, Winslow immediately reported to Bradford all that had happened. Then came a man from Wessagusset, having escaped pursuing Indians, with the news that "they would be all knokt in the head shortly." Some indeed had already become as servants to the Indians while others had died of cold or hunger. One man was so weak that when his feet stuck in the mud while gathering shellfish he could not pull them out, but died where he stood. Others had spread out into the country, settling like savages wherever they could find ground nuts to abate their hunger. They were often visited by Indians who, despising their weakness, would eat up the miserable pottage they had cooked or walk off with the blanket that was their only covering.

John Sanders, the Wessagusset leader, had meanwhile come to Plymouth, borrowed more corn, and gone off to Maine where he hoped to get food from a plantation of Sir Ferdinando Gorges at Monhegan. When the twenty-third of March (1622/3) came around, Bradford brought the matter up at the yearly court day —the progenitor of all New England town meetings. From Winslow's *Relation* we gather that the governor made a full report of events to his constituents and, after declaring himself unwilling to undertake war without the consent of the majority and reluctant to shed the blood of those whose good the colony had in mind as one of its principal purposes, asked for guidance. After long debate the voters handed the responsibility back to the governor, as they were to do so frequently in the years to come, authorizing him to take whatever steps he thought necessary after consulting Standish and Allerton, his assistant.

The conclusion was that Standish was to take eight men and go to the Massachusetts pretending trade, to fall upon them when he saw opportunity and to return to Plymouth with the head of Wituwamat. Reaching Wessagusset, Standish warned Weston's men of his intention and advised them to send for those of their party still wandering about in the woods. The captain was soon visited by a brave named Pecksuot and then by Wituwamat, both of whom if we are to believe Winslow were insolent and threatening—and also aware of Standish's intentions.

"Though you are a great captain," Pecksuot is supposed to have said, "yet you are but a little man. Though I be no sachem, yet I am a man of strength and courage."

Pecksuot could scarcely have chosen a tenderer spot to tramp on. The next day when Pecksuot, Wituwamat, his eighteen-year-old brother and another brave were in a room with Standish and some of his men, the captain ordered the door barred and "began himself with Pecksuot, and snatching his own knife from his neck, though with much struggling, killed him therewith." Wituwamat and the other brave were also killed, the youth captured and hanged. "It is incredible how many wounds these two Pueeses [pineses] received before they dyed," Winslow observes, "not making any fearful noise, but catching at their weapons and striving to the last." The sentence somehow brings that bloody and shameful encounter to life—the unnatural quiet in the room, then the sudden cry of Standish, the flurry of activity, the heavy breathing of men struggling for their lives, the desperate contest of muscles so evenly matched that often there was no motion at all, then the vicious stabbing, the eyes widened by hate and fear and blood lust, the body's surprise and disgust at its violation, the sticky feel of blood on the hands.

What must Standish have felt when with the dead and dying men at his feet he stood over them with a faint dizziness in his head while he recovered his breath and noted the pools of congealing blood on the floor? Had he a moment of doubt, of remorse, of wonder for the meaning of life which was impregnated in ecstasy, brought forth in pain, sustained with so great difficulty and so quickly ended? If he had, there is no record of it. Recovering his breath, he picked up his fine Damascus blade and hacked the head of Wituwamat from the still warm body. Wituwamat was the same brave by whom he had felt himself insulted at Manomet, so the captain was satisfying a personal grudge as well as carrying out the governor's orders—which he may have done much to influence.

How did he carry the head back to Plymouth? Did he casually grab it by the long hair? Did he impale it on the end of his sword or wrap it in a bit of cloth? Winslow does not tell us. After some other actions in which three more Indians were killed the men of Wessagusset headed for the Maine coast to seek passage home while Standish returned triumphantly with his trophy and was "received with joy, the head being brought to the fort and there set up."

The foreign tribe of head-hunters had proven its superiority over those who took merely scalps.

Winslow goes to great pains to prove the necessity of this action and the certainty that the Pilgrims would themselves have been destroyed if they had not acted first. It is easy now to condemn their brutality. Even then their pastor John Robinson when he heard of it wrote over from Leyden: "Oh! how happy a thing had it been, if you had converted some, before you had killed any!" Bradford himself omits the whole episode as if he preferred to forget it. To us there is something disgusting about the attention given the head as a trophy. Since Bradford authorized it, it upsets all our notions of his character—his kindness, his patience, his religiousness. Like a sudden flash of lightning it makes grotesque what we had thought familiar and substantial. It exposes shadows, remnants of medievalism that shock us—as Bradford would be shocked by the twentieth century savagery of atomic warfare. We are accustomed to commit our legal murders impersonally and wholesale, by the pressing of a button in a plane and the dropping of a bomb which wipes out a city. In the action just described the Pilgrims killed seven men. But each one had to be killed personally and with nearly equal risk. The man who was capable of taking this sort of risk himself was not likely to be too squeamish about cutting the head off a dead body. As for setting the head up on the fort—where incidentally it remained until it was no longer recognizable—it is but fair to

remember that in that day London Bridge was generously deco-
rated with heads lopped off by the executioner, a custom not to
be given up there for over a hundred years. And it is but just to
remember that the Pilgrims after long discussion, on evidence
they thought unanswerable, and with the advice of Massasoit
had moved against the Massachusetts in order to avoid being
wiped out themselves.

The action had immediate results throughout the district.
Other tribes, which according to Winslow were in the conspiracy, were so terrified and amazed that "they forsooke their
houses, running to and fro like men distracted, living in swamps
and other desert places, and so brought manifold diseases among
themselves, whereof very many are dead." The dead included
three friendly sachems—Canacum of Manomet, Aspinet of Nauset and the gentle, hospitable Iyanough of Mattachiest (Cummaquid) whose transmuted name survives today in Hyannis.

The Pilgrims had their victory. Standish had demonstrated
his personal courage and zeal. But to Bradford remained the
moral responsibility of having permitted the action. Whether
or not it was an error of judgment no one now can say. Yet we
know enough of Bradford to be sure that he approved the plan
only because he thought Plymouth would otherwise be wiped
out. Hunger, the smallness of the colony, the vastness of the
wilderness and of unknown tribes throughout its length and
breadth no doubt pressed him to a decision. He may have exaggerated the dangers. Yet his sense of stewardship and moral responsibility was such that he would have agreed with Robinson's
sharp criticism: "It is a thing more glorious in men's eyes than
pleasing in God's, or conveniente for Christians, to be a terrour
to poore barbarous people."

By this time Plymouth was again so straitened in provision
that Standish had taken from the seed corn to relieve the men
at Wessagusset. As the third planting season approached it was
obvious that if Plymouth was ever to rise above a starvation
standard, something drastic had to be done. While this critical
problem was occupying Bradford's mind an event as dramatic
and unexpected as the first appearance of Samoset befell the
colony.

A bedraggled, ill-clothed Englishman walked up the street of neat unpainted little houses inquiring for the governor. Bradford stepped out to see a stranger who introduced himself as no other than the once prosperous, self-confident, persuasive Weston! Having come to New England with a fishing ship "in the disguise of a blacke-smith" to see what had happened to his colony, he had been cast away in a storm on his way to Wessagusset and had barely escaped with his life. Then he had been stripped to his shirt by Indians. After borrowing a suit at Piscataqua he had somehow made his way to Plymouth. If Weston behaved toward the owner of the suit as he was to behave toward the Pilgrims, that owner never saw suit or payment.

At Weston's sad tale Bradford gave in to his request for some beaver to trade with, doing so secretly for fear of displeasing the adventurers who were now at outs with Weston, and probably for fear of what the other colonists would say to such kindly treatment of a man who already had cost and cozened them far more than they could afford. Yet Weston not only failed to repay them for the beaver, but made trouble for them with the adventurers over their generosity. If Bradford could be stern enough to order the assassination of Wituwamat, what made him so tender toward a man who had done them so much harm? His own explanation is that he "pitied his case, and remembered former curtesies." Was it in part, perhaps, a revulsion from too much sternness toward the Indians and an unrealized desire to compensate?

Or was there a connection between Weston and the Southworth family toward whom Bradford now had special cause to feel attracted?

Sometime during the previous year—perhaps with the mail brought in the *Swan* or the *Charity* in the summer of 1622— William Bradford had learned of the death of Edward Southworth in London. Either on the *Charity* or the *Discovery* which sailed for London in the fall, he had sent a tender and urgent message to Alice Carpenter Southworth to come to Plymouth. For months now he had been awaiting a reply, never knowing whether the letter had reached its destination (for even if the ship arrived safely the lack of official mails left the delivery of a letter pretty much to chance), never knowing whether Alice favored his suit, or was on her way, or had been lost at sea—or had married another before his proposal reached her.

As members of the Leyden church they had known each other well. She was the same age as Bradford and had married South-worth six months before William had married Dorothy. The promptness with which he had begged her to come to Plymouth suggests that he had admired her in those early days and was confident that she had the qualities the wilderness required of a wife.

Well, there was nothing he could do but wait and hope, count-ing on work and responsibilities to absorb his abundant male energies.

The greatest responsibility facing him in the spring of 1623 was how to assure the food supply. Another hungry summer lay before them, and Bradford knew that one more poor harvest would mean the end of the plantation, which would join the roll of other failures that so far had ended every attempt to colonize New England. Something drastic had to be done.

The trouble, Bradford was convinced, lay in the insistence of the adventurers that the colony be operated on a communal basis, everyone working for "the general" rather than for him-self. The Pilgrims, in fact, were perforce experimenting with communism. As things stood, no matter how hard a man worked or how much he loafed he got the same diet as everyone else. The colonists could not own land. Theoretically they were al-lowed no time at all to work for themselves. The houses they had built were not their own, and any improvements they might make would pass to the merchants at a division to be made seven years hence. Private property, except for a few non-pro-ductive personal belongings, was abolished. In effect, the Pil-grims were bond servants for those seven years—forbidden to profit from whatever talents or initiative they might possess.

If all the colonists had been of the calibre of Bradford, Brew-ster, Winslow and Standish perhaps even this handicap would have been overcome. But there were plenty of young men who resented the fact that their labor went to feed other men's chil-dren, while men of age and experience thought it hard that their counsel and wisdom should count for nothing. Husbands were irritated by the sight of their wives washing and cooking for bachelor strangers as if they had been servants. Men simply did not produce under such a system. Under such a system they were even capable of starving themselves to death, thus proving to Bradford "the vanitie of that conceite of Plato's and other ancients, applauded by some of later times, that the taking away of propertie, and bringing in communitie into a comone wealth, would make them happy and florishing; as if they were wiser then God."

When all had equal portions regardless of their contribution to the community, Bradford reflected as he turned it over and over in his mind, the less talented got the notion that they were as good as the better endowed, which was upsetting to "those relations that God had set amongst men." There is no pride of class in this conclusion; simply a hardheaded recognition of the fact that men vary in abilities and are therefore unwilling to do their best unless these talents are recognized. "Let none objecte this is men's corruption, and nothing to the course it selfe. I answer, seeing all men have this corruption in them, God in his wisdome saw another course fiter for them."

Knowing that he was breaking the agreement with the adventurers yet willing to take the responsibility upon himself, Bradford "with the advise of the cheefest amongest them" announced that every man should raise his own corn. Every family was assigned a portion of land according to its size, and all the unattached youths and boys were assigned to families.

"This had very good success," Bradford soon noticed with delight, "for it made all hands very industrious, so as much more corne was planted then other waise would have bene by any means the Governor or any other could use, and saved him a great deall of trouble, and gave farr better contente. The women now wente willingly into the feild, and tooke their litleons with them to set corne, which before would aledg weaknes, and inabilitie; whom to have compelled would have bene thought great tiranie and oppression."

But now, having set all their seed corn, there was not a kernel left to eat. They had no bread, nor grain of any kind to make it with. "All ther victails were spente, and they were only to rest on Gods providence; at night not many times knowing wher to have a bitt of any thing the next day." Hard as their trials had been before, they had never been so close to death as this. There appeared now to be little hope that the adventurers would send any supply. Nor would the Indian tribes who had lost their sachems be likely to rush in with offers of food, even if they had any to spare.

By now the Pilgrims, who had never been expert sailors or fishermen, had but one boat left. Yet life itself depended on their taking food from the ocean. So dividing all the men into several companies of six or seven each, Bradford sent them to sea on a regular schedule. "No sooner was the boate discharged of what she brought, but the next company tooke her and wente out with her. Neither did they returne till they had cauight something, though it were 5 or 6 days before, for they knew ther was nothing at home, and to goe home emptie would be a great discouragemente to the rest." Somewhere the colony had at last acquired a proper net. But even with the net they sometimes failed to take enough fish. Then the whole colony went to digging shellfish out of the sands at low water. Plymouth Harbor with its acres of sand flats was a lifesaver to the Pilgrims, yet they grew heartily sick of the diet it provided and would feel no enthusiasm at all for the shore dinners Plymouth provides today to the thousands who come to see the place where they lived and worked. They would ask for bread, beef and beer.

By keeping one or two of their best hunters ranging through the woods they were able once in a while to satisfy their craving for red meat. When a deer was brought in, it was divided amongst them all.

From the middle of April until the end of May (1623) the colonists were busy with planting. After the ground had been prepared they hauled heavy buckets full of alewives up from Town Brook as Squanto had taught them, placing them spokewise in each hill of corn and setting a guard each night to fend off the wolves. Nearly exhausted by their labor because of the lack of food, the planters began to dream of an ample harvest from a larger planting than they had ever undertaken. But from the end of May until the middle of July their plans and plants were blighted by such a drought as they had thought impossible in this country. "The stalke of that was first set," Winslow wrote, "began to send forth the eare before it came to halfe growth, and that which was later, not like to yeild any at all, both blade and stalke hanging the head, and changing the colour in such manner, as wee judged it utterly dead. Our Beanes also ran not up according to their wonted manner, but stood at a stay, many being parched away, as though they had beene scorched before the fire."

As if this were not enough there now came news of a supply which had been sent out from London only to be twice driven back by weather and ill luck of the most persistent sort. Yet— wheels within wheels—there was worse news contained in the very nature of this supply. For the ship on which supply and passengers were to come had been chartered by John Peirce, a London merchant and one of the adventurers, in whose name the Gorges patent for the colony had been taken out. And Peirce, working behind the backs of all the other adventurers, had persuaded the Council for New England to void the earlier patent and to issue in its stead one which gave all the Plymouth lands and more too to himself and his heirs forever. Under this patent the Pilgrims were his tenants and he their feudal lord. The only thing that had prevented Peirce from enforcing the patent was the loss and discouragement arising out of the damage done his ship. This had made it possible for the other adventurers to buy him off "with great trouble & loss" * so that once more the Pilgrims had a right to the ground beneath them.

With all this bad news came some that was good: a ship called the *Anne* was to leave England for Plymouth at the end of April, with sixty passengers and sixty tons of goods.

No doubt among the letters that reached Bradford was one from Alice Southworth, telling him that she would come in the *Anne.* By this time he must have wondered why he had been so mad as to invite a woman to share the miseries of this impoverished place. It wrung his heart to look at his people, they were so lean with hunger, so ragged in apparel. Worst of all, they no longer flared up against their fate but accepted it with a dulled consciousness. Even the children walked sedately instead of running and shouting. When their work in the fields was ended,

* The adventurers had expended for goods, passage-money, and subsistence £640, for most of which they had a claim on Peirce. In part payment of this claim he surrendered his stock as an adventurer, and assigned his patent to the Company.—Goodwin, *The Pilgrim Republic,* 236.

they had no strength for games. How beautiful now must Leyden have seemed in retrospect, far beyond even the extravagant praise of Polyander.

Now as a result of all these misfortunes there came into Bradford's mind the thought which to a man of his convictions was the darkest, the most frightening of all possible experiences. Could it be that the hand of God was against them? Had He determined to destroy them?

Search as he might, and often as he talked it over with Brewster, he could not see how as a church they had failed to comply with the commands of God, or how as a civil community they had failed to come closer than any people in Europe to the pattern suggested in the Bible. God's displeasure then must be directed toward those amongst them who were not of the church. Once you understand this point of view, the forbearance and tolerance of the Pilgrims toward the non-church colonists is truly remarkable—formed and tempered no doubt by the biblical admonitions regarding the stranger within the gates.

One thing they could do: they could "humble themselves together before the Lord by fasting and prayer."

Bradford appointed the day. It was cloudless, hot, dry—one of those sizzling July days of which New England is capable, as if to balance out the zeros of February. As on a Sunday they marched solemnly up the hill to the fort which was their meeting house, dressed in their best clothes. At the rear of the procession marched Bradford in a long robe, Brewster on his right and Standish on his left—embodiment in their three persons of the civil, religious and military arms of government. All day the men of Plymouth spent in prayer and meditation, with such success that "before our departure the weather was over-cast, the clouds gathered together on all sides, and on the next morning distilled such soft, sweet, and moderate showers of rayne, continuing some foureteene dayes, and mixed with such seasonable weather, as it was hard to say whether our withered Corne, or drouping affections were most quickned or revived. Such was the bountie and goodnes of our God." An inquiring Indian who happened by was much struck by the particularity of the English God in sending such gentle rain. Likely as not, he said, when their medicine men asked for rain it came "mixed with such stormes and tempests, as sometimes in stead of doing them good, it layeth the Corne flat on the ground." While the skeptic may wonder why the Pilgrims failed to pray sooner and what would have happened if they had, the important fact for history is that they now felt themselves sustained by God and able therefore to go on.

Now if only the promised supply from England would come . . . But there was reason to fear for the safety of the *Anne*. A ship which had put in at Plymouth toward the end of June had brought news of meeting a supply ship—presumably the *Anne* —at sea. They had been separated thereafter in a storm, but if the ship had come through safely she should have reached Plymouth before this.

For the first two weeks of July Bradford added to his other burdens the fear that the *Anne* and with it Alice Southworth had been destroyed. On that day of prayer and fasting his own petitions must have gone more toward the safety of the ship than the need for rain.

Then, on a day not long after the season of gentle showers began, a ship was sighted.* As always, a ship from home was the signal for a general rush to the shore in the hope of finding wife or children aboard, or at least letters and news from those left at home, as well as good English bread, beef and beer—even if the bread be hard-tack and the beef salted.

As Bradford waited with the rest, watching the boat as it was swung over the side and rowed slowly—too slowly—in, he felt almost as much fear as joy. For the colonists standing around him were a ragged lot, "some litle beter than halfe naked," all looking pinched and hungry. As governor, the responsibility was his. Those who came ashore could not know how great a miracle it was that the settlers were alive at all, and in good health too despite their thin waists and pinched cheeks.

As the passengers came ashore he could see the shock in their faces. Some wept at what they saw, others wished themselves in England again. But for the old friends from Leyden the pleasure of being together was sufficient.

Brewster and his wife wept gladly at the sight of their daughters Patience and Fear, now young ladies of twenty-three and

---

* Bradford places the date about July 14, Winslow at the end of the month.

seventeen. Francis Cooke embraced his wife Hester and his three children aged from five to eight, of whom only the oldest remembered him. Sam Fuller found his wife in the crowd now filling the beach, Thomas Morton his son and namesake, while a number of the strangers who had come over on the *Fortune* in 1621 found wives and children—Thomas Flavell, Robert Hicks, William Hilton, William Palmer. Richard Warren, a *Mayflower* passenger, got the largest parcel of all—a wife and five daughters. Standish got himself a girl whom he married so quickly that her maiden name has been lost. Allerton gained a sister, the former wife of Degory Priest who had died in the first sickness. She was now married to Godbert Godbertson (Cuthbert Cuthbertson), a Walloon hatter from Leyden.

But amidst all these friends, each of whom deserved and received a hearty welcome, Bradford was looking for one—for Alice Southworth. He had put on his best suit for her, the one with silver buttons, perhaps—it is an error of the nineteenth century to suppose that the Pilgrims went always in drab-colored clothes and tall hats, and after the country custom then prevalent in England he may have given her a kiss of welcome.

It revived his heart to see her; it replenished his spirit to know that she had been willing to come. Now he could look forward to having a home again. Now he could look forward to living in a state befitting a governor. Yet even as he offered his arm to lead her up the hill, a twinge of shame struck him at the thought that the best he could offer her was a lobster (always indifferent fare to the Pilgrims) and a cup of fair spring water with never a morsel of bread.

"Abused, Traduced, Calumniated, Overthrowne & Undone"

THOUGH William Bradford had reason to regret the gaunt and bedraggled appearance of the colonists, he was proud of one thing to which he now impatiently led Alice Southworth. This was the governor's house, standing inside its own fence at Plymouth's only crossroads and occupying the northwest corner of what is now the junction of Main and Leyden streets. It stood in a larger plot than the eleven other houses, and though small enough it looked large by comparison with the rest. West of it at the foot of Fort Hill were the homes of Standish and Alden and beyond, atop the hill, was the plain, solid cube of the building which served as defense and meeting place.

Leading Alice up to the house now, his hand may have trembled on the latch string as he bowed her in before him. The moment was important. Alice's first impression was important. Strong though he had proven himself in every test, he must have trembled with anticipation. It was not likely that she would refuse him, having come so far. And yet—well, a man must tremble after waiting so long, enduring so much, and hoping so greatly.

Bradford had done the best he could to make the place attractive with Dorothy's household goods. But there had been little room on the *Mayflower* for furniture, so that the long, rough-hewn trestle table and benches, the few stools and the large bed

were all of native make. He had placed a turkey-work carpet on
the table, hoping that this touch of the mode would hide the
marks of the adze. He had carefully placed a few pewter dishes, a
couple of silver spoons and an iron rush-light holder on the
carpet. In the fireplace, which nearly filled the north wall, burned
a small fire for cooking. One commodity the Pilgrims never
lacked was wood, and men arriving from Old England never
failed to be impressed by their lavish use of it. No one in England, wrote an early settler, is "able to afford to make so great
fires." The fireplace was without mantelpiece, a huge oak beam
being laid across the top of the opening. Trivets, a large iron
pot, and a few other cooking utensils lay on the hearth. Except
for the silver spoons and the turkey carpet there was little
appearance of luxury, to be sure, yet the house had a certain
snug and cozy look about it. A woman's eye would immediately
see what was needed, a woman's mind would immediately begin
to assume ownership and devise plans. Likely as not, it was this
challenge, and her wonderfully habitual acceptance of it, which
bridged the first gap of embarrassment when Alice Southworth
came face to face with what the new world meant, and when
William Bradford stood awkward and overwhelmed with what
he had asked of her. We can hope that they had a moment to
themselves now, though the governor's advice was needed everywhere at once with all the new arrivals to be accommodated and
the ship to be unloaded. We can hope that Bradford was able to
repeat what he had written and Alice to grant what he asked.

The arrival of the *Anne* with more than ninety passengers
again taxed living accommodations to the limit. Building must
have gone forward at great speed, for not many months later
there were thirty-two houses at Plymouth for a hundred and
eighty residents.

Alice Southworth, though leaving her two children behind,
had not come without family. Her older sister Juliana had come
with her husband George Morton and five children. As G. Mourt,
Morton had fathered the first published account of Plymouth,
known as *Mourt's Relation*. As leader of the *Anne* company and,
even more important, a native of Harworth near Bradford's
own birthplace, Morton would certainly have been invited to
share the governor's home. The arrangement also made it pos-

sible for Alice to move directly into Bradford's house without waiting until they were married.

The marriage was delayed just long enough to suggest that the couple waited for Morton to get enough of his house built so that he and his large family could move out.

On August 14, then, Alice and William were married—not by Brewster, but by Isaac Allerton, the deputy governor. The marriage of a man so well liked, so deeply respected must have been a public affair. The feeling for young Governor Bradford was not like the usual respect for a public official seen at a distance and formally acknowledged as the symbol of government. Bradford had worked and sweat by the side of the poorest colonist. Every child in the colony knew his moods and manners. To Englishmen, accustomed to class distinctions, this was a new kind of magistrate—one who could be dignified, clothed with the majesty of the law, yet who could put off his long robe to hoe and hack and saw with the rest. Necessity may have dictated this. Or Bradford's rural upbringing. Yet there was something essential and deep in the man, too, that could respond to this concept of a governor. Here a new attitude toward law and government was in the making. Unconsciously, Bradford was forming the model of the self-made man, the public officer as servant of the people, which was to leave its mark upon future generations.

Yet more than this, William Bradford had become a symbol in the popular mind—a symbol of survival and fatherhood. To some degree all public figures undergo this unconscious transmutation in the minds of the people. To a child, parents are of such overwhelming importance that they carve in the mind the patterns by which all future relationships are judged. Thereafter teachers, bosses, policemen, presidents come to be loved or hated (or both) with reference to these parental symbols. So Bradford as head of the struggling little colony had become the psychological father of all. His strength, his vision were relied on to pull them through, just as the real father of childhood had provided and protected. The price of this protection—Bradford's superiority in command—they were willing to pay, as they had paid it in childhood to their parents. Yet something new and sweet entered into the relationship, something that did not quite correspond with the ambivalent symbol of the father who was loved for his protection but hated for his authority. Bradford acted like a brother, an equal. He brought into play that other symbol—of the brother who helped but did not exert absolute authority. Fatherhood and brotherhood—through these two simple, basic, psychological formulas men habitually regard their relations with other men, and governments are patterned on them, whether autocratic or democratic. The secret of Bradford's lasting success at Plymouth was his ability to give the protection of fatherhood and the equal spirit of brotherhood, and thus to fulfill in himself the requirements of these two basic symbols governing the reactions of men to those they work with and for. It is a secret still but little understood by those who would be governors of men.

So when Bradford led Alice Southworth up the hill to the fort, his act inevitably had in it something of the ancient fertility rite (as does the marriage of a prince or princess even today), the marriage of the father-governor somehow guaranteeing increase and plenty to all.

It was in no sober garb that Bradford set out. He may have chosen his turkey grogram suit and cloak, or the lead-colored suit with silver buttons, set off by a violet cloak and a colored hat. Alice would have been wearing a gown, perhaps of purple, turned under and looped back from the front to show her petticoat. Perhaps she permitted herself a gathered sleeve, a bit of lace at cuff and collar, but remembering the infamous affair of Thomasine Johnson's finery with its disastrous effects upon the church at Amsterdam, she would have been mighty careful. Simple declarations were given, an entry was made in the record (subsequently lost) of births, marriages and deaths, and that was all. The memory of a similar experience when he had stood before the Dutch magistrate with Dorothy must have run through Bradford's mind, and a twinge of regret for that pure, earnest and youthful love. Such a love was irrecoverable. It could happen but once. With Alice it would be a different thing—mature, not shy, experienced rather than adventurous. But they were still young, still zestful, still able to delight in the pleasures of marriage as their pastor had assured them they had a right to do according to nature and God's plan.

He had waited long and endured much, and now he could be a whole man again.

A week or ten days after the arrival of the *Anne,* the *Little James* came in. She had started out with the *Anne,* separated from her in a storm, and had been despaired of when she appeared off Manomet Point and stood in for shore. "A fine new vessell of about 44 tune," Bradford observed, she was built to stay in the country and to perform the duties for which the *Speedwell* had been intended. Fishing and trading had from the beginning been planned as Plymouth's economic base—not subsistence agriculture. Now at last the Pilgrims could work according to plan. Or so they thought.

But first the *Anne* must be laden and sent home to gratify the London adventurers. And this must be done while houses were a-building so that the passengers could be accommodated ashore. Meanwhile there were the fields to be tended and the day's fare to be sought at sea or in the mud flats of the harbor.

Warned by previous experience, the old planters were afraid that their corn would go to feed the newcomers. After the agreement Bradford had made with them, this would have been disastrous. But since the newcomers were equally afraid that the others would consume the provision they had brought, an agreement was arrived at whereby the *Anne* passengers were to have all the provision that had come over with them, the old planters to enjoy exclusively the fruits of their labors even though this meant going on short rations until harvest time.

About the twenty-fifth of August the *Anne* departed, well laden with furs and clapboard (lumber for barrel staves), an important item of commerce in those wine-bibbing, beer-drinking days. She also carried Edward Winslow whom Bradford was sending back to give first-hand information to the adventurers. He was instructed to arrange for their pastor to come to them (the adventurers had been obstructing this), to see that the next supply contained useful trade goods and fishing gear, and to prevent the coming over of any more unqualified strangers (of which the *Anne* had brought a sufficient number) or "particulars."

For the *Anne* had brought ten men who, according to instructions from the adventurers, were not to share the work of the

colony but were to be "on their own particular." It was an arrangement calculated to make trouble. So when Bradford had
bid farewell to Winslow and the friendly ship's captain William
Peirce, he had to address himself to the problem of fitting these
men into the life of the colony. An agreement was drawn up
by which they were to have "competente places for habitations
within the towne." * Though subject to all laws, they were ex-
empt from work for the colony except military and other public
service. They were not to trade with the Indians and each male
over sixteen was to pay a bushel of corn a year, or its equivalent,
for the maintenance of the government.

Next Bradford had to busy himself about the harvest, though
with each man responsible for his own this was less burdensome
than it had been before. With his young charges—Thomas Cushman, Joseph Rogers and William Latham—he gathered up the
ripe ears of corn and the bean pods which would provide their
winter staple, and perhaps a few Indian askutasquash, soon to
became a familiar item of New England diet under the simpler
name of squash.

Harvest was scarcely over when a new surprise descended
upon a colony which by now must have been almost immune
to shock. Captain Robert Gorges, son of the indefatigable
old colonizer Sir Ferdinando, put into the harbor (after first
settling at Wessagusset) and was soon ashore exhibiting a commission which in effect put an end to Bradford's governorship!
Appointed general governor of New England by his father's
Council for New England, he was to have almost unlimited
authority, though Bradford was to be one of his advisers and
assistants for the time being.

Despite this blow, Bradford entertained him for two weeks—
long enough for the two men to become thoroughly acquainted
in the close quarters Plymouth afforded. Gorges confided to
Bradford that one of his jobs was to apprehend Weston, who
had cozened his father by getting a license for exporting ordnance to New England and then selling the guns for his own
profit abroad. Weston having the ill luck to return to Plymouth
at this point was called before Gorges and let off only on Bradford's plea. Whereupon, as soon as Gorges had left, Weston be-

* It is worth noting that the concept of a town is already present.

gan talking behind Bradford's back. "Though they were but
yonge justices, yet they wear good beggars," he said of the Plymouth men who had shared their rations with him, provided him
with beaver, and saved him from punishment. Weston, like
most men, was quickest to see in others the very fault of which
he was himself guilty. In any case this is his last appearance, for
he set sail for Virginia in the *Swan* while Gorges returned to
Wessagusset by land—leaving Bradford to wonder how long he
would remain governor of Plymouth.

The *Swan* also carried away several of those who had just
come over on the *Anne* "on their perticuler, some out of discon-
tente and dislike of the cuntrie, others by reason of a fire that
broke out, and burnt the houses they lived in, and all their
provisions." It also came near to burning down the Plymouth
storehouse which contained all the trade goods, supplies and
provisions for the colony. Apparently there was treachery, for
in the midst of the uproar, the street full of half-drunken sailors
from the ship getting in the way of frantic colonists running up
with buckets and wet cloths, a voice cried:

"Look well about you, for all are not friends that are near
you."

When the worst of the fire was over, a wattled shed of the storehouse was found to be smoldering, and investigation showed that
a firebrand an ell long was lying against the dried leaves of the
wattles, in such a position that it did not seem possible it could
have come there except by a human hand.

While the departure of Weston and some of the "particulars"
(including Timothy Hatherly who was one of the adventurers
and is to be heard from again) had brought some relief, the
threat to their autonomy hung heavily over the Plymouth colonists during the winter of 1623. Also the pinnace, *Little James,*
was a disappointment. An unruly crew, sent over to work on
shares, finally had to be put on wages on Bradford's responsibility, and when they went around to Narragansett to trade
"they made but a poore vioage of it." The Dutch, who had
settled during this year at New Amsterdam, were beating them
out of the Indian trade, and it was several years before the Pilgrims would solve the mystery of their success. Then at the har-

bor's mouth on her way home, the *Little James* was caught in a storm and had to cut her main mast away to keep from being driven on the flats.

In the midst of these misadventures came one major piece of good news. Gorges had departed for England, leaving Bradford once more to govern without interference. "Haveing scarcly saluted the cuntrie," Gorges had found that it did not "answer his quallitie & condition." There is a tone of irony in this quiet observation. For Bradford, experiencing the exhilaration of a talented man set free in a wide new world, knew that the old qualities and conditions counted for nothing here. A man stood or fell by what he was and what he could do. And Gorges by this test had proven himself inferior to the yeoman's son.

For three years Bradford had been governor, bearing the brunt of all the blows that had threatened to extinguish the colony—hunger, Indian attack, wasting disease, the failure of a supply, dissension, and the usurping of his powers. There had scarcely been a moment free of crisis since, weakened by illness, he had first taken up the job. He was tired. He wanted rest. He wanted to be relieved of the constant interruptions, the habit the colonists were falling into of dropping their problems on him and leaving them there, the lack of any leisure to spend with Alice. This time, he told her, he would flatly refuse to go on.

So at the annual meeting toward the end of March he stood up before the men who for three years had followed him as leader and told them to find another governor. "If it is any honor or benefit," he said, "it is fit others should be made partakers of it. If it is a burden, it is but equal others shall help to bear it." Then he told them that they should give the next governor more assistants than he had had.

But the colony would not let him off. There was not another man amongst them who matched their concept of governor, not another man they would consent to put in his place. Much as he wanted to quit, Bradford could not help being moved by the tribute. Conscious of the bond of suffering which bound him to them, humbled to tears at the realization of their regard, he finally consented to carry on for another year though with five assistants serving him as a council in which he would have a

double voice. And so, somewhat sheepishly no doubt, he had to
return to Alice after all his brave talk of getting off and admit
that they had talked him into it once again.

Anyone who has filled a position of responsibility knows how
Bradford felt—how the desire to put down a sometimes intolerable burden conflicted with a need for the genuine admiration it
also brought. Perhaps a leader is only a man who needs love and
challenge more than he needs peace. Certainly Bradford's success
as a leader came partly from the high valuation he put upon the
father symbol as a result of his fatherless youth, and from his
ability to be a nearly ideal father to his people. "A common father to them all," Cotton Mather was to write of him, never
guessing how precise and how suggestively right his choice of
the word "father" was.

Only a week or two before the election Bradford had passed his
thirty-fourth birthday. Yet already he was old in experience, the
only man in the world who had succeeded in making a new world
colony sustain itself. He had learned a good many things about
human nature and the governing of men. He had the courage
of Standish, the diplomacy of Winslow, the dignity of Carver
and the spirituality of Brewster. His contemporaries found many
things in him, and their variety is a measure of the man. He
had a "cherfull fram of sperit," he was "loving unto all," he was
"a person of great gravity and prudence . . . and for one of
that persuasion very pliable, gentle, and condescending." He
was "discreet and grave," "prudent and godly." Even the enemies
of the colony, though they lampooned Standish, left Bradford
alone.

Like Franklin, he had that fortunate combination of the intellectual and the practical. He was the sort of man who could convert ideas into acts, being intelligent enough to grasp big ideas
and practical enough to beat them out upon the anvil of experience. He was an Admirable Crichton whose power of leadership seemed instinctive, whose energy inexhaustible. In early
Plymouth there was no distinction between the various branches
of civil government. Bradford exercised them all. As executive
he handled the food rations, dealt with visitors and neighboring
tribes or settlements, handled the accounts, supervised the military and arranged for the importation of food. As magistrate he

sentenced those who had done wrong and saw the sentence carried out. As business agent—for Plymouth was half government and half business firm, with very little formal distinction between them at first—he traded with the Indians, saw to the lading of ships, the inventorying of supplies, the movements of ships, the assignment of jobs. Yet he could hoe and saw with the rest of them on week days, and prophesy on Sunday.

That a man could be all these things, exercise all these authorities, and still be loved by those he ruled is close to a miracle. That he could be all these things and still avoid dictatorship is more remarkable still. He knew how to be both firm and kindly. He knew when to be stern and when to break the tension with a joke. Above all, he had integrity—that hardest of all virtues to define though most quickly perceived in its absence.

When you add to these things the fact that he was a linguist, a scholar, a writer of charm, a man having wide familiarity with the written culture of the past and of his own day, you have shown that he was, even at thirty-four, a great man. Not a perfect one, God forbid. He took an Old Testament delight in the downfall of the colony's enemies. And he was both indefatigable and ingenious in cutting down those he thought injurious to the colony he had kept alive with the breath of his own body. The most famous of these encounters we are now about to see.

Not long after Bradford's re-election Captain William Peirce brought the *Charity* again into Plymouth Harbor with four important passengers—Edward Winslow, a ship's carpenter, a saltmaker and a man who was soon to come near destroying the colony, the Reverend John Lyford. More exciting to the colonists than the appearance of any of these gentlemen, however, were the three heifers and a bull which Winslow brought with him. The first cattle in the land, they were to do more for the Plymouth economy than all the expensive and ill-starred adventures in fishing which, as Bradford truly observed, was "a thing fatall to this plantation." The ship's carpenter proved capable and industrious, quickly building several shallops and other boats that served the colony for many years, though he died before he could complete the program. The saltmaker turned out to be a windbag with little skill at his craft. He finally burned down the building and ruined many of the pans with which he had been supplied, so that the attempt to make the colony self-sufficient in the producing of salt fish for the English market came to nothing. Nor did the Pilgrims ever succeed as fishermen despite the large and continuous investments the adventurers made (at heavy cost to the Pilgrims) in ships, supplies, and English crews. This was a business they never got the hang of, and it must stand as Bradford's most conspicuous failure.

At planting time the colonists begged Bradford to assign them lands on a permanent rather than a yearly basis, so that they might have the benefit of fields they had already worked hard to clear and improve. Calling to mind an observation of Seneca's, "that a great parte of libertie is a well governed belly," Bradford agreed, assigning an acre to each person. Thus the superiority of private venture over communal labor was recognized and adopted as a permanent principle.

As for Lyford, a minister of the Anglican church, Bradford and Brewster accepted with the best grace they could this flouting of their desire to have their own Pastor Robinson sent over. But a faction among the adventurers had consistently opposed it, sending Lyford as a substitute. Lyford, on his first coming ashore, behaved in a manner so humble as to embarrass Bradford. He bowed and cringed, "and would have kissed their hands if they would have suffered him; yea, he wept & shed many tears, blessing God that had brought him to see their faces." Though he came with a large family which the colony would have to feed, Bradford welcomed him with the best entertainment Plymouth was capable of and invited him to sit with the assistants who, together with Brewster, made up the governor's council. Soon Lyford was asking to be received into the church. After making "a large confession of his faith, and an acknowledgemente of his formerly disorderly walking," he was accepted, the Pilgrims little guessing as yet what these "disorders" were. Soon Lyford was preaching on Sundays, dividing the labor with Brewster. John Oldham, one of the "particulars" who had been a thorn to the governor, now came forward "out of some sudden pange of conviction" to ask forgiveness for past sins and was promptly taken into the council. Thus unwittingly Bradford had given the fifth column an advantage they were soon to use.

In time Oldham returned to his old ways, showing "a spirite of great malignancie," and trying to build up a faction against the church among men like Billington, with many "private meetings and whisperings amongst them." Now Lyford, joining forces with Oldham, was observed to be much busied with his pen as if he were writing a book, whispering such things to his adherents "as made them laugh in their sleeves." When Captain Peirce made ready to depart, Lyford handed him a stack of letters.

It was clear to Bradford that some sort of conspiracy was brewing. The London adventurers were already quarreling amongst themselves, and such ammunition as Lyford was sending might lead them to break with the colony entirely. Gorges' departure had left Bradford in an equivocal position, a governor more by default than by authority. Any stirring up of mistrust might bring the whole Council for New England down upon them, might even bring annulment of their patent and a prohibition of their worship. That this was no idle fear was plain from the fact that Gorges had brought with him an Anglican priest, William Morrell, who—the Pilgrims learned only at his departure—had been granted authority to superintend all churches in New England. To Bradford it looked as if Lyford's activities were simply part of a plan to annul the present government of Plymouth and destroy its church.

Speaking a word to his friend Peirce, therefore, he waited until the ship had put to sea, then followed it out in a shallop, boarded, and with the ship hove to, opened and read all the letters Lyford and Oldham were sending back to England. As expected, the letters were full of slanders and accusations. With the help of a few trusted friends who had come with him he therefore copied out most of what Lyford and Oldham had written, and in some cases kept the originals while forwarding copies. He also found that Lyford had done some letter purloining of his own, for enclosed in one of his letters were copies of letters by Winslow and a friend of Brewster's which he could have got only by opening them while they lay "sealed in the great cabin" as the ship was outward bound from England.

After returning the letters to Peirce, Bradford came back to Plymouth. The copying had been a great labor. It was night when the shallop glided up to the dock. The next morning Lyford and Oldham looked somewhat guiltily at the governor. He gave them a grave good morning and went on about his business, willing to wait until they set a trap for themselves.

When Oldham picked a quarrel with Standish, calling him a beggarly rascal and even drawing a knife on him, it looked as though the trouble had begun. Bradford, hearing the noise, sent him word to be quiet, but when he ranted more, calling them all traitors and rebels, the governor had him jailed at the fort.

Then Lyford, without saying a word to Bradford, Brewster, or any others in authority, held an Anglican service. The brethren had now endured enough. Bradford summoned the whole company to a general court at which he accused Lyford and Oldham of "disturbing their peace, both in respecte of their civill & church state, which was most injurious; for both they and all the world knew they came hither to injoye the libertie of their conscience and the free use of Gods ordinances." For Lyford to join the church and then seek their ruin, said Bradford, was perfidy. As for Oldham, who had enjoyed the protection of the colony while unable to stand alone, he was like the hedgehog in the fable who, after begging a cony to let him into her burrow, ended by forcing her out and having it to himself.

When Lyford denied the charges in an injured manner, Bradford pulled out the letters and began to read them, whereupon Lyford, as well he might be, "was struck mute." But Oldham jumped up in a rage, threatening to drag Bradford through all the courts of England. Then, turning to the company, he called:

"My masters, where is your hearts? Now show your courage. You have oft complained. Now is the time; if you will do anything I will stand by you."

No doubt Standish and a picked group stood to their arms at the fort's one door while Bradford stood his ground in front of the assembly. As the Pilgrims always went armed to church it is likely they took the same precaution at a town meeting, so if trouble should break out now there would be no lack of arms to make it bloody.

But there was not even a muttering to break the dramatic silence. Not a man rose to stand beside Oldham. Not a man spoke in his support.

Bradford then turned his attention to Lyford, asking whether he thought they had done evil to open his letters. It was a master stroke, for Lyford, knowing well enough that his own rifling of the ship's mail had been discovered, was wise enough to make no reply. Bradford next explained to the people that he had intercepted Lyford's letters under his authority as a magistrate and to prevent the colony's ruination. After having some more of the letters read he invited Lyford to defend himself. Billington, said Lyford, had told him many of the things he had put in his letters. But Billington, who seems to have been many a man's scapegoat, denied that he had ever said such things as Lyford had set down. Bradford then took up, point by point, every item in Lyford's letters, giving him opportunity to justify himself if he could. His only defense was that he had been misinformed. Then Bradford came to what was obviously the sorest point of all— Lyford's ministration of the Anglican sacraments after becoming a member of the Plymouth church.

Bradford's conduct of the examination must have been devastating. Indeed the whole plan of attack from the deferred accusation to the open meeting shows a sense of drama and timing quite in keeping with the age of Shakespeare but rather surprising in men who scorned the stage. Already the Pilgrims were learning that as a substitute for the theater a town meeting was hard to beat. Lyford, a character straight out of Molière, now began blubbering and begging forgiveness.

"I have so wronged you as I can never make amends," he cried. "It was all false—all false and nought, both for matter and manner."

Convicted, Oldham and Lyford were sentenced by Bradford to be expelled from the colony. Oldham was to go at once even though it was winter. His family might stay until he was able to care for them. Lyford might remain for six months. If he behaved himself, sentence might be revoked.

When Lyford followed his first confession with an even fuller one in church, he was allowed to teach once more. Gentle Sam Fuller was all for having his sentence revoked at once. Yet within a month or two he was caught at his old tricks again, writing to England that everything he had said in his earlier letters was true though he had been forced to deny it. When Lyford's six months had expired and he was to be turned out of the colony, his wife was so concerned that she confided to one of the deacons and several of her friends the fact that Lyford had not only had a child out of wedlock but had lied to her about it, and after their marriage had been found several times with the housemaids in circumstances which required no imagination as to what he was about. She now feared, she said, that God's anger would overtake them once they were turned out of town, and that she would be defiled by Indians as her husband had misused others. (She might have been spared that worry. The Indians never violated a white woman.)

When Winslow returned from England in the spring of 1625 he brought further news of Lyford. Outraged friends of the minister had demanded an investigation of his banishment, in the midst of which "two godly and grave witnesses" had testified that while in Ireland Lyford had seduced a girl whom a godly young parishioner with ideas of marriage had asked him to confer with. Not only had Lyford "satisfied his lust on her." He had also "indeaoured to hinder conception." Then he had commended her highly to the young man, who had married her. Troubled by conscience, she had finally confessed the whole thing. Thus the investigation of Lyford in England had ended with the recommendation that he be unfrocked.

Meanwhile March election court had come around again, and with it had come Oldham, though without permission to return to the colony. If he behaved as Bradford says, he must have been a mad bull indeed, for even the friends he had brought along were ashamed of his behavior though they were unable to restrain him. Bradford had him locked up until he calmed down, then ordered him to be passed through a guard of musketeers. "Ever one was ordered to give him a thump on the brich with the but end of his musket." After which he was "conveied" to a boat—still struggling, no doubt—and bid "goe & mende his maners." And, perhaps, his breeches.

In time Oldham did mend his manners, to such an extent that he was permitted to come and go at will. As for Lyford, he became pastor to a new settlement on Cape Ann near what is now Gloucester. Roger Conant, one of the "particulars" who had left Plymouth, was superintendent while Oldham was in charge of trade.

This new settlement was to lead to still further trouble. For one of the prizes Winslow had brought back from his first trip was a patent for a piece of land on Cape Ann. There the Pilgrims in 1624 had set up a stage and otherwise hopefully prepared once again to make money in the fishing business. But when they returned in 1625, it was to find the outcasts Oldham and Lyford in possession! They had appropriated the Pilgrim stage for the use of a fishing ship friends had sent out from England, and when the Pilgrims tried to take possession Oldham refused to give it up. The dispute moved briskly from taunts and accusations toward blows and battle until Captain Peirce at last arranged a compromise. Back to Bradford in Plymouth went an appeal for more manpower. Then the two parties joined forces and built a new stage for the Pilgrims, leaving Oldham and Lyford in possession of the old.

Relations with the adventurers in London, however, were not so easily rebuilt. Already the irate adventurers were calling them "contentious and intolerant, negligent, careless, wasteful, unthrifty." You "suffer all the general goods and affairs to go at sixes and sevens," they complained, "and spend your time in idleness." News of the exiling of Lyford and Oldham created such a storm that "the Company of Adventurers broake in peeces here upon, and the greatest parte wholy deserted the colony in regarde of any further supply." Disastrous as this seemed to the Pilgrims at the time, it opened the way toward a new deal (negotiations for which were begun by Standish on a trip home in 1625 and completed by Allerton in 1626) whereby the Pilgrims bought out the adventurers for £1,800, a sum equivalent to at least $130,000 (1951). They were to pay two hundred a year for nine years, beginning in 1628. "In which they rane a great adventure," says Bradford, "as their present state stood, having many other heavie burthens allready upon them, and all things in an uncertaine condition amongst them."

Meanwhile their harvests were good and they were able to trade corn for furs as far north as the Kennebec. But when Standish returned from England in the spring of 1626 he brought news that saddened the Pilgrims far more than any of their economic disasters. John Robinson, their beloved pastor, was dead. That King James and the Netherlands Prince Maurice had also died at about the same time was to them of far less importance. There came news of still one more death which touched Bradford closely —that of Robert Cushman whose son had been a part of the Bradford household since 1621.

In Thomas Cushman, now a young man of nineteen, Bradford must have seen himself as he had been during the first year in Holland. Having had the care of Thomas from his early teens, Bradford had led him through his most critical years, finding in him many of his own qualities and reliving through him those awakening years, now so distant, in the meadows around Auster-field and in the fellowship of the little congregation at Scrooby. As Brewster had been to Bradford, he was now in turn to Thomas Cushman. As events were to show, he managed to impart to Thomas some of his own fine qualities—a love of learning, concern for the church, and an ability to bring men together and heal their differences. Thomas was to follow Brewster as ruling elder (in 1649), a post he retained until his death in 1691—the year when Massachusetts Bay Colony succeeded in swallowing up Plymouth.

Surely Bradford's care of Thomas had in it a desire to make up for what he had failed to give his own son John, still unaccountably remaining in Holland and now a lad of eleven. Perhaps it was the realization of Thomas' loss which now spurred Bradford to insist on his own son's coming over, for not long after John did arrive—to confront a father who was a stranger to him and to meet a new mother, a half brother born in 1624 and an infant sister. By this time Bradford had also adopted Thomas Cushman as his own son, so that John suddenly found himself part of a large and utterly strange family. Did Bradford see in his features the girl-wife of his young manhood? Was it Dorothy's parents who had kept him in Holland, unable to give up the child who looked so much like their lost daughter? No one knows, or will ever know. But we do know that John failed to measure up to the rest of the family. While Thomas Cushman and William Junior became men of consequence in the colony, John, after marrying Martha Bourne for whose family the town at the base of the Cape is named, moved from Plymouth to Duxbury, from Duxbury to Marshfield, and finally to Norwich in Connecticut. The break during the years when he was growing from five to twelve had been too critical. For while Bradford, looking at the grown lad who was his son, could remember with a tug at the heart the youngster he had once held in his arms and kept from falling overboard into a Dutch canal, John had no such memory—only the vaguest recollection of a father whose actual appearance somehow did not jibe with this blurred memory at all. Moreover, he had lost a mother. In an irrational way he perhaps held this against his father.

So, in a family which was warmly bound together, he felt himself a stranger. Despite his father's efforts, despite gentleness and understanding, John remained withdrawn. And Bradford, understanding the tragedy out of the memory of his own orphaned childhood, could do nothing to change it. Memories he had thought dead came back to him—the feeling of desertion, the sense of being in but not of his uncle's household. How closely John's life paralleled his own—the early loss of parents, the necessity of depending on substitutes who however kind could never quite fill the need, the life in a household which was already a unit and where in little, unintentional ways—the necessary removal of someone else's clothes from a peg, a changing of places at table—the newcomer was made aware of his newness. Nothing Bradford was able to do wiped out the gap of those seven absent years. John kept moving around in search of that lost home whose memory, along with that of his young mother Dorothy, kept echoing in his mind. Though he never became a leader of men and left no children of his own, we may hope he found what he sought in Norwich, Connecticut.

Perhaps it was a sudden realization of what had happened to John that led Alice Bradford to send for her two children, for they came over about a year later. Constant Southworth (born about 1615) was the same age as John. Both he and Thomas, a year younger, became distinguished leaders in the colony.

Not long after his arrival in 1624 Bradford's friend George Morton had died. So until 1627 when his widow (a sister of Alice Bradford) married Menassah Kempton (sixteen years her junior), Bradford also took the responsibility of providing for this family of five children. Whether they lived at the governor's house or had a separate establishment we do not know. But in any case the oldest son, Nathaniel, continued to live with Bradford after his mother's remarriage. Almost the same age as John, he served as another hurdle to John's relations with his father. Under Bradford he learned to write and keep records, becoming his clerk at the age of eighteen. He went on to be clerk of town, colony and church. In a day when clerical abilities were rated higher than they now are, he received a good many grants of land and died a rich man—as wealth was then reckoned in those relatively unacquisitive days. As author of *New England's Memoriall* (1669) he preserved what for many years was the chief source of the information about Plymouth contained in Bradford's lost manuscript.

By 1628 the Bradford household consisted of the following assortment of children:

John Bradford (c. 1615–1678), son of Dorothy and William
Thomas Cushman (1607–1691)
William Bradford, Junior (1624–1703/4)
Mercy Bradford (c. 1627–   )
Nathaniel Morton (1616–1685), son of George Morton and Juliana Carpenter
Joseph Rogers (c. 1608–1678), son of Thomas who died in the first sickness
William Latham (died about 1645), Carver's servant boy
Constant Southworth (c. 1615–1679), and his brother
Thomas Southworth (c. 1616–1669)

No wonder John may have felt as if he had been superseded!

Once the Plymouth men gave up the idea that they could make a killing in the fish trade and began to concentrate on furs, their luck improved. In the summer of 1626, hearing that a plantation at Monhegan was to break up—for of the many colonies planted along the New England coast only Plymouth had so far had the grit to hold on—Bradford made up a crew and departed with Winslow to see what he could get hold of. A David Thomson who had settled at Pascataway (Piscataqua) insisted on going along with them, much to Bradford's disgust since the Monhegan men, "perceiveing their joynte desires to buy, held their goods at higher rates." Finally Bradford agreed with Thomson to make an offer for the whole lot, after which they would split. In this way over £500 worth of goods were purchased, including the contents of a French shipwreck which contained "Biscaie ruggs & other commodities." Bradford made payment chiefly in furs. Thomson now found that he had undertaken more than he could pay for and wanted to resell some of his share to Plymouth. Bradford, with a sharp eye to values, refused unless it was to buy the French goods only. Thomson, recognizing a shrewd trader when he saw one, soon gave in.

For the first time since the Pilgrims' arrival it now began to look like clear sailing ahead. They had another good harvest, they were well provided with trade goods, they had been able to pay their debts on time, were even able to reclothe their tattered people, and had extended their trade with the Indians.

Such good fortune proved but short-lived. For others (by which Bradford no doubt means to include Thomson and Oldham) gave the Indians twice as much for their furs, forcing the Pilgrims to do the same.

With Allerton's return in the spring of 1627, a new era began at Plymouth. Now that the tie with the merchant adventurers was dissolved—except for the debt which had to be extinguished—there was a danger that colonists who were not church members might consider themselves free of working "for the general," might try to go to trading on their own and thus make it impossible for the colony to pay off its heavy debt. Still suspicious of some of the "strangers" in the colony, Bradford realized that the only way to gain their allegiance was to give everyone an equal stake. All heads of families and all single young men who were free (that is, not bond servants) and of proven ability and discretion were therefore allowed to share in the division of the colony's property, which until now had been held in common. Each single man would have a share, while the head of a family could purchase as many shares as there were persons in his family. The trade would be retained as a monopoly, managed by the officers of the colony in order to pay off the debt.

The company, when called together, agreed to the plan. The next step was an actual division of land, houses and cattle. The residents of Plymouth were divided into groups of thirteen, to each of which was assigned a cow or heifer, and two of the goats brought back from the Monhegan trip. Each person was next assigned twenty acres of land in addition to the single acres he already had. Both cattle and land were chosen by lot. To Bradford and his household fell a heifer "of the greate white back cow."

As for the houses, each man was to keep the one he was in, but any inequalities were ironed out in such fashion that "he that had a better alowed some thing to him that had a worse." Bradford, for his services as governor without pay, had his house given him as did four or five others. These must certainly have been Standish, Brewster, Winslow and Allerton.

So at last Plymouth had cut loose from all outside control, and unless Gorges should take a notion to send over another governor for New England, or the new king begin to meddle in their affairs, the Pilgrims were at last free to manage themselves. More than ever the responsibility was Bradford's to develop a stable and prosperous government. His interpretation of the proper spheres of religion, politics and business is worth a close look.

Church, Town and Colony

THE governor's house stood at the center of Plymouth, on the corner where the street, passing from oceanside to fort, crossed the coastwise road which within the eye's reach became but a trail. That was the way the Pilgrims distinguished them—the street, and the road. No names were needed for there was but one of each. For Plymouth in 1627 was little if any larger than Plymouth in 1624. With its hundred and eighty people and its thirty-two houses it was about the size of Austerfield. From his doorway William Bradford could see all of Plymouth—its houses, fort, storehouse, wharf and graveyard. On the diagonal corner but a few feet away was the home of his well-loved foster father, William Brewster, in whose yard was the sweet spring where at most times of the day you could see a child or a woman dipping up water.

When William Bradford walked out of his house he knew everyone in sight, down to the youngest child. He knew the character and condition of every resident, knew not only the state of his pocketbook but the state of his soul. It is this intimacy which gives a special charm to Plymouth—the warmth of good neighborhood, the security of the known, the honesty and plain dealing which exist where nothing can be hidden for long, but most of all the personal quality entering into every transaction, every piece of business, even into the law. Something of the same quality remains in small New England towns and town meetings to this day. It is a condition in which the community has not been swallowed up by the state—in which the state is a *function* of the community.

The government of Plymouth was a personal affair, and the personality was William Bradford. At all times and seasons people came to the house which also served as his office and as impromptu court. If there was a deed, a will, an inventory to record, they came to Bradford.* He kept the books in his own hand. A couple who had made up their minds to marry came to him so that the contract could be recorded. Disputes over boundaries, quarrels seeking legal solutions came to him. Edward Dotey, often in trouble, has drawn blood of Josias Cooke, and Josias comes to complain. Helen Billington has slandered John Done. She will have to be fined, set in the stock and whipped. (Bradford was always hard on the Billingtons.) Stephen Hopkins has been letting servants sit drinking in his house and playing shovel board. And so it went. If the case required a jury, Bradford as magistrate would set the wheels in motion.

Often Standish would drop in to discuss the poor condition or small quantity of the colony's firearms, Fuller to report on an ailing patient, Allerton to discuss a trading trip. Often the inner council of half a dozen met there to tackle with their combined faculties a question of major importance such as the division of lands.

Yet simple and intimate as the Plymouth government seems, it was a very special instrument. Scholars, misled by its apparent simplicity or scorning its tininess, have paid it scant attention, preferring to concentrate on the larger and later colony of Massachusetts Bay. Some, bogged down in a semantic confusion which has led them to brand the Plymouth colony government irrelevant to a study of town government, dispose of the beginnings at Plymouth with a footnote. Yet Plymouth is one of the most interesting experiments in government the world has ever seen, and in many ways—even to such details as the calling of town meeting on the first Tuesday in March, a custom still alive in New England—it served as the foundation for American democracy. It was the essentially democratic Plymouth rather than the essentially theocratic Boston which held the key to the future.

The nature of Plymouth's government, on the surface so decep-

---

* Plymouth was six years ahead of Massachusetts Bay in recording deeds and wills.

tively simple, is difficult for us to grasp because religion, business and politics were approached through a common instrument. This was the idea of contract. Plymouth was built on three contracts—the religious covenant of the congregation at Scrooby, the political compact signed on the *Mayflower,* and the business contract with the adventurers in London. The commercial contract, because of an essential disagreement between the merchants and the colonists, was the source of many difficulties until the Pilgrims finally freed themselves of the adventurers in London, whereupon they made another compact among themselves to cover their business dealings. This arrangement was a success.

The very essence of the three compacts was their voluntary nature. In the religious covenant lies the secret of the Pilgrim concept of human relationships. And in the constant bickering and bitterness engendered by the contract with the London merchants lies the secret of the whole motivation of Plymouth. The Pilgrims could not stand the deal they had with the adventurers because their hands had been forced. The contract, they felt, was not voluntary. And volition was a sacred thing. It was the essence of their religious lives, it was the germ and seed of the Congregational way. It was even an attribute of God Himself. For the Pilgrim God was not the arbitrary tyrant of Calvin, but a father who had *voluntarily* placed Himself under the restraint of a covenant so that all who voluntarily covenanted with Him might be saved. Their chief objection to the Anglican church, remember, was that it forced all men together into one church, the good with the bad. It gave a man no choice. It destroyed the only true path— that of a compact or covenant—by which he could join himself to God. "Every particular soul must enter into a particular covenant with God; out of this way there is no life."

The next step was political. If the relation between man and God was through a covenant, the relationships among men for social ends should be by compact too. Plymouth in its modest way was a forerunner of Cromwell and the Commonwealth. The difference—and it is an important one—between Plymouth and Boston is that Plymouth never fused, or confused, these two compacts, the religious and the political. The leaders of Boston felt themselves divinely ordained to be rulers. Bradford, a yeoman, never did. His personality—for he might easily have been dictatorial—saved Plymouth from the fate of theocracy. The impetus behind the Pilgrim church was of course Calvinism, with its determination to purify not only the individual but "to renew society by penetrating every department of life, public as well as private, with the influence of religion." The Pilgrims always had in the forefront of their minds the desire to attack every problem both private and social with uncompromising idealism. They had a religious motivation, therefore, in everything they did about government. But they did not confuse the religious covenant and the political compact as others did. This is one of their great though unrecognized achievements in politics. Robert Browne, in *The Life and Manners of all True Christians*, the first English defense of a full measure of religious liberty, insists that the magistrate is to have no ecclesiastical authority. It was this Brownist conviction which made the Pilgrims radicals to the men of their own day, and which made Boston always a little suspicious of them even while borrowing their form of church government. For Boston realized that the theory of covenant and of social contract led on to the Plymouth way, led on to democracy. And Boston's leaders could not accept this loss of magisterial authority or admit that there was anything good in democracy.

In Plymouth, however, through the Mayflower Compact "the democratic Church had grown into a democratic State." Governor and council were chosen by the votes of all free men, without property restrictions, and the governor was always subject to examination or criticism by a popular assembly of the whole electorate. In Massachusetts Bay this vital spirit of true independency, of separation of church and state, was missing.

The love of local law, of self-government was therefore implicit in Separatism. Bradford and his friends had suffered too much from absolutism to repeat its errors. In the Netherlands, moreover, he had seen at work a system which acknowledged the importance of religion in the state without attempting to control it. There the state supported the churches but did not interfere with them. And there a man's voice in government was distinguished from his voice in the church. As early as 1568 William of Orange had acknowledged the contractual nature of the relationship between ruler and ruled, while local self-government in Holland was a vigorous thing. Fynes Moryson while traveling in Holland noted that "they love equality in all things, so they naturally kick against any great eminency among them." And Plymouth like Holland remained caste-free. There was no attempt here to set up a hierarchy of infallible ministers and uncontradictable magistrates. Blessed with a complete absence of blue-bloods and titles, Plymouth's leaders brought with them no aura of inherited authority to impose upon the rest. In the new world where land was free and plentiful, there was no occasion to divide men into land-owning and landless. There was no need of classes. Nor was there a division between a land-owning aristocracy and a rising class of merchant capitalists as in England.

To make certain that neither church nor state should exceed what properly belonged to each, no overlapping offices were permitted. When John Done was chosen as a deacon in 1633/4, he was immediately relieved of his job as assistant to the governor. In so small a colony and where the need of leadership was great, it would not have been surprising if Bradford had been chosen a deacon or Brewster, with his experience in matters of state, had been elected a deputy or assistant. But this never happened. Nor was the church permitted to meddle with marriage—another contractual relationship. Even with death and burial the church had no concern. Most, though not all of Plymouth's political leaders were members of the church, yet church membership was not a qualification for voting. And not until after Bradford's death was a property qualification applied. Only when the old leaders dropped off did Plymouth succumb to the less democratic influence from Massachusetts Bay.

So the church, under its own covenant, existed as a vital influence upon, but apart from the civil government. You could live in Plymouth and be an active partner in all three contracts—religious, civil and commercial, or you could be outside the church or for that matter outside all three. Obviously, you would be a more useful person if you took a full part in the life of the community. But it was not required.

The form of government at Plymouth, indebted first to Separatism and then to the extension of the covenant idea into the political or social contract, reached back into England as well as Holland for its ways of working. Although the New England town (and Plymouth was for administrative purposes first a town and later a collection of towns under a colonial government) can trace its origins back to the Teutonic mark, the Pilgrims knew nothing of this. All they could do was to borrow what was useful and what they could remember of local government as they had seen it in Holland and England. Much that they remembered from England they did not like, and much had to be improvised anyway because they were engaged not only in local government but in operating a tiny republic, surrounded by men of a totally different culture and cut off from the home government to which they owed at least a nominal allegiance.

But government as it developed in Plymouth showed several resemblances to that of the English parish or manor. True, the parish was both temporal and spiritual—which was chiefly what the Pilgrims did not like about it. Yet its vestry was chosen at a parish meeting which all might attend. As well as with church matters, it concerned itself with the care of the poor and repair of the roads, functions still handled by New England towns in a similar manner. Because the responsibility of office was little sought after, offices tended to rotate.

With their known attitude toward the Anglican church the Pilgrims would have been inclined to copy as little as possible of a political unit in which the rector was presiding officer, so any resemblances between Plymouth and an English parish are likely to be coincidental rather than purposeful. Of course any small local governing unit is bound to resemble small units in other times and places, and rural conditions everywhere promote a kind of primitive democracy. The important thing about the Pilgrim republic is its accent on voluntary association—on the idea of a contract freely entered into. In this the Pilgrims anticipated Rousseau.

The Plymouth men wanted to be sure about this, so they kept emphasizing it. In 1636 they passed a declaration that "no imposicon law or ordnance be made or imposed upon us by ourselves or others at present or to come but such as shall be made or imposed by consent according to the free liberties of the State and Kingdome of England and no otherwise." Thus Plymouth—which according to some modern scholars of government is of no political interest—had established that government by free choice of the governed which in England was but a theoretical dream in the minds of a few statesmen and philosophers.

The Pilgrims had to rely on their memories for what law they knew. Fortunately, since this was very little, they made their laws according to need rather than according to custom and precedent. There were no lawyers in Plymouth, which may account for the fact that Plymouth enacted a simple legal code which any man could understand. In England, as a matter of fact, the lawyers were against the idea of codification. As a result the laws there were in a chaotic state very profitable to lawyers. The Pilgrims, having begun to establish a legal basis for government before stepping off the *Mayflower,* carried on the process by enacting various laws and orders as the need arose. These were entered in Bradford's notebook, which unfortunately is lost. But the colony's record book, which probably came over in the *Anne,* preserves all the laws enacted beginning December 1623. The first entry there provides that "all criminal facts, and also all matters of trespasses and debts between man and man, should be tried by the verdict of twelve honest men, to be impanelled by authority, in form of a jury, upon their oath."

In 1636 Plymouth enacted the legal code which together with its form of church organization is, according to a legal scholar, Plymouth's major achievement. The code was enacted a year before Massachusetts Bay began real work on its laws and is based upon the custumals, or abstracts of local or borough laws such as the Yorkshire men would have been most familiar with.

Naturally one of the chief concerns of these yeomen was a clear title to the land. Bradford could remember how carefully the "counter where the evidences are" had been guarded in his uncle's household because the lack of any system of deed recording could result in loss of title if the papers were lost. And he remembered the excellent system of recording used in the Netherlands where he had bought his own house. Plymouth followed Holland in this regard, and in the laws of 1636 there is a provision requiring all sales, gifts and conveyances of houses and lands to be recorded. To own land outright was almost a compulsion with anyone of yeoman stock. So the Pilgrim land deeds are freeholds, and the first of them are in Bradford's hand. The grants are called "meersteads"—a term used only around Yorkshire. It was the free land of the frontier, plus the yeoman thirst for it and the Dutch manner of recording it, that laid the groundwork of a free society.

In addition to providing for trial by jury and proper handling of land deeds, the early laws of Plymouth listed civil and criminal offenses and made a number of efforts to control the economy. In 1626 it was made illegal to transport timber out of the colony, craftsmen were not to work for strangers and no corn or peas were to be sold abroad. The next year a law was passed against thatch roofs because of the fire hazard. Flax was to be grown and cared for (1639), and for killing a wolf a man was entitled to four bushels of corn—a pretty good bounty (1636). In 1638 the Pilgrims tried wage fixing—at twelve pence a day. They repealed the law as fast as they could.

Capital punishment was decreed for treason, murder, "conversing with the divell by way of witchcraft conjuracion or the like" (though no one was ever convicted at Plymouth under this law), sodomy, rape and buggery. Fornication before contract or marriage was to be punished "at the discretion of the magistrate according to the nature thereof." The Pilgrims, apparently, considered this aspect of human behavior capable of refinements and variations meriting various fines. Considerable freedom was permitted those who had agreed to marry, but any woman who bore a child short of the nine months' term from the date of her marriage was presumed to have been guilty of fornication. Many a husband and wife were punished at Plymouth for the crime of having a premature child. Carnal copulation before contract was subject to a fine of ten pounds; after contract it cost five. And of course after marriage it was free—which, with the pound worth about seventy-five dollars, sets a pretty definite estimate on the pleasures of the pre-marital bed.

Carnal relations without intent of marriage came higher. Arthur Peach, one of three men hanged for murdering and robbing an Indian, had previously stolen something else from Dorothy Temple, the Hopkins' servant, so that she gave birth to a child after his death. For this she was sentenced to two whippings, but was excused from the second after fainting at the first.

The close surveillance of sexual behavior inevitably forced desire into other channels. John Allexander and Thomas Roberts were found guilty in 1637 of "lude behaviour . . . by often spendinge their seede one upon another." Allexander, regarded as the chief offender, was severely whipped, burnt in the shoulder with a hot iron, and banished. Worst of all the Plymouth scandals was that of Thomas Granger, a seventeen-year-old servant

to Love Brewster, who was found guilty of buggery with a mare,
a cow, two goats, five sheep, two calves and a turkey. He was sentenced to be hanged. The animals, under Levitican law, were
first killed before his eyes and thrown into a pit, then he himself
was executed. "A very sade spectakle it was," Bradford remarks,
at the conclusion of a long passage in which the intimate details
of similar crimes are discussed with many citings of authority
and lapses into Latin for modesty's sake. The case of the man who
took out "his instrument of nature that hee might prevaile to
lye with Ann Hudson in her owne house," is by comparison quite
innocently refreshing.

Other Plymouth laws show a concern for the care of the poor
and destitute. If a man died bankrupt, for instance, his family
was to be left enough land for its support. Bond servants were
protected against careless or cruel masters. Alcoholic beverages
were controlled and a drunkard is defined as one who lisps or
falters in his speech, staggers in his going, vomits, or cannot follow
his calling.

As you read the dusty pages of the court orders, the patience,
justice and plain dealing of Bradford as magistrate begin to grow
clear. When Francis Sprague was fined 6 shillings 8 pence
for assault on William Halloway, Halloway was fined five shillings for provoking him. Or you may be rewarded after much
reading with such a judgment as that against Thomas Burnes.
John England having drowned while using his canoe, the canoe
is declared forfeit to the colony!

Plymouth never made such sumptuary laws as the Bay was to
do, though there is a curious regulation in 1645 against "wearing
visors and strange apparel to lascivious ends, a recent cause of
abuses."

Simplicity remained a trait of the colony throughout its
seventy-two years. Until 1624 Bradford and his assistant were
the only officials. Then four more assistants were added, and in
1633 two more. A clerk, a treasurer, a constable and a marshal
completed the roster. There were few if any salaries. Finally in
1639 the court allowed twenty pounds to Bradford "because his
service impoverishes his estate." To this the towns were invited
to add "what every man shall think meet."

The first list of freemen or voters, made in 1633, shows sixty-eight names. In such a community, government could be intimate indeed. Somehow the manner of handling the wolf bounty brings this intimacy to life. "Every householder shall pay half a penny for every person in his family to him that shall kill a wolf. The skin is to be brought to Mr. Jenney and there receive corn for his pay, but Mr. Jenney shall have the skin for his pains in delivering forth the corn." How appealing, to men who must fill out income tax forms!

The legal code of 1636 gave Plymouth a brief, sensible, understandable rendering of the law by which it governed itself. With such a written body of laws a man knew where he stood and how far he could go—even how drunk he could safely get. In the General Fundamentals of 1636 there was also a restatement of the basis of that law—the laws themselves to be made by free men and therefore subject to alteration by them, an annual free election, justice to be impartially administered, trial by jury with the right of challenge, the testimony of two witnesses needed to convict. Incidentally, the Pilgrims gave women more property rights than they would have had in England, and here too Holland probably led the way.

For the first twelve years there was one government for the whole colony. Three times a year the entire electorate met in general court. Then, as the population grew and scattered in search of land, separate communities were established and town governments were required in addition to colony government. The change took place with so little fuss that it is very difficult to say when separate town government began. Plymouth itself was never incorporated, its boundaries not fixed until 1640. Perhaps 1633, when the office of constable was established, is as good a date as any, for in this year it was agreed "that the chief government be tied to the town of Plymouth." Yet this does not mean that Plymouth's experience in local government waited until 1633. It had begun in February of 1621 when Standish was chosen captain at a meeting held in the common house.

Meanwhile Scituate had been settled about 1632, Duxbury— or Ducksburrow as Bradford prefers to write it, in 1631. About the time of Bradford's death there were twelve towns in the colony. In 1636 representatives of the three towns then existing were chosen to assist the governor and to revise the colony laws, and the laws they wrote gave the towns the right to dispose of their own lands. At the March court in 1638 deputies or representatives from each town finally replaced the whole body of freemen, who now met in their individual town meetings to order their affairs. Now the towns began to do a number of things for themselves. In 1639 the court gave them the right to levy taxes, to make necessary orders for the control of cattle. Each town was expected to establish a church if it was too far away from Plymouth for worshipers to come in.

Meanwhile Plymouth was having troubles enough of its own to maintain a pastor. At first, of course, the congregation awaited the arrival of its own beloved pastor with Brewster filling his place. But Robinson's coming was consistently blocked by a group of the adventurers, and finally his death ended all hope. The congregation then begged Brewster to become pastor, but he refused out of some notion of insufficiency which does credit to his modesty but which was hard on the church. Perhaps, having left the university before graduation, he felt that he would afford a convenient scourge to the critics of the Plymouth church. Once the reverend divines of Massachusetts Bay began to arrive this would have been true enough.

As a result, Plymouth was without a pastor for seven years. Then in 1628 a Mr. Rogers was sent over. He was "crased in his braine" according to Bradford, and was packed off again the following year. Ralph Smith lasted seven years (1629–1635), but he was less vigorously Separatist than the church liked. Bradford found him somewhat wishy-washy. Roger Williams, however, who assisted Smith from 1631 to 1634, was far from wishy-washy. He clashed with the church of Plymouth as with other congregations he served in New England. The young Williams apparently had the intolerance of the young and brilliant—a very different spirit from that for which he later became noted. It is clear that Bradford admired him and was sorry to see him go. In 1636 John Reynor came, remaining eighteen years. Thereafter the Plymouth church spent fifteen years looking for another shepherd, finally choosing John Cotton in 1669, long after Bradford's death.

Reynor had an assistant, Charles Chauncey (or Chauncy), who later went as pastor to Scituate and thereafter became the second president of Harvard College. Chauncey had been one of the best known Hellenists of his day at Cambridge, one of the two Greek lecturers in Trinity College when George Herbert the religious poet was the other. Harvard's first president, incidentally, was Henry Dunster. Forced out of office for holding that infant baptism was nowhere indicated in the Bible (which indeed it is not), he fled from the wrath of orthodox Massachusetts to Scituate, where he ultimately took Chauncey's place. Though Plymouth may not have been tolerant by our standards, it was a haven for many whom the Bay would not tolerate.

Under Reynor the first permanent meeting house was built in 1637, on the north side of Town Square. There, within a stone's throw of Bradford's house, the congregation met as it had met in Leyden, on one week day evening and twice on Sunday. From the open windows, on a pleasant day, came Pilgrim voices chanting the wooden verses of an Ainsworth psalm to a pleasant enough tune which completely disregarded the natural rhythms of the words:

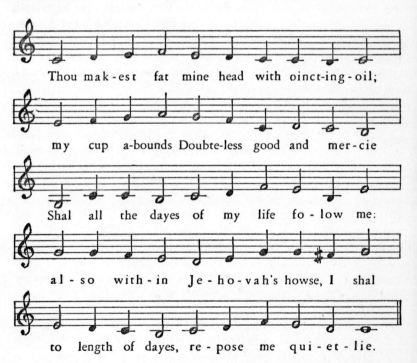

It was a nice sentiment. But quiet repose was one thing the Pilgrims almost never had.

There was not a lawyer, a university graduate, or a magistrate among the plain men who established Plymouth. Yet they originated the distinctive form of New England town meeting and town government, based on the "politically active congregation" and distinguished by a peculiar agrarian policy. They established a caste-free government with annual elections and with the power to make and revise their own laws. They established the covenant or contract idea as the basis not only of their religious bond, but of the political and commercial aspects of their community, and—through the marriage contract—of the family as well. While in Boston the political and religious compacts coalesced into theocracy, Plymouth managed to keep them separate but associated. Yet at Plymouth, government was always subject to moral purpose and religious faith. Its contractual origin was a child of the church covenant; its purpose was to bring the laws of God to life on earth. It is much too easy for us to forget or ignore this constant conviction of the Pilgrim that he was doing God's work and that God took a personal interest in his plantation.

Cotton Mather tells about a minister who preached to a congregation in the area now known as Maine. When he urged them to be religious, as "otherwise they would contradict the main end of planting in this wilderness," a member of the congregation shouted, "Sir, you are mistaken. Our main end is to catch fish."

The Pilgrims had learned to their sorrow that they were not to succeed in that apostolic calling. But they did know that the covenant with God was the basis of and the reason for their political and social organization—that the community they had built was rooted deep in religious faith. They intended to keep it so. This is the essence of the Congregational way.*

We think of them as conservatives, but to their contemporaries they were rebels, they were setting aside precedent, tradition, constituted authority, the majesty of things long established. What they were doing, of course, was revaluing, as every age

---

* A fascinating revival of this concept took place when New England missionaries invaded Hawaii, with consequences to be narrated in a subsequent book.

must do, the place of man in society. How much of a man belongs to himself and how much to the community? What restrictions must a man accept in order to be free? They did not make the modern blunder of thinking freedom an absolute, for they knew that before a man can be free he must accept obligations—to God "whose service is perfect freedom," to the community. In the four contracts (if we include marriage) they had found the equation which provided the maximum of happiness, freedom and usefulness as they understood these words. They had found an instrument by which all the vital relations of man could be regulated.

As leader of the colony, Bradford deserves a large part of the credit for this distinguished concept of government. It is a large concept, taking within its sweep not only the relations of man to man but of man to God. The church was a brotherhood, a family of the faithful. The state was to be an extension of this brotherhood yet distinct from it, founded on a separate compact. As long as Bradford was in control at Plymouth the separate administrations of church and state were maintained.

The dreaming youth at Austerfield, the eager student under Brewster had joined with the craftsman and business man of Leyden to produce a person apt for action as well as reflection. No better combination could be wished for in a public man, particularly in one who had no precedent to follow but must build as he went along. The intellect and the organizer in Bradford made Plymouth what it was and gave America a tradition and a concept of freedom and responsibility, of the relation between church and state, and of the contractual nature of all man's relationships which—though hidden for a while by the less liberal concepts of Massachusetts—have been "a lanterne unto our fete and a light unto our pathes."

The Trials of Monopoly

IF William Bradford thought that all the crises were behind him, once the agreement for £1,800 was made with the merchants in London, he was soon disillusioned. Plymouth staggered from one crisis to another throughout its whole seventy-two years, each one seeming more insuperable than the one before. All of these crises Bradford met with "answerable courages," but in the one we are now to explore he failed dismally. Great in many ways, Bradford was apparently too ready to trust his friends to be a success in business. Yet the cause lies not in a defect but in a virtue—in the one fundamental, pervasive concept which appears in all the corporate actions of the Pilgrims.

To these men a contract was a sacred thing, the basis of man's walk with God. Such was their church covenant. Something of this sacredness clung also to the social contract by which men agreed with each other regarding law and government, to the marriage contract, and to the business contract which by providing food and clothing completed and rounded out their contractual world. The Pilgrims were not, except within the proper limits of their own definition, saints. They were capable of shrewdness, evasion, even cruelty. But belief in the sacredness of contract was their rock, their foundation. It was the core of Bradford's concept of the beloved community, the creation of which was the overmastering purpose and ambition of his life. So when the "undertakers" had agreed with the merchants and had chosen Isaac Allerton, one of their own congregation, to act as business agent, they felt that they had a firm basis to go on and would soon be out of debt. Even when Allerton's behavior grew so outrageous that any sane man should have seen where it would end, they continued to trust him. Nothing but Bradford's faith in the sanctity of contract can explain or excuse his failure to prevent Allerton from leading Plymouth into a hole which almost proved its grave.

Yet things started out very auspiciously. In addition to the £1,800 for which the London merchants were willing to settle, there were other debts amounting to about £600 more. Remarked Bradford: "Thus all now is become our own, as we say in the proverb, when our debts are paid." Bradford, Allerton and Standish, to whom the trade monopoly had been granted, took in five others—John Alden and John Howland, young men whose merit had gained them the confidence of the leaders; William Brewster and Edward Winslow, and Thomas Prence—another young man who at twenty-one had come over on the *Fortune*. Three years later (in 1624) he had married Patience Brewster shortly after she reached Plymouth on the *Anne*. These were the undertakers as they called themselves—with a significance for us which almost came to be realized, since they came close to burying the colony in debt. They were to operate the trade monopoly for six years, in which time they hoped to extinguish a debt which they had nine years to pay. Again Allerton was sent off to England, with authority to take some of the merchants there into partnership for trading purposes (he took James Sherley, John Beauchamp, Richard Andrews and Timothy Hatherly), and secret instructions to arrange for the transportation of those in Leyden who still wished to come. Aware of the storm that would have arisen if the Plymouth people not of the congregation should learn that profits from the trade monopoly were being used to transport members of the Leyden congregation, Bradford and his associates decided to put this one over without asking a consent they well knew would be refused.

A new spurt of energy now activated the men of Plymouth. Boats were overhauled, trading goods were carefully sorted, inventoried and stowed, and expeditions were soon dispatched both north and south to catch the fur trade where it looked most promising.

In 1622/3 Bradford had been at Manomet, where he had discovered how easily the long and dangerous trip around the Cape could be avoided by sailing up the Scusset River to a point where a short portage would lead to the Manomet River and the ocean—the route of what is now the Cape Cod Canal. By keeping boats on both rivers, trade to the west and south would be opened up. Now, in 1627, a trading post was built at Aptucxet. It was a sturdy building, with hewn frame, hand-riven shingle roof, and leaded glass windows. Like many New England buildings, it was a simple rectangle to which a smaller rectangle was joined, yet its right proportions suggested snugness and stability. The circular stone pavement entrance was still in place when an excavation was made in 1926—three hundred years later. Two men were kept there all the time, raising corn and caring for swine when not otherwise occupied but always ready to go out with the bark when there was likelihood of trade. "All which tooke good effecte," Bradford noted with satisfaction, "and turned to their profit."

Northward went a party under John Howland to establish a trading post on the Kennebec where Augusta now stands, and where Winslow had first traded in 1625. To trade with the Abenaki Indians they took corn, coats and shirts, rugs and blankets, biscuits, peas, prunes, and the usual knives and beads. Business soon prospered here too.

Then from another quarter came motions for trade. The Dutch, having settled at Manhattan in 1623, wrote a letter in March 1627/8 full of compliments to "the noble, worshipful, wise and prudent Lords" of Plymouth to suggest trade. Bradford, looking about him at the little houses clinging to the sandy slope like bugs on a branch, must have smiled ruefully at the salutation. But he returned, in Dutch, a friendly answer with a graceful acknowledgment of the "freedome and good contente" he had enjoyed in Holland "for which we, and our children after us, are bound to be thankfull to your Nation, and shall never forgett the same, but shall hartily desire your good & prosperity, as our owne, for ever." The warmth of the words lets us see him bringing his pen to a pause while the past floods in on him—Dorothy with the child in her arms, and the sun falling across the floor in the little house on the Achtergracht just as in a painting of Vermeer; the cleanliness and beauty of Leyden, the great solid buildings, the air of prosperity and established well-being. A wave from the past sweeps over him, a warm and tender yearning for the life and youth that can never be recalled. Dorothy would be living yet if he had been content to stay in Leyden. As for the privations of life there, they had been but flea bites by comparison with what had since been endured. But then, shaking off his reverie, he may have recalled that Leyden itself had once gone through a siege so bitter that even the trials of Plymouth had not matched it, and that "all great and honourable actions are accompanied with great difficulties, and must be both enterprised and overcome with answerable courages."

As for trade, though they were fully supplied for this year, "hereafter it is like we shall deale with you, if your rates be reasonable." Bradford then inquired what prices they would give for furs, what commodities they would accept in trade and what they had to sell. Not long afterward the signer of the Dutch letter, Isaac de Rasier (de Rasieres), secretary and chief trader of New Amsterdam, arrived at Aptucxet with a large company, "a noyse of trumpeters," and several samples of trading commodities—linen, Holland and other stuffs, and a chest of sugar. After learning that it was a twenty-mile walk to Plymouth, de Rasieres asked that a boat be sent for him. Unlike the Pilgrims who were lean and sinewy from years of enforced fasting, he had apparently lived too amply on Dutch beer and victuals to be fit for the frontier.

Bradford met the shallop which brought him right up to the pier at the foot of the hill where Town Brook joined the ocean. The Dutch trader must have been puffing by the time he reached Bradford's house, where Alice would have set out some refreshment including plenty of liquid, in her best pewter dishes and tankards. The conversation was in Dutch, and though it must have come awkwardly at first to Bradford and his wife, it brought too that glow of achievement mingled with surprise which is peculiar to the man who finds himself speaking another's language. At night they showed him to the parlor where, as in England, the best bed was placed. With its green rug, its table and cupboard and settle, it was well furnished for visitors and may have surprised Rasieres. The affable and observant Hollander spent several days at Plymouth, sending home to Holland a description which provides one of our few intimate first-hand accounts of Plymouth. Back with him to his bark went some of the Plymouth undertakers (Bradford was apparently too busy with the multiplying affairs of the colony to go), to trade tobacco for cloth. Tobacco had been raised in Plymouth almost from the beginning, and the several regulations against its use on the street or where there was a fire hazard shows that it was popular with the Pilgrims. Even Elder Brewster made use of it, if we may judge from the tobacco box, tongs, case and pipes in the inventory of his estate. For several years now the Pilgrims made good money on the tobacco they traded to the Dutch, until Virginia nosed them out.

Another strange item the Dutch offered them they would at first have none of. It was nothing but pieces of white and purple-black shell in cylindrical form, bored through and strung together. The Pilgrims were persuaded to take £50 worth of it and were sure they had been cheated, for it took them two years to get rid of it. Then suddenly it caught on, and the secret of the Dutch success in trading with the Indians was explained. For the Indians could not get enough of it. So now, instead of having to cart bushels of corn to their trading posts (for it was the Pilgrims now who had a corn surplus), they had only to carry the light, easily transported "wampampeake" or wampum to their distant posts. Furthermore, since the fishing ships from England and the straggling settlers along the coast were not acquainted with it, Plymouth for a while had a practical monopoly on the Indian trade. Once again the Dutch had been a present help in time of trouble.

Now, when all seemed to be going well, trouble struck from a totally unexpected source. Isaac Allerton, a member of the Leyden congregation and one of the most trusted of Bradford's assistants, began to speculate on his own. Bradford had known Allerton from the early days in Holland. Allerton's two boys were almost the same age as John Bradford and had been his playmates in Leyden. A few years hence his daughter, Mary, was to marry Bradford's adopted son Thomas Cushman while she was

still in her teens. Allerton himself had just married (1626) as his
second wife Fear Brewster, herself only twenty and the daughter of Bradford's revered foster father. Four years Bradford's
senior, Allerton was a shrewd business man, with an apparent
gift for high finance and complicated business deals which impressed his associates. It was incredible that he should do anything hurtful to the colony. Moreover he was bound by a solemn
contract with all the rest of the undertakers to keep all trading
under a joint account for the colony's benefit. He was furthermore bound by letters of authority which specified what he was
to do and how far he was to engage the colony's credit. It was simply inconceivable that a pillar of the church should fail to live
up to these sacred obligations. So his action "was not much lookt
at, but past over."

This, apparently, was what he was waiting for. In 1628 he
brought back a greater quantity of things from England, "so in-
termixte with the goods of the generall, as they knew not which
were theirs, & which was his, being pact up together; so as they
well saw that, if any casualty had beefalne at sea, he might have
laid the whole on them, if he would; for ther was no distinction.
Allso what was most vendible, and would yeeld presente pay,
usualy that was his." Still, "because love thinkes no evill," the
undertakers sent him to London again, though with double caution that he was not to exceed his instructions, or mix up any
other goods with theirs.

Meanwhile Bradford had been forced to deal with another and
unrelated crisis. Back in 1625 a Captain Wollaston had settled
not far from Weston's former plantation of Wessagusset. Disap-
pointed in the failure of the new world to make him auto-
matically wealthy—a dream still boiling in many minds as a result of the extravagant literature about America—Wollaston
had gone off to Virginia, taking some of his servants with him.
The market for servants was so good that he soon sent back for
more. At this point Thomas Morton,* his partner, proposed
instead that the men ignore their bonds and remain with him.
He would give them their freedom, they would join him as partners in trading and planting, and all would lead a merry life.
Naturally they consented. Plenty of liquid refreshment, a may-

* Not to be confused with Thomas Morton the Pilgrim, brother of George.

pole, and poetry composed for the occasion by Morton himself soon made Mare Mount, as he renamed the plantation, a merry place indeed. Moreover, Morton was a clever manager. He beat the Pilgrims to the Kennebec in 1626, thus spoiling their trade. He gave the Indians guns and let them do his hunting for him. He invited the squaws to join in the general merriment, and must have seemed to the natives a far more amiable person than the men of Plymouth.

The men of Plymouth, naturally, were outraged at Morton's heathenish merriment, his supplying the Indians with guns—and his stealing their trade. In 1628, having obtained the consent of some other plantations (or having, as Bradford claims, been urged forward by them), Plymouth sent Miles Standish to apprehend this competitor who had ignored their warnings. Standish accomplished his mission and brought Morton before Bradford and his council, who exiled him to the Isle of Shoals —without a gun or sufficient clothes, Morton complained. A few months later they shipped him back to London. To London also went a letter from Bradford to Sir Ferdinando Gorges, begging him "as a most special beginner and furtherer of the good of this country" to deal with Morton. Poor Bradford!—he could scarcely have chosen less happily, for Gorges and Morton were on friendly terms. The chief result was to bring them together to plot against Plymouth.

While Allerton was on his way back to England, the first of two groups of Leydeners sent by Allerton had set sail for the new world, both arriving in 1629. When the undertakers finally got a look at Allerton's accounts, it proved an expensive business, including in addition to £550 for transportation some rather amazing items for cloth and shoes. Nor was this the end of it. For sixteen months or more the Plymouth people had to feed the newcomers before they could raise crops of their own. Most of them, moreover, were very poor. They had no kindred or relations amongst the Plymouth residents. In fact, says Bradford, most of them were entirely unknown to the first-comers.

Naturally enough, the Plymouth residents who had not come from Leyden began to complain against these expenses laid on the general account. To quiet them, Bradford announced that the tax of three bushels of corn a year which had been agreed to when the lands and houses were divided would not be collected if the undertakers could possibly do without it. Despite what happened afterward, they never demanded it.

One of the errands laid upon Allerton this year (1629) was an enlarging and confirming of the Kennebec patent and a royal charter for Plymouth. Gorges—presumably for a price—granted what the undertakers desired. The patent as signed by Gorges and the Earl of Warwick on January 3, 1629/30, made Bradford in effect the lord of the manor over all the colony's lands. With bribes all along the way, Allerton then pushed the affair up through the king's officers. Disregarding his instructions, he had inserted a clause that would cancel all customs for a period of "7 years inward, & 21 outward," and this the king would not swallow.

Bradford was furious. It was now obvious, he thought, that Allerton was purposely making difficulties so that he would be sent back to London again the following year. To crown insult with injury, he then brought home with him as his secretary the one man in all the world the Pilgrims least desired to have amongst them—Thomas Morton of Mare Mount, who was invited to go elsewhere as soon as the undertakers had recovered from their astonishment.*

Allerton, who really seems to have been a victim of megalomania, had again brought goods to be sold for his private profit, and had also cooked up another deal in London which he now (1629/30) sprang upon the confused partners. He and the London undertakers had taken a patent to a piece of land along the Penobscot and had hired a man named Edward Ashley to run a trading post there. The Pilgrims knew Ashley, for he had been in the country before, having lived naked among the savages as if he had been one of them. Allerton now invited the undertakers to join in this venture, knowing very well he had them in a corner. For if they failed to join, the Penobscot post would draw off much of the trade from the Kennebec. If they joined, they would have to supply Ashley with corn and other commodities.

---

* Morton came again in 1643 and was allowed to remain for several months, the Pilgrims fearing to offend him because of his powerful connections in England.

So, with a sense of involvement which must have looked to Bradford exactly like the days and devices of Thomas Weston, they plunged in, sending young Thomas Willet, who had arrived on the second *Mayflower* in 1629, to keep an eye on things. They soon discovered that while Allerton had supplied Ashley with plenty of trade goods, he had left them short.

And now Allerton's operations began to multiply at a dizzying speed. He had taken up large sums at high interest in England, claiming the necessity of getting the trade goods transported at the proper time. He picked up a bargain of salt—there must have been a mountain of it since he paid £113 pounds. Winslow and some of the other partners, who seem to have been infected by Allerton's financial wizardry, now suggested another venture which involved hiring a ship from England to come fishing on shares, bringing instead of the usual salt cargo a supply of trading goods which could thus be obtained without freight charges.

When this was proposed to Bradford, he exploded. Hadn't they learned from sad experience that every time they had tried fishing it was they who got hooked? But they insisted and at last he gave in. Back to London went Allerton in the spring of 1630 to carry out his multiplying assignments. In due time Ashley received some trade goods, but not Plymouth. Hearing that his old friend Captain Peirce had sailed into Massachusetts Bay, bringing passengers for a new colony there, Bradford sent for news of the fishing ship that was to have supplied them. It had been forced back to England by storms, Peirce revealed, and the voyage given over. But Allerton had bought another ship, in which he was returning, to fish for bass.

Now it was clear that one of the other undertakers must go to London. With intuitions of approaching disaster, Bradford fixed upon Edward Winslow whose skillful dealing could always be counted on in an emergency. Winslow had not been long dispatched when who should arrive in Massachusetts Bay but Timothy Hatherly, one of the four London partners, sent over to investigate them! (This was the same man who had returned to England after a brief stay in Plymouth in 1623.) Hopefully sending to Boston to inquire what goods he had brought, Bradford learned that he had nothing but two packs of rugs and two hogsheads of metheglin * which when opened turned out to have been "drunke up under the name of leackage, and so lost!" Hatherly also sent a letter from Sherley (Plymouth's London agent) which added to the confusion by describing two ships which had been set forth—all, apparently, at the expense of Plymouth, one having been purchased outright. Sherley hinted at debts rising toward six thousand pounds.

Thoroughly alarmed, Bradford impatiently awaited Allerton's arrival from England. He came at last with Hatherly whom he had picked up at Boston, plausible as ever and promising great profits. But the partners had by now had enough. Since he claimed that the ship for bass fishing was not charged to their account, they let him go off with it on his own affairs, having at last put an end to his service as agent. When Hatherly returned to London they sent a good supply of beaver with him as well as a letter stating that Allerton had discharged them of any responsibility for either of the two ships, and that Winslow was to replace Allerton as agent. Sherley continued to insist, however, that one of the ships was on the general account, and finally (in a letter of January 2, 1631/2) that they should both be so handled. According to Sherley, Allerton had had £7,103.17.1! This was where the undertakers stood, having begun four years before with a debt of £2,400 and having sent over mountains of beaver, otter and mink!

Allerton's accounts, when looked into, were full of gross charges—£500 for the patent which never got the royal sanction, £50 spent on a journey, £200 set down against Brewster "because he knew they would never let it lye on the old man, when, alass! he, poore man, never dreamte of any such thing . . . but thought that many of them [things brought over from England] had been freely bestowed on him & his children by Mr. Allerton." Sherley's accounts, when finally produced, claimed debts against the Plymouth undertakers of £4,770.19.2, not counting £1,000 still due on the old debt. Many items were charged twice, large sums were included without explanation. Most of this debt Allerton with the help of the London partners had managed to pile up in the short space of two years, 1629 and 1630.

* Metheglin was mead, an apparently delectable drink brewed from honey.

In 1640/1 Andrews and Beauchamp entered a bill of complaint in a chancery suit to compel an accounting for the joint venture at Plymouth. Each put in for £1,100, claiming that Sherley had paid them nothing since 1631 when each had put that sum into the joint account. Sherley, they claimed, had said "he will first dye & rott in prison before hee will give your orators any accompte." To which Sherley returned that the orators were liars, that Allerton was the one to go after, and that anyway he doubted Beauchamp had put in that much. The Plymouth partners now sent a load of beaver direct to Beauchamp and Andrews instead of to Sherley. Beauchamp sold his share for £400, Andrews lost his through poor judgment—and again charged the Pilgrims! At last in 1641 the London partners settled for a sum of £1,200—all but Beauchamp who went on demanding more than was his due, according to Sherley, until he was finally quieted in 1646. To achieve this, Bradford had to sell one of his farms, and the other undertakers had to dispose of property, unjust as the claims appear to have been. "Thus were they abused in their simplicitie, and no beter then bought & sould, as it may seeme."

It is impossible to calculate how much the manipulations of Allerton and the greed of the London merchants cost the Plymouth partners, but the sum runs into six figures. Yet in the years 1631 to 1638 alone they had sent almost 14,000 pounds of beaver and 1,156 other skins, having a value far higher than their alleged debts. To Bradford there must have been bitter irony indeed in Sherley's opinion that "had ther been an orderly course taken, and your bussines better managed, assuredly (by the blessing of God) you had been the ablest plantation that, as we think, or know, hath been undertaken by Englishmen."

The shock of Allerton's behavior was not the only burden Bradford had to bear during these years. To chronicle all the losses and discouragements Plymouth suffered as a trading company would go far beyond the scope of this book. But the fate of the trading posts in Maine must be described.

When the Pilgrims first came to the North Atlantic coast they were inhabiting a wilderness where settlements had been many times attempted and had always failed. But once they had proved that Europeans could settle and hold on, the gradual peopling of the coast was inevitable. The Dutch made a permanent settlement at New Amsterdam in 1623. Settlers came into Massachusetts Bay long before the well-known influx of 1630. A man named Jeffrey was on the site of Manchester-by-the-Sea. Samuel Maverick, an Anglican, had built himself a fortified house at East Boston while Thomas Walford had a palisaded house at Charlestown. William Blaxton had a house and orchard near the site of Boston common, and out in the harbor David Thompson had established an island plantation. There were settlers at Weymouth, and at Nantasket which Roger Conant had abandoned for Naumkeag (Salem) after a brief stay on Cape Ann in 1625. And from the north the French began to sift down into Maine.

With Allerton dismissed and Ashley sent back to England for having sold powder and shot to the Indians, the Penobscot post of Pentagoet was now entirely in the hands of Bradford and his partners with Thomas Willet in charge. In 1632 while Willet was in Plymouth getting supplies a small French ship came into the harbor. The men who came ashore, pretending they were newly come from the sea and did not know where they were, begged permission to haul their ship up on the beach to stop her leaks. Let into the trading post by the three or four "simple men that were servants" left in charge, the visitors politely fell to admiring the muskets lying in racks along the walls and took them down to examine them, asking whether they were loaded. Advised that they were, the Frenchmen turned the weapons upon the surprised servants, forcing them to carry the contents of the trading post to the ship. Thereupon they released the servants and departed.

"Tell your master when he comes," they said, "that some of the Isle of Rey gentlemen have been here."

The loss to the partners was about £500 in goods and three hundred pounds of beaver.

Three years later, in 1635, the French returned. Still polite, they caught up with some of the leaders who were at sea in a shallop and persuaded them to pilot the French ship into the harbor (means of persuasion not noted!). Monsieur de Aulnay, the leader, then took possession of the post in the name of the king of France, forced Willet to sell his goods, set the value of them to suit himself, and told Willet he would pay when it was convenient if Plymouth would send after the money. Of course no payment was ever made. As for the house and fort, said de Aulnay, it was built on French ground and therefore forfeit. "So thus turning them out of all (with a great deale of complemente, and many fine words), he let them have their shalop and some victualls to bring them home."

When Willet reached Plymouth with his story, the partners were outraged. Happening upon a Captain Girling who had brought a fine big ship of three hundred tons into their waters, they hired him to shell the French into submission, for which he was to have seven hundred pounds of beaver. If he failed, however, he was to have nothing. Standish and twenty men went along in their own bark as a landing party. But Girling bungled things from the start. He would not allow Standish to summon the French to parley but began heaving his cannon balls in on them from so great a distance that he did no hurt at all. By the time Standish had persuaded him to move in, he had used up all his powder which, it now appeared, amounted to only a barrel despite his fine show of ordnance. After this comic opera assault the good captain had to draw off again while Standish went off in the bark to see if he could get powder from the nearest plantation. Hearing that Girling planned to seize the Plymouth beaver without dispossessing the French, Standish sent the powder but headed for Plymouth with the beaver. Girling, once he had received the powder, sailed off for England without firing another shot. And that was the end of the Penobscot trading post.

Just the year before, disaster had struck also at the Kennebec. A man named Hocking from the plantation of Piscataqua went up into the Kennebec to trade, thus trespassing on the Plymouth patent. Warned off, he insisted on going up the river above the trading post, where he could effectively cut off the trade that should come down to them. John Howland, who was then in charge, discussed the matter with John Alden who also happened to be there. Both were assistants to the governor, both were undertakers, and with the heavy debts that had been laid on them they knew the Kennebec trade to be a vital necessity to the colony. Again they warned Hocking and again he defied them.

Now Howland decided to cut the cables of Hocking's boat so that he would float downstream. Two men set out in a canoe and had succeeded in cutting one of the cables when Hocking picked up his musket and shot one of the two men dead, whereupon his companion killed Hocking.

This disposed of the threat to their trade, but it put Plymouth in a dangerous position. For several great men including the Lord Say and Sele and the Lord Brooks had a hand in the Piscataqua plantation, and the Pilgrims' patent was never so secure that they could afford to provoke displeasure in high places. In fact, this incident—though it could not have been avoided —threatened to open up again the whole question of Plymouth's rights and gave encouragement to designs even then going forward in London to wipe out their autonomy. As usual, Bradford was asked to step into the breach. This being one of the five years when he did not serve as governor, he was sent up to Boston with Winslow in July to see what could be done. (He went again with William Collier in August.) For Boston, the new plantation in Massachusetts Bay, had intruded itself into the incident in a way that alarmed and angered the Plymouth men.

Plymouth's relations with the Bay communities had begun in friendliness and grown into caution. There were many reasons why Plymouth should have a kindly feeling toward "the Bay." It was Plymouth's success which had encouraged the first settlement out of which the Massachusetts Bay Company developed. In 1626 Roger Conant became manager of the little colony at Naumkeag (later Salem). Then in 1628 came John Endecott and forty others to prepare the way for a still larger settlement. By this time a patent had been issued to an influential group of men, some of whom came from the town of Boston in Lincolnshire where Bradford had once been thrown into prison. They included Alderman Thomas Leverett and Richard Bellingham the borough recorder, Thomas Dudley, steward to the Earl of Lincoln and a parishioner of John Cotton, and Simon Bradstreet who took Dudley's place when he left for America, also marrying his daughter. Other men of influence who joined the venture were John Winthrop, Isaac Johnson who had married Arabella, the Earl's sister, John Humphrey who had married another sister, and Sir Richard Saltonstall.

With such backing, Endecott might have expected to fare much better than the Pilgrims. But his company suffered from lack of adequate housing, a hard winter, and an infectious fever of which many died. Lacking a physician, Endecott wrote to Bradford begging the assistance of Samuel Fuller. Fuller not only helped the sick, but gave so good an account of the Pilgrim way in religion that Endecott sent a very gracious letter of thanks to Bradford in which he expressed himself "satisfied touching your judgments of the outward forme of Gods worshipe." Much to his surprise, such had been the common report of Plymouth, they turned out to be the same which he himself professed. Certainly it did nothing to hurt Endecott's reputation with Bradford that he had also got rid of Oldham and Lyford who until his arrival had been members of Conant's colony.

Still more delighted were the Pilgrims to learn in the summer of 1629 that Naumkeag, renamed Salem, had taken to itself their own way of church government, using the same form of covenant, choosing a teacher and pastor and fulfilling the prophecy of John Robinson that "there will be no difference between the conformable ministers and you when they come to the practice of the ordinances out of the kingdom." Invited to attend a service at which the church members would solemnly declare their acceptance of the covenant, Bradford set sail for Salem and though failing to arrive in time for the ceremony, was able to extend "the right hand of fellowship."

Arriving in 1630, the new governor John Winthrop moved the seat of government from Salem to Charlestown and then to Boston, which was so named in September. In July he had sent to Salem to ask advice regarding the form of church government to be established, urged on by the mortality amongst his people which he concluded must be the result of God's displeasure. Fuller, Winslow and Allerton all happened to be in Salem at the time. They quickly wrote Bradford to advise him that the Plymouth way was being recommended to Boston too, asking him to set aside a day of prayer for the new settlement. Soon word came from Boston that the advice had been followed.

"Thus," wrote Bradford in one of his noblest sentences, "thus out of smalle beginings greater things have been prodused by his hand that made all things of nothing, and gives being to all things that are; and as one small candle may light a thousand, so the light here kindled hath shone to many, yea in some sorte to our whole nation; let the glorious name of Jehova have all the praise."

There was a good deal of suffering and sickness in Boston during the first winter (a mild one) despite the solid foundation which had been laid in England, so different in scope and support from Plymouth's origins. Over a thousand settlers had come to the Bay, more than Plymouth had accumulated in ten years. Nonetheless, they were soon on rations of salt junk and hard tack, smelt, clams and mussels. A hundred and eighty servants had to be turned loose to fend for themselves.

But by 1634 when Boston stuck its nose into Plymouth's business with regard to the Kennebec affair, Massachusetts Bay Colony was strong and healthy and beginning to feel its oats. When Alden put in there on business, the Boston magistrates locked him up on the strength of his having been present at Kennebec at the time of the double murder. Plymouth's pride in Boston took a sudden fall at this evidence of an intention to meddle without jurisdiction or authority. Bradford immediately sent Standish off to Boston to obtain Alden's release. As everyone in Plymouth knew Standish's character and how he was likely to handle the matter, it is evident that they were in no mood for compromise. Word soon came back that Alden had been set at liberty (on his promise to reappear when called) but that Standish had been bound over to the June court! There is a hint of reproof here for the captain's undoubtedly blustering behavior, as also in the letters Dudley sent back to Plymouth with their reference to "this unhappie contention betweene you and us" and the faith that "time cooleth distempers."

Bradford makes it clear that the men of Plymouth now decided to abandon the Standish policy of bluff and bluster for one of conciliation, asking Winthrop and the other Boston magistrates to advise them what to do next. Write to all the neighboring plantations, especially that of the dead man at Piscataqua, said Winthrop, and request them to send representatives to consult, determine, and take any action required. This was done. Boston was named the meeting place and the time was set a month ahead. But when the day came only Bradford and Winslow, with their pastor Ralph Smith, appeared in Boston. Since Piscataqua had failed to send representatives and since all the evidence, when reviewed, supported Plymouth, the colony was exonerated while Winthrop and Dudley both wrote to Lord Say and other gentlemen interested in the plantation.

"And thus was this matter ended," Bradford concludes, "and ther love and concord renewed."

Yet it was to be strained many times again. Though Plymouth had fathered the churches of Massachusetts Bay, the Bay had no intention of following the basic principle of Separatism, which was that the church covenant and the political compact were things apart. Too, Boston was always conscious of its superiority in numbers, wealth, and birth—and so was Plymouth. Though in religion there was little to separate them, in government there was a good deal. What the differences were became more apparent as time went on. In spite of the love and concord just professed, there was a sharp conflict in the offing.

The Beloved Community

WHILE Bradford, trying to oversee the colony's trade, was having his difficulties with Allerton and Sherley, his work as governor was greatly complicated by the establishment of the colony in Massachusetts Bay. The scattered settlements along the New England coast before 1630 had been too small to cause any great concern, though Thomas Morton had threatened the Kennebec trade and there was always the danger that indefatigable old Ferdinando Gorges would some day succeed in getting a strong colony planted. But the Massachusetts Bay Company meant business. Proud of the fact that Plymouth's example had brought about the new settlement,* Bradford was still a little doubtful of the effects on Plymouth, being shrewd enough to see that the stronger colony would be likely to show an appetite for the other's trade and lands.

Encouraged and gratified by Boston's decision to follow the Plymouth way in church government, Bradford was now faced with a problem which gave him an opportunity to show an equal faith and confidence in them. The occasion, however, was not a pleasant one. John Billington, who had been in and out of trouble ever since he had been tied up by the neck and heels for cursing Standish, had quarreled with a man named John New-

* Thomas Hutchinson says: "Whether Britain would have had any colonies in America at this day, if religion had not been the grand inducement, is doubtful." *History of the Province of Massachusetts Bay*, 1765.

comen and murdered him in a fit of rage. A jury was formed, a trial held—presumably with Bradford as judge—and Billington found guilty. Knowing that Winthrop was not only a Cambridge man but a lawyer, Bradford wrote to him for advice. Winthrop agreed that Billington must die, and die he did—probably at the hand of Standish, the only Pilgrim whose stock in trade was death.

This was in the fall of 1630. The next affair that led Bradford to consult Winthrop involved a spectacular character named Sir Christopher Gardener. Gardener turned up at Massachusetts Bay with a couple of servants and "a comly yonge woman whom he caled his cousin, but it was suspected she (after the Italian maner) was his concubine." He had come to America, so he said, in order to forsake the world and live a plain, private and godly life. Soon in trouble with the Boston authorities, he fled into the woods where he joined up with the Indians in Plymouth's jurisdiction. Unable to catch him, the Boston magistrates promised a reward to anyone who could.

Some of the Plymouth Indians now came in to ask Bradford whether they might kill Gardener. Bradford told them to bring him alive to Plymouth, where they would be rewarded.

"He has a gun and a rapier," they told him. "He'll kill us if we go about it."

"Watch your opportunity and take him," said Bradford.

And so they did. They found him at a river side with a canoe close by. When they tried to grab him he jumped into the canoe and pushed off. Then as they pursued and he raised his piece, the stream carried his canoe against a rock and tumbled him, his rapier and his musket into the water. Nimble as a chipmunk, Gardener jumped up with a dagger in his hand and kept them all at bay. Finally they brought long poles with which they beat the dagger out of his hand and brought him, complaining about his swollen, aching arms, to Bradford.

"We did but a little whip him with sticks," the Indians said, with hurt surprise.

Mindful of the courtesy owing to a Knight of the Sepulchre, with or without a concubine after the Italian manner, Bradford sent Sir Christopher to a lodging where his arms were bathed and anointed. The Pilgrims gave him such attentive care that they were able to relieve him of a little notebook which had slipped out of his pocket and fallen into the bed where it might have made the worthy knight uncomfortable. The notebook contained a record of Gardener's reconciliation with the pope and the church of Rome—this in spite of his having earlier declared his intention of following the New England way. The notebook was brought to Bradford who sent it to Winthrop with the officers who conducted Gardener to Boston.

Bradford also wrote to Winthrop asking clemency for Sir Christopher—whether because of the whipping with sticks or because he had taken a liking to him does not appear. Before long he was shipped back to England, presumably with his servants and his "cousin," where he immediately busied himself against the colonies. The cause was heard before the Privy Council itself, with Ferdinando Gorges (who by now had a large design of his own for destroying the Bible commonwealths) backing up Sir Christopher. Much to everyone's surprise, the Privy Council made a declaration so favorable to Massachusetts Bay that it practically amounted to a censure of Gardener and Gorges. That it only prodded stubborn old Sir Ferdinando the more, Plymouth was in due time to learn.

Bradford's first meeting with Winthrop face to face must have been in the late fall when he went up to Boston to pay his respects to Mistress Winthrop who had just arrived on the *Lion,* skippered by Bradford's old friend William Peirce. Maybe there was another motive in Bradford's visit, for in September a pinnace from Salem had been forced into Plymouth Harbor on its way to trade for corn on the Cape. Now one thing the Pilgrims were willing to die for was their right to everything that pertained to the Cape. Bradford had written a sharp note to the government at Boston, saying that Plymouth would resist any interference of this sort, "even to the spending of our lives." These were strong words from the head of one state to another. Though tiny, Plymouth in effect was a sovereign state, and in his dealings with Boston Bradford was acting the part of a foreign minister. Shaky as its patent was, Plymouth had always acted like a sovereign power, entitled to wage war against any who encroached upon its property.

Yet because their contact with the Massachusetts Colony had

begun in love and friendliness, ripening into Christian brotherhood based on a flattering emulation of the Plymouth church, Bradford was uneasy about the sharp rebuke he had administered and eager to meet face to face the man who had written him so lovingly.

John Winthrop was only a year or two older than Bradford. The son of a country squire, he had entered Trinity College, Cambridge, at the age of fourteen (the usual age in those days), left without graduating, followed the law and done well at it. But somewhere—perhaps at Cambridge, that seedbed of Puritanism—he had begun to have a concern for his soul. In 1629 he had joined the "Cambridge Agreement" which pledged him to remove to New England if the government and patent of the Massachusetts Company should be moved there. In October he was elected governor, and the next March he sailed in the *Arbella,* reaching American waters in June where the first person to greet him in the new world was none other than Isaac Allerton, busied about the bass fishing which had caused such a furor at Plymouth.

Winthrop's portrait shows a man capable of asceticism—though with his four wives and fifteen children it is but fair to state that he did not exactly achieve it. It shows a man of dark and rather pointed features, with eyes deep for reflection and darkened as if with the world's sorrow. Quick intelligence and sharpness in contest are there too, though it would be stretching things to find the conservative, aristocratic temperament which his political acts made amply clear. Or the sweet and gentle spirit shown in the letters sent back to his wife in England.

The two men took to each other from the start. While Bradford deferred to Winthrop with the pathetic and superfluous respect of the self-educated man for the formally educated, Winthrop was quick to appreciate Bradford's qualities. "Discreet and grave" he calls him—thus revealing as much about himself as about Bradford since men always seek in others the qualities they would like to find in themselves. Yet the judgment comes close enough to Roger Williams' "prudent and godly" to give us a very important reflection of Bradford's character from the minds of discerning men who knew him. It is fashionable today to dissemble the larger traits of character in a rather amorphous and equalizing good fellowship fortified by the theory of winning friends and influencing people and a very false set of ideas about democracy. In Bradford's time there was no such dissembling. Largeness of character was honored wherever it was genuinely manifested. The theory of human freedom had not then been debased by the false deduction that while in business a man could be as sharp as he liked, in politics he must pretend to be as dumb as the dumbest. So Bradford, fulfilling for himself an unconscious father symbol, looked and acted like a leader of men to those who elected him year after year.

In the struggle that lay ahead between Plymouth and the Bay he would need to be discreet and prudent. He would need all the discretion and prudence at his command.

But now, at the first meeting of these two leaders who a century and a half before the formation of the United States demonstrated quite amazingly the Hamiltonian and Jeffersonian points of view, there came after the first tentative politeness a warm and mutual response as each realized the worth in the other. The qualities of leadership are self-stimulating, but they are also isolating. A man who knows himself for a leader, as Bradford did by experience, is quick to recognize leadership in another. Allied, as in this case, with a strong sense of brotherhood in Christ, the two men formed a firm friendship from the start. For each the experience was something like that of meeting a home-town citizen in a foreign land. The Puritan spirit in religion had that quality for men of the seventeenth century, but with an impact far beyond the understanding of a secular age such as ours.

Bradford lodged in the ship, as Winthrop's *Journal* tells us without saying why. This would mean, not the little shallop Bradford sailed up in, but Captain Peirce's ship, the *Lion*. Peirce, who made more trips to New England than any other master of the time,* had become an old friend to Bradford and had even become associated with the undertakers in some of their business affairs, such as the Penobscot trading post. On many

---

* In the *Anne*, 1623; *Charity*, 1624; *Jacob*, 1625; second *Mayflower*, 1629; *Lion* twice in 1630 and again in 1631 and 1632; *Rebecca*, 1634; *Desire*, 1636-8. Peirce took Indian slaves away to Virginia, 1637, was fatally wounded in West Indies, 1641.

occasions Bradford would have entrusted letters and errands to him, for delivery or execution in England. It is more than likely, for example, that the sturdy, vellum-bound volume in which Bradford wrote *Of Plimoth Plantation* was brought over by Peirce in the second *Mayflower,* for it was in 1630 that Bradford began to write his book.

More important than any commodity he brought over in cabin or hold, however, was what he brought in his head. The importance of news from Europe to these dwellers between the two wildernesses of forest and sea cannot be exaggerated. Lengthy and remarkably full as were many of the letters from friends, they could not report events and impressions as a live observer could do it. Anyone who has ever been irritated by the things so surprisingly left unsaid in letters will understand how important it was to talk with a man who had just come over, to question and exchange opinions with him. So Bradford, sitting in the snug little captain's cabin with a glass of wine mellowed by long carrying across the oceans of the world—Bradford savored each morsel of news as he savored each sip of wine, with time for meditation. The troubles of Europe would be a welcome relief from the troubles brought upon him by Allerton's behavior.

After their first meeting, Bradford and Winthrop frequently wrote back and forth. In February 1631/2, for example, Bradford replied to a complaint about Plymouth's handling of those who wished to remove to or from Boston. The Bay Colony seems to have suspected Plymouth of trying to lure Boston men down, and to prevent Plymouth men from leaving. Better situated and better capitalized than Plymouth, Boston should have had no need to fear—except that Plymouth was beginning to look attractive to men who chafed under Boston's more rigid and less democratic government. For the Bay Colony was rigidly controlled by a small court of assistants, six of the nine also being magistrates or judges. Governor and deputy governor were elected by the assistants from among themselves. Church membership was very early made a qualification for voting. Political rights were thus limited to a small group.

"For John Pickworth," wrote Bradford in answer to a particular complaint, "he came but as a sojournour to worke for a few weeks, in wch time he goate a wife, and so is longe since returned duble, and hath no cause to complaine, excepte he hath goot a bad wife."

Discreet, sober, grave—why did no one ever bother to remark that Bradford also had a sense of humor?

It was not until the fall of 1632 that Winthrop, accompanied by Endecott and Pastor John Wilson, visited Plymouth. Nothing quite like it had ever happened to the little commonwealth, except possibly the visit of Isaac de Rasieres in 1628. Captain Endecott represented the military, Wilson the church, and Winthrop the civil government, and their combined visitation was a mark of deference, a tribute in a way to Bradford himself. Leaving their boat at Wessagusset, they reached Plymouth on foot where—apparently forewarned by a chain of messengers, Bradford, Brewster and the other leaders came out to meet and conduct them ceremoniously into the town. Endecott with his long nose and sharp, depending chin beard, his beautifully wrought sword clanking at his side, was brusque and punctilious. He soon paired off with Standish and fell to talking of military matters. Winthrop—dark, tall, aristocratic—greeted Bradford with gentle courtesy, and walked by his side up the narrow forest path, while Brewster attended Wilson. In honor of the occasion Bradford wore his long magisterial gown, the same in which he marched to church. Led up to the governor's house, Winthrop was shown to the old parlor with the wainscoted bedstead, and feasted in the "great rome" with its long trestle table and benches, its great fireplace. "They were very kindly entertained, and feasted every day at several houses." So Winthrop himself reports it, adding one of the best descriptions of a Plymouth Sunday that has been preserved. The morning service in which the Boston men shared the sacrament with their Plymouth brethren did not interest Winthrop so much as that in the afternoon. Here Roger Williams, Plymouth's "teacher" since the previous year, proposed a question to which the pastor, Ralph Smith, spoke briefly. "Then Mr. Williams prophesies (or explains); and after, the Governor of Plymouth (who has studied the Hebrew language and antiquities) speaks to the question; after him, the elder (a man of learning); then two or three more of the congregation." Winthrop, apparently, was impressed with Bradford's knowledge of Hebrew, as well he might have been considering the fact that Bradford had taught himself.

Winthrop himself was next invited to speak and was followed by Pastor Wilson. Then, "the deacon, Mr. Fuller, puts the congregation in mind of their duty of contribution, whereupon the governor and all the rest go down to the deacon's seat, and put into the box, and then return."

What the Pilgrims were able to put into the box was in large part owing to their visitors from Boston. For Plymouth, though still stricken with the results of Allerton's high finance, was in the midst of a boom brought about by the demand for cattle in the Bay. In former times it would have been hard to find a loose shilling in all of Plymouth, the whole economy including the payment of taxes being on a barter basis. But now "the people of the plantation begane to grow in their owtward estats, by reason of the flowing of many people into the cuntrie, espetially into the Bay of the Massachusetts; by which means corne & catle rose to a great prise, by which many were much inriched, and commodities grue plentifull." Fear of war between king and Parliament was to swell the population of New England to about twenty thousand by 1640, when the opening of the Long Parliament eased the grievances of the Puritans. Even as early as 1634 there were twenty villages around the shores of Massachusetts Bay, each with an average population of two hundred.

But the sudden prosperity in Plymouth had effects that worried Bradford. "For now as their stocks increased, and the increse vendible, ther was no longer any holding them togeather . . . And no man now thought he could live, except he had catle and a great deale of ground to keep them; all striving to increase their stocks. By which means they were scatered all over the bay, quickly, and the towne, in which they lived compactly till now, was left very thine, and in a short time allmost desolate. And if this had been all, it had been less, thoug to much; but the church must also be devided, and those that had lived so long togeather in Christian & comfortable fellowship must now part and suffer many divissions.

"And this, I fear," Bradford adds in the most solemn reflection of his whole book, "will be the ruine of New-England, at least of the churches of God ther, & will provock the Lords displeasure against them."

There is no clearer evidence of what Plymouth meant to Bradford than in this interesting passage. Here was Plymouth prospering at last after ten years of short rations, sickness, and poverty. Yet to Bradford that prosperity spelled ruination. Why?

Bradford's vision of the good life was based upon the small, tightly knit community, bound together in Christian brotherhood as firmly almost as a family is bound. Arising in the church, the spirit of brotherhood would also control the operations of government and the getting of a living, and all would prosper under contract—the form of agreement by which man dealt even with God. If prosperity was a threat to community, prosperity was a bad thing. Here is a remarkable sense of social values very different from that of a civilization dominated by the nation-state and "economic man", though still alive today in New England villages. If Bradford had given us nothing else, he would be remarkable for this alone.

When Winthrop and his attendants had been almost a week at Plymouth (October 26 to 31), they set out in the dark of early morning for home. Bradford, Brewster, Smith, Williams and others went with them half a mile to start them on their way, while Lieutenant William Holmes * with two others and Bradford's mare went another ten miles to "the great swamp." It had been a memorable visit, serving to tie the two colonies closer together through personal esteem. But it never prevented little Plymouth from delivering a sharp rebuke to its younger though larger rival whenever a rebuke seemed in order. It is easy for the strong to show strength. Plymouth exercised the rather more admirable strength of the weak.

Of the men who walked out in the morning dark with Bradford and Winthrop, quite the most remarkable was Roger Williams, well enough known to every schoolchild for his founding of Providence, but rarely remembered as the Plymouth "teacher" for about three years.

His meeting with Winthrop at Plymouth had a dramatic background. A young man, still in his twenties, Williams had gone

---

* Holmes' wife was one of the two women Plymouth tried for witchcraft. Both were acquitted.

first to Boston, where he had refused to take communion with Winthrop because the church there was not separated. When Williams was called to the Salem church as teacher, Winthrop was furious. Finally he applied such pressure that Williams had removed to Plymouth where he made a good impression on Bradford as "a man godly and zealous, having many precious parts." Soon he was a member of the church and then teacher, his teaching well approved until his opinions began to run ahead of Plymouth's. It is true enough that Williams in his early years and with his quick changes of belief was a very unsettled man to follow. Brewster, remembering the trials of the Separatists under John Smyth at Amsterdam, foresaw the same kind of confusion in the making for Plymouth. And Brewster was right. For Williams also came to question the validity of his first baptism, had himself baptized again, and then was soon questioning the validity of the second. Thereafter he forsook all church ties and became a "Seeker," founding at Providence the first American community where complete religious toleration existed. Anyone who thinks, however, that Williams had no strong opinions of his own should read his pamphlet on the Quakers, *George Fox Digged out of his Burrowes.*

It is clear that Bradford liked young Williams—liked his democratic attitude, his tolerance reminiscent of John Robinson's, his young enthusiasm and utter earnestness. They must have had many a hot argument over religious matters, Bradford smarting a little under the youthful impatience of Williams' "sharpest admonitions & reproufs," and lighting upon him in return for his "unsettled judgmente."

When Williams began to "fall into some strang oppinions," then, the church at Plymouth with Brewster's advice was willing to let him go, and "he left them some thing abruptly," returning to Salem for two years until he was banished by the Bay Colony.

About the time Williams was leaving Plymouth, Bradford and Winslow were on their way to Boston again. Winslow had recently been investigating the possibilities of trade along the Connecticut—partly on a suggestion made by the Dutch several years before and partly at the request of Indians who had been driven out of their homes there by the warlike Pequots. The prospects looked good, but Plymouth was reluctant to operate on its own, well aware that its patent did not extend that far from the coast. According to Winthrop's *Journal,* Bradford reached Boston on July 12, 1633, remaining just a week. Bradford says some of the chief men in Boston had already proposed a joint trading post, and that it was to complete such an agreement that he went up to Boston. Winthrop implies that the initiative was with Plymouth. Both colonies and both leaders were somewhat tender in the matter of pride and precedence.

Boston immediately began to hedge and equivocate. They had no trade goods. All right, said Bradford, "We will put in sufficient for both, provided you become engaged for the half, and prepare against the next year." The Boston men "conffessed more could not be offered, but thanked them, and tould them they had no mind to it." Bradford and Winslow then inquired whether it would be any offense if Plymouth should go on without the Bay. Not at all, said Boston—an answer the Pilgrims were soon to remember with bitterness.

Winthrop says his government "thought not fit to meddle with it" because of warlike Indians and rivers either too turbulent or shallow or icy for convenient trade. As a result, the Pilgrims rather than the Bay "were the first English that both discovered that place, and built in the same, though they were litle better then thrust out of it afterward as may appeare."

While the Pilgrims were making ready, the Dutch—who had now decided they would like the Connecticut trade for themselves—in 1633 made a small fort at what is now Hartford, planting two cannon to control the river. The Pilgrims, having got word of what was going on, built what must have been the first pre-fabricated house in America. Stowing the knock-down frame and other materials aboard a bark, they sailed up the river, knowing that if they succeeded in getting past the Dutch they would have enemies in the Pequots. Ordered to settle above the Dutch—a trick they were soon to suffer from themselves on the Kennebec—the Plymouth men sailed boldly past the fort despite threats that they would be shot at. But the threats were not carried out. By the time the Dutch could send off to Manhattan for reinforcements, the Pilgrims were snugly settled in their house behind a stout palisade. Soon a little army of seventy was sent against them—an army brave with banners. But the sensible Dutch, who knew a fait accompli when they saw one, "came to parley and returned in peace." Early in 1634 a Plymouth bark was trading with the Dutch, so the breach must have been quickly healed.

One reason for the restoration of friendly relations was the aid given to several Dutch traders by the Plymouth post. At the beginning of the winter three or four Hollanders had gone up the river above the Plymouth trading post at Matianuck to trade with an Indian tribe living in a palisaded village. Sickness soon carried away most of the Indians and the Hollanders nearly died of cold and hunger before struggling back through ice and snow to the Pilgrim post, where they were nursed and fed. Then in the spring the Indians around Matianuck were suddenly stricken with smallpox. In a realistic passage which rivals (and precedes) Defoe's *Journal of the Plague Year,* Bradford says:

"For wante of bedding & linning [linen] and other helps, they fall into a lamentable condition, as they lye on their hard matts, the poxe breaking and mattering, and runing one into another, their skin cleaving (by reason thereof) to the matts they lye on; when they turne them, a whole side will flea of at once (as it were), and they will be all of a gore blood, most fearfull to behold; and then being very sore, what with could and other distempers, they dye like rotten sheep." Even though the English fetched wood and water for them, built their fires and got their victuals while they lived, most of the tribe died. By the marvelous goodness and providence of God, says Bradford, not one of the English grew sick though they tended the Indians for many weeks together. As for their Christian care of the poor savages thus stricken by white men's ills, "their masters here [at Plymouth] did much comend & reward them for the same."

Yet the end result of these mass deaths among the Indians soon confronted the much enduring Pilgrims with another crisis. For as soon as the Bay settlements learned that the Indians they feared had been swept away, "hereing of the fame of Conighte-cute River, [they] had a hankering mind after it." Under Brewster's son Jonathan the Connecticut post had been doing well for the undertakers. Soon it was overrun with men from the Bay. First came John Oldham with ten other men, settling in 1634 just below the Dutch at a place soon named Wethersfield. By the summer of 1635, Brewster reported to Bradford, "The Massachusetts men are coming almost dayly, some by water, & some by land, who are not yet determined wher to setle, though some have a great mind to the place we are upon."

Bradford wrote a sharp letter of complaint to the government of Massachusetts Bay, recalling the fact that they had refused Plymouth's invitation to settle the Connecticut jointly and had given the Pilgrims a free hand. It was too much, argued Bradford, that after braving the double danger of Indians and Dutch and establishing a trade along the river, they should now be crowded out.

Brewster, following Bradford's instructions, was meanwhile treating the interlopers with Christian kindness. The first arrivals would have starved if he had not fed them. He supplied them also with canoes and guides, introduced them to the Dutch, stored their supplies—all at the expense of the undertakers. Yet no sooner had they been strengthened by Plymouth's aid than they began to settle in Brewster's very dooryard and on land the Pilgrims had bought of the Indians.

Correspondence between Boston and Plymouth grew noticeably sharper.

Plymouth: "We tould you before, and (upon this occasion) must now tell you still, that our mind is other wise, and that you cast rather a partiall, if not a covetous eye, upon that which is your neigbours, and not yours."

Boston: "We at first judged the place so free that we might with Gods good leave take & use it, without just offence to any man, it being the Lords wast."

Plymouth: "If it was the Lords wast, it was them selves [Plymouth] that found it so, & not they; and have since bought it of the right oweners, and maintained a chargable possession upon it al this while."

Yet in the end Plymouth gave in as it always did, for "to live in continuall contention with their freinds & brethren would be uncomfortable, and too heavie a burden to bear." A settlement was patched up by which Plymouth was to retain its trading post and one sixteenth of the land it had bought from the Indians. The men from New-towne (Cambridge) were to have another sixteenth, and the rest was to go to a group from Dorchester who had come out with their Pastor, John Wareham, to escape the Boston oligarchy. All Plymouth received was repayment for the purchase price of the land. Today the fact that Plymouth pioneered the Connecticut country is all but forgotten.

Thus ended the honeymoon between Plymouth and Boston. From now on there was a constant jockeying for power, with little Plymouth constantly on its guard to avoid being swallowed up. For Bradford this meant that having overcome the problems of hunger, disharmony and commercial legerdemain, he must now tackle the problem of political survival. It must have seemed to him as if he had been climbing a ladder from which he would only be forced to leap into space when he reached the top. The basic struggle to survive had been won. Next the proper motivation for economic health had been found. Attempts to nullify the Plymouth government had been averted. A successful trading monopoly had been established which, if it had not been for Allerton's manipulations, would have wiped out the debt in short order. The church had been preserved from Lyford's designs and strengthened by the providential decision of Salem and then Boston to follow Plymouth's form of church covenant. The trade in cattle had brought an unexpected prosperity, though it had also brought the problem of dispersal. The Connecticut trade had seemed to be a solution to the barrenness of Plymouth, a recompense for the loss of the Penobscot post and a convenient area for Plymouth's future development.

Yet the end result of all these crises overcome was that Plymouth was in danger of being swallowed up. From now on Bradford would have to give more and more of his time to statesmanship, and like the foreign secretary of a small power seek ways to beat off the grasping hands of its big neighbor.

Returning good for evil, he was able in 1636 to save the cargoes of two Massachusetts shallops which were cast away in a storm near Plymouth on their way to Connecticut. The goods, strewn up and down the shores, he caused to be picked up, inventoried, washed and dried, and restored to their owners.

Massachusetts was soon having graver troubles than this in its Connecticut venture. John Oldham having been murdered by Indians in a quarrel at Block Island, Captain John Endecott—whose personality in some ways resembled that of Standish—was

sent on a punitive expedition. Of course Oldham's murderers
had fled, so after "punishing" the inhabitants, Endecott went
to the mainland where he killed and burned among the Pequots
without getting the men he sought. He then returned to Massachusetts. The expedition had been launched without informing
either Plymouth or the Connecticut settlements. As a result, the
Pequots began to cut off the English wherever they found them
along the Connecticut, catching them when they went out fowl-
ing or as they passed in boats. Soon Massachusetts was begging
Plymouth's help—after having virtually deprived the Plymouth
men of Connecticut and refused to help them against the French
at Penobscot. Bradford seized the occasion to remind Massachusetts of Plymouth's grievances and to suggest that the Bay
had so far shown little inclination to help Plymouth. Therefore
how could Plymouth be sure, if it now aided Massachusetts, that
it could count upon her aid at some future time?

Winthrop answered: "Wheras you desire we should be in-
gaged to aide you, upon like occasions; we are perswaded you
doe not doubte of it; yet as we now deale with you as a free people, and at libertie, so as we cannot draw you into this warr with
us, otherwise then as reason may guid & provock you; so we desire
we may be at the like freedome, when any occasion may call for
help from us."

It is easy to imagine the wry smile with which Bradford read
this lawyer's equivocation. But his jaw must have tightened at
the veiled threat with which the letter ended: "If the Lord shall
please to blesse our endeaours, so as we end the warr, or put it in
a hopefull way without you, it may breed such ill thoughts in our
people towards yours, as will be hard to entertaine such opinione
of your good will towards us, as were fitt to be nurished among
such neigbours & brethren as we are. And what ill consequences
may follow, on both sids, wise men may fear, & would rather
prevente then hope to redress."

Somewhat reluctantly, Plymouth decided to ally itself with
Massachusetts and prepared to send fifty men—a sizeable army
for the little colony. Meanwhile the Pequots had almost persuaded the Narragansetts to join them in a war of extermination
against the English. But Roger Williams, now settled at Provi-

dence where he was highly regarded by the sachem Canonicus for his fair dealing with the Indians, managed to turn his tribe to the English side—a fair return indeed after his banishment by Massachusetts.

Guided by the Narragansetts, an army of Massachusetts and Connecticut men fell upon the palisaded town of the Pequots before daybreak. While some of the attackers surrounded the town to prevent escape, others thrust their way in and set the highly inflammable bark houses afire, so that more were burned to death than otherwise slain. "It was a fearfull sight," Bradford reports, apparently on the basis of a conversation with someone who had been there, "to see them thus frying in the fyer, and the streams of blood quenching the same, and horrible was the stinck & sente ther of."

The Narragansetts, leaving the dirty work to the English, took no part except to catch any who tried to escape the flames. "O brave Pequots!" they cried with savage humor, mimicking the phrase the Pequots used in their songs of triumph. A large part of the remnant was wiped out when they tried to retreat into a "hideous swamp." The sachem Sassacus escaped to the Mohawks, who promptly killed him and sent his head to Boston. About seven hundred were either slain or taken, the prisoners being divided between the Connecticut settlements and Massachusetts. One of these was the wife of the sachem Mononoto who begged that "the English would not abuse her body." Apparently she had cause to fear, for the girls and women were in much demand among the soldiers though there is not a single recorded instance of a white woman being abused by an Indian. All the male prisoners were shipped off to the West Indies as slaves, under none other than Captain William Peirce. As for the brave English who had done the slaughter, Winthrop reported that "they found them selves so fresh as they could willingly have gone to such another bussines." The frying in the fire, the streams of blood and the stench were apparently all in the day's work.

Even Bradford, though believing the Bay men somewhat to blame in bringing on the war, could write that "the victory seemed a sweete sacrifice, and they gave the prays therof to God."

Then suddenly we realize that there are contradictions in the
spirit of the man which have lain hidden to us—that the Old
Testament delight in a mighty God of war who delivers His
chosen people from all their enemies is a part of Bradford's
character too, along with his kindness, his tact and his vigor. The
men of Plymouth, even the men of Boston are God-protected
and God-endowed. Their triumph over the Pequots is therefore
but an aspect of predestination, an inevitable outcome of divine
law.

"O that you had converted some before you had killed any,"
we hear John Robinson's voice echoing. But the sound of his
voice was lost in the waters of the Atlantic and in the deep forests of the vast new world. The frontier created a situation too
like that of the ancient Hebrews and their enemies, it evoked
too clearly the phrases of the Psalms to escape so earnest a student of the Bible as Bradford. He shows none of the zeal for
conversion which moved John Eliot, and Plymouth never made
any great success of converting the heathen though a later minister at Plymouth, John Cotton, was superior even to Eliot in
his knowledge of the Indian tongue. Nor is there in Bradford's
writing any glimmer of appreciation for Indian folkways, except
as they made the survival of Plymouth possible. In this respect
Bradford must give way to Roger Williams, whose sense of the
brotherhood of man was truly universal.

By 1640 Plymouth was as well off as it had ever been, and the
prospects ahead looked bright. It was true that the fur trade
had fallen off because of competition in the north with the
French, and in the west from the new settlements at Providence
and along the Connecticut. Despite the vast quantities of fur
sent over to England, the London partners were not yet satisfied
nor the last debt discharged. Too, the political and economic
center had shifted from the Old Colony to Massachusetts Bay.

But trade in corn and cattle was brisk and prices almost un-
believable. Cows brought as much as £28—two thousand dollars! * Calves, milk goats, kids and other livestock were equally
profitable while corn now brought six shillings or about $3.75
a bushel. At last the Pilgrims had found a trade to replace their

* As of 1951.

always unsuccessful efforts at fishing. Many of them had been born to husbandry and were glad to return to it. Other trading now began to be neglected. The old partners decided to sell out the Kennebec post; it was bought by Bradford and a few others, who promised the purchasers * one sixth of the income.

As Bradford reviewed the events of the decade, there were other hopeful signs. It had been in many ways an exhausting experience for him—the dishonesty of Allerton which hurt most because it hurt his beloved William Brewster, the encroachments of the Bay upon Plymouth's rights and bounds, the dispersal of the people beyond reach of the mother church. Yet they had escaped major disaster, they had brought their laws into a code, they had preserved their long peace with the neighboring Indians (Massasoit in 1639 had asked that the ancient league with Plymouth should remain inviolable), and they were beginning to build up a firm economic foundation in flocks and fields. Yeoman that he was, Bradford felt the need for this kind of security. Whenever possible, he took up more land for himself just as his ancestors had done. Even if he could have foreseen that from circumstances beyond his reach the boom in cattle was soon to suffer a ruinous drop, he would have wanted land.

Although during the thirties he had four times been relieved of the governorship (and would be relieved only once again as long as he lived), it had made no great difference in his affairs. Still an assistant governor and an undertaker in the trading monopoly, his time was cumbered with public affairs. In or out of office, the people persisted in thinking of him as governor. They preferred him to all the rest, and by 1639 he had given up the struggle and accepted their preference. By then the early exhilaration of finding the qualities of leadership within himself had worn off. He accepted leadership as a duty. Perhaps he even came to think of it as a right, until his once strenuous objections to re-election weakened and grew perfunctory, hardening at last into pure formality; for this fate even the great seem unable—perhaps the least able—to escape.

The twenties had been a struggle for survival, the thirties for economic independence. With a glance northward, Bradford

* That is, all the Plymouth residents who had signed the 1627 articles of agreement with the "undertakers."

could see that the forties would bring increasing pressure upon Plymouth's political independence. Or rather, its independence as a community of God. For it was the community, the organism that concerned Bradford, not its merely political aspect, or the economic. Plymouth too had a soul—a soul to be saved. He would save it—if he could.

The Bradford Household

WHILE William Bradford was governing, overseeing the colony's trade, serving as judge, trying to settle with the London merchants, marrying the young couples who were growing up, negotiating with the new colonies springing up about him, managing his farms and livestock, convening and presiding at the general courts and the courts of assistants, writing a book and prophesying of a Sunday in church, he was also looking out for a confusingly large household of his own.

In addition to Dorothy's John, there were his three children by Alice Carpenter Southworth—William, Mercy and Joseph (1630–1715). There were Alice's two sons, Constant and Thomas, and her sister's son Nathaniel Morton who remained in the Bradford household and was closer to Alice than to his own mother. And there were four orphan boys—Joseph Rogers, Thomas Cushman, William Latham and Samuel Godbertson or Cuthbertson. From the fact that both John and William wrote a hand remarkably like Bradford's it is easy to see that he had another duty added to all his others—that of schoolmaster.

The lack of schools in Plymouth Plantation was a matter of deep concern to Bradford. True, there were many parents who like himself were capable of educating their own. Mistress Fuller, and other women as the colony spread out, operated "dame schools." But those who most needed educating were least likely to get it. A sound congregation required a people able to read the word of God for themselves.

When the colony had been struggling for its life, when every man, woman and child had been needed to raise a wall of corn against the threat of starvation—then there had been a good excuse for deferring the establishment of public schools. But Plymouth had come a long way since those early years. Now, in 1640, it was prosperity more than poverty which was like to prove its ruin.

Yes, they had come a long way. It had been a bitter struggle. Yet like any man who has survived the struggle and had time to pause and look back, William Bradford had begun to idealize it a little, almost to wish it back. Providing for a family of thirteen had not been easy, and with so many boys of about the same age his household had looked more like a boarding school than a home, yet now that they had begun to marry and move away he was sorry to see them go. If, with memories of his orphaned childhood, he had wanted a child-filled home of his own, he had got it with a vengeance. Yet it must have been hard on Alice, with no one but little Mercy to help her in the household chores.

The marriages began in 1634. Patience Morton, a member of the Bradford household from 1624 to 1627, was first. After the death of her father George Morton she, her sister, three brothers and her mother had lived with the Bradfords. Marrying John Faunce, she became in 1647 the mother of Thomas Faunce whose memories as an old man are the sole basis for the legend that the Pilgrims, at their landing, first set foot on Plymouth Rock. The next year her brother Nathaniel, Bradford's secretary, married Lydia Cooper. Nathaniel was clerk of the colony for nearly forty years and author of New England's Memoriall, an important sourcebook of Plymouth history until Bradford's lost manuscript was discovered. Not long afterward Nathaniel's brother John married a girl named Lettice, and at about the same time Thomas Cushman married Mary Allerton, daughter of the man who had nearly wrecked Plymouth's economy. Whether Allerton came to the wedding we don't know, but it is unlikely since by this time he had been asked to leave Marblehead where he had been in the fishing business and had taken himself off to New Amsterdam. And since this is the last we shall see of him, it may be as well to record that he later went to New Haven, prospered as a trader, married again (his wife Fear Brewster having died in 1634), built himself a grand house—and died insolvent. Certainly Bradford, who without doubt officiated at all these marriages, must have noted the irony of his joining Cushman's son to Allerton's daughter, remembering too that it was Allerton who had joined him to Alice.

In 1637 both of Alice's sons were married—Constant to Elizabeth Collier, daughter of one of two London adventurers who had settled in Plymouth, and Thomas to Elizabeth Reynor, the pastor's daughter. As Collier's other daughters married Love Brewster and Thomas Prence (whose first wife, Patience Brewster, had died in 1634), most of the leading families were now interconnected. Both of the Southworth boys went on to become leaders in the colony—Constant as a deputy from Duxbury (they were preferring that spelling now to Bradford's homelier Ducksburrow), colony treasurer (1659–1679) and assistant governor (1670–1678), Thomas as deputy from Plymouth (1651), assistant governor (1652–1653, 1657–1669) and commissioner of the New England Confederacy. In 1640 Bradford's own John married Martha Bourne—whose name has been preserved on the map of the Old Colony though Bradford's has not, and whose father did more to Christianize the Indians than anyone else in the colony.

So before he was out of his forties Bradford's large household had shrunk to a mere five or six. Joseph Rogers had married a girl named Hannah at an uncertain date and was soon to move to Eastham down on the Cape. William Latham had gone back to England. Sam Cuthbertson (or Godbertson) who had become Bradford's ward at his father's death in 1633 was apprenticed to a tailor (Richard Higgins) the next year. After the custom of the time he was taken into his employer's household—along with a calf of which Higgins was to have half the increase at the end of the seven-year apprenticeship. What happened if the increase came out an odd number was not specified. Perhaps the unlucky odd was converted to beef.

In addition to all these marrying young people, the Bradford tribe—thanks to the marrying Carpenter sisters—also included the Kemptons, the Fullers, and the William Wrights. Wright

and his wife Priscilla Carpenter had come over on the *Fortune*
in 1621. Both Wright and Sam Fuller were carried off in the epidemic of 1633, along with Cuthbertson and his wife (Allerton's
sister). Francis Cooke, Peter Browne and Francis Eaton of the
Mayflower, John Adams of the *Fortune,* Thomas Blossom and
Richard Masterson of the second *Mayflower* had also succumbed.
Brewster's two daughters, Fear and Patience, were taken the following year. It was a sad blow to little Plymouth, but as it was
the first epidemic to strike since the winter of 1621, it is clear
that the chance of staying alive in Plymouth was far better than
in London.

Of all these unscheduled departures, Bradford would have
felt most keenly about Deacon Samuel Fuller, a friend since the
early Leyden days where they had been married the same year.
More than any other man, Fuller had been responsible for drawing the new settlements of Massachusetts Bay into the same
church fold, and his double ministry of physic and prophecy had
been a mainstay of the Plymouth community. Though he had
walked often to the burying ground in these thirteen years, Bradford had never felt a deeper sense of loss. "The Lord gave and
the Lord hath taken away"—the words must certainly have run
through Bradford's mind as he tarried a while at the grave, for
they well express his philosophy: "The Lord gave and the Lord
hath taken away; blessed be the name of the Lord." The privations suffered at Plymouth could scarcely have been endured on
any other basis.

The next year Fuller's wife was keeping a small "dame school"
in her home.

Where the Bradfords were able to bed down their large family
is anybody's guess, for the governor's house at Plymouth was
never very large. Probably the whole parcel of boys were jumbled
together in the upper story under the low eaves. The inventory
of Bradford's estate gives us a hint, at least, of what his Plymouth house must have looked like. The old house had been extended, its planks probably covered with clapboard. We may
safely imagine an unpainted, undecorated building with a large
central chimney and small windows of leaded glass in diamond-
shaped panes. The extension included the "new chamber" where

Bradford and Alice slept. Since the parlor was old, either the "great rome" or the "studdie" must have belonged to the newer part.

It was in the great room that meetings of the assistants were held and other public business done. Two great carved chairs, a smaller chair, a long table and "forms" or benches furnished the room, with carpets for the tables and a large number of cushions which suggests either that the floor was used for larger meetings or that the fathers liked to ease a little the hardness of the plain benches. Around the huge fireplace, capable of taking four-foot logs, were kettles and skillets of brass and iron, with a row of pewter plates in a near-by open-shelved cupboard where Alice also kept four dozen trenchers. (A trencher was a wooden dish about ten inches square, and two people often dined from it at once.) A corselet and headpiece hung on the walls, probably rusting from disuse since the early years of Indian alarms.

In the parlor, just as in Austerfield, was the best bedstead—wainscoted, with a feather bed, bolster and pillow, where Winthrop and Rasieres had slept. Extra guests could be accommodated on the canvas bed. The cupboard and settle show that this was the room the family liked to use when there was no company to be entertained. For nothing, on a cold winter evening, could compare with a settle, its high back collecting the heat thrown off by the fireplace, its base snug to the floor cutting off the cold air that poured like a stream around one's feet. But Bradford's work room was the "studdie" where the most noticeable items were the desk and a large moose skin brought back from one of the many voyages to Maine. The study was stuffed with trading goods—cloth of all kinds in lengths from two to ten yards, and large quantities of shoes. Nearly three hundred books filled a case of shelves, for next to Brewster Bradford had the largest library in Plymouth. And probably on the desk lay the large, vellum-covered volume in which whenever he could find a spare moment Bradford wrote down the history of his lifework —Plimoth Plantation.

After 1647 room had to be found somewhere in the house for Alice's sister, Mary Carpenter. An old maid, she had returned to England from Leyden in the thirties and settled at Wrington near Bristol in Somersetshire, her old family home. When her

mother died, Bradford in 1646 wrote her a warmly hospitable
letter inviting her to come and make her home in Plymouth,
though warning her of unsettled times. She chose to come, and
was part of the household until her death many years later.

In the new chamber—obviously the one he and Alice used except perhaps on a cold winter's night when with no guests in the
house they would crawl into the parlor bed for better warmth
—in the new chamber were the governor's clothes. Anyone who
thinks the Pilgrims drab and colorless will be surprised by the
variety and extent of Bradford's wardrobe:

A cloth cloake faced with taffety and lined with baies [baize]
A sad colored cloth suit
A Turkey grogorum suit and cloak [grogram was a coarse fabric
    of silk and mohair]
A red waistcoat
A suit with silver buttons
An old green gown
A violet colored cloak
A leaden colored suit with silver buttons
A broadcloth coat
A pair of black breeches
An old serge suit
Three more coats
Three cloaks
Old doublets and waistcoats
Four hats, some black, some colored
Two pair of stockings.

Another surprise is the large number of weapons—muskets,
pistols, cutlass. No one will be surprised to find chamber pots
listed in the household inventory; however, three seems like a
very modest number for so busy a household! A brewing tub
and a "great beer bowl" worth £3 makes clear enough what the
chief item of entertainment was. The sixty-four pieces of pewter
and the thirteen silver spoons are those of a man moderately well
to do.

But Bradford's real wealth was in his land. Like his great-great-
grandfather Peter, like all his other yeoman ancestors, he had
an urge to own land, to own it outright and to see it well stocked
with cattle. Old Peter's ewe lamb had made a long journey from

Bentley-cum-Arksey to the pastures of Plymouth. It was a basic part of Bradford's heritage, and it had made the voyage in such a way that it could not sicken or be destroyed, for it had come in his head. Because of his loss in Holland, because he had seen the Bentley lands partly swallowed up there, a compulsion was on him to bring them back again, to recover literally the ground he had lost and for which his family had fought. Much as he loved the challenge of his governorship, he loved in a more intimate way, a way wound in with the past and with youth, to walk out into his fields, to plant, to hoe, to stack hay. He liked to see his eight sheep browsing of a summer's afternoon while the shadows of clouds played over them and over the rolling green hills. He liked to see young William shepherd them, as once he himself had done in the tight, neat little homeland he would never see again. And he liked to calculate the increase in his cattle and what it would bring him in the Boston market.

When Winthrop had visited Plymouth in 1632 Bradford had been able to send only one mare for three distinguished visitors. Well, the mare had done her duty and there were more horses now. (There would be five at his death.) What a marvelous help the horse was, to a man often wanted in half a dozen places at once! Really an epochal step in Plymouth's transportation system, making them much less dependent on wind and water. In an afternoon he could easily ride over to his three-hundred-acre farm at Jones River (Kingston) to take a hand in the haying. In summer the whole family might be over there for weeks at a time, for he had built a house near Stony Brook around 1637.* Even Bradford, who hated to see Plymouth depopulated, had become a victim of economics, for though he had agreed with the law passed by the court in 1633, that the governor's residence should be tied to Plymouth, yet he too had in effect moved out so far as his income-producing activity was concerned. In 1647 he was trying to operate the farm through tenants. Apparently it was not a success, for the court in October authorized him to seize their goods and grain until they paid what they owed him.

The Jones River farm, with its house looking out across salt marsh and bay to the sea, was not all. In addition to the orchard

* The site of Bradford's Kingston farm and house is marked with a boulder and tablet.

and garden adjoining his Plymouth home, Bradford owned the land extending from his house northward to where Pilgrim Hall now stands. He owned land at Eastham, Bridgewater, Sawtuckett, Coaksett. He had rights in the town land at Punckatessett. In 1637 the court ruled that he might "take in" his acres at Strawberry Hill. An island lying in Green's Harbor (Marshfield) was granted him in 1639. In 1649 the court granted him a parcel of meadow to winter ten cattle on the further side of "Raged Playne" west of the Weymouth path. At the same time he also received a parcel of meadow at the end of John Faunce's land, and another at Jones River. (These last two Bradford gave just before his death to his son John.) In 1650 he got forty or fifty acres for his children at Barnstable, with the right to bargain with the Indians for it if any living should lay claim to it.

He was ready to go to court to protect these holdings when he had to. In October 1636, for instance, he entered an action of trespass against four young men, and was given £5 and costs. But then, in an act which lights up the neighborly, intimate quality of government at Plymouth and the lack of any barrier between the law which punishes and the law which grants land, the next court entry says: "All such young men or others as wanted land should repair to the Governor and assistants the next morning." The four who had trespassed all got land. An easy solution: but why hadn't the young men thought of it in the first place?

A more serious trespass took place in 1638, when Bradford got £45 in damages from John Combes. Since most of the trespass cases were for cutting hay or retaining animals that belonged to other people, this was probably John Combes' offense. For £45 (more than $3,000 in 1951) he must have made a lot of hay.

While Bradford, during the thirties, was far from the richest man in the colony—Allerton had that distinction in the tax list of 1633, as everyone must have noted with malicious delight —he kept on adding to his land holdings. In 1634 Winslow (the highest taxpayer), William Collier, Allerton, and Hopkins drew a heavier tax. But Bradford the yeoman went on acquiring land. At his death he owned more land than any other man in Plymouth, even though to satisfy the London merchants he had had to sell off—and much it hurt him to do it—three hundred acres. Since any man keeps on through life measuring himself by home-town standards, it must have been one of Bradford's great inward satisfactions that he owned far more land than anyone in Auster-field, and owned it outright too, with none of the feudal "by your leave" on which even the best of Austerfield titles was suspended.

With the increase of lands and cattle the Plymouth folk could now have the beef, bread and beer they had longed for in the twenties. Still most meat was eaten salt, and so heavily seasoned with saffron that Pilgrim fingers—not at all hostile to touching their food—were stained yellow. Since cooking methods were primitive—performed in great kettles hanging from a rod or green pole, or in tall-legged skillets set in the coals—the Pilgrim fare was simple. Soup, porridge, hash or stew—something that could be cooked in one dish—was most prominent. Breakfast might consist of a hasty pudding followed by pea soup or stew. For dinner pork and beans and a dish of vegetables boiled together. Supper would probably be breakfast warmed over. Dried peas and beans, corn meal and salt meat were the winter staples —all washed down, even by babes just weaned, with beer. The summer season brought vegetables in variety, all of them familiar to us, though the likelihood is that the Pilgrims cooked them to death. Bradford, in a poem which we may hope contains more of truth than poetry, listed wheat, rye, barley, oats, beans, peas, roots and herbs, onions, melons, cucumbers, radishes, parsnips, carrots, turnips, skirrets (a kind of turnip), beets, cole-worts, cabbages, berries, pears, apples, cherries, plums, quince, peach, nuts and grapes. The sandy soil of the Cape was hospitable to berries, and in season Bradford's family took their fill of wild strawberries as much as two inches around, raspberries, huckle-berries, gooseberries, "bilberries," "treackleberries" and currants.

Every housewife had her preference in herbs, whether for cooking or dosing. Marjoram, purselaine, sorrel, pennyroyal, yarrow, sarsaparilla—they were all here or soon growing in kitchen gardens. With catnip, sage, spearmint, and a good many others they were gathered while in bloom and hung in the rafters to dry. Cowslip, violet, primrose and liverwort were at hand to make salads—a new thought perhaps for the present-day housewife.

With the passing of Sam Fuller, Plymouth's women had to rely more than ever upon their own remedies. It was part of a girl's upbringing to concoct these. Alice had certainly learned a few of Sam's secrets from him. He seems to have had a real fondness for her, even to remembering her in his will. His first wife was Alice's sister. He and Alice had each witnessed the other's betrothal at Leyden. Perhaps she learned from him the formula for Venice treacle, supposed to be good for nearly anything that ailed a child. It consisted of snakes pounded—presumably after their decease—with white wine and twenty different herbs plus a dash of opium. Or the common drink for throat distemper (diphtheria)—pounded snails and earthworms boiled in ale. She would know that basil eased a woman in childbirth, that dill was good for breeding milk in nursing mothers, that hyssop was good for a cough and killed worms, that sage prevented abortion. She would have a piece of salt beef ready to lay on a child's cut, bedstraw to stop bleeding. And though she would have known that mint hinders conception and nettles provoke lust, she would have resorted to neither.

There were, of course, more exotic ingredients in the pharmacopœia—filings from a dead man's skull, the milk of a nurse giving suck to a male child, cat's ear, goose dung, male urine, wolf guts and the hair of a virgin. Bitter rivalry went on in the seventeenth century between the followers of Galen who believed that virtue resided only in vegetable substances, and those of Paracelsus whose mineral preparations had a much more dramatic sound. On the whole, Alice Bradford probably stuck to the herbs and simples that could be concocted from her own garden.

Her kitchen was also full of tools for the many other trades a housewife was expected to practice—brewing, spinning, weaving, butter churning, candle making.* Her hams and bacons hung in the chimney, her corn and apples from the ceiling. She had no sink, stove or refrigerator, and we would probably have found her cooking monotonous, but to Bradford who remembered the lean years it was as good as a feast.

* Pine knots and rush lights in time had given way to Betty lamps and candles.

Comfortable as his household had become, William Bradford had only to look out the diamond-shaped panes of his study window to be unhappily reminded of the changes that had taken place at Plymouth during the thirties. The home of his beloved old foster father across the street was now a tavern operated by James Cole whose name still identifies the hill which was the Pilgrim's first burying place. Brewster, his wife dead and his daughters married, had moved to Duxbury with his two younger sons. John and Priscilla Alden had gone there too with their large brood, as had Standish and his whole household including the still faithful Hobomok. Winslow was at Marshfield, Allerton departed, Sam Fuller dead. Whenever he thought of it, Bradford shook his head. The community—that sweet, tightly bound communion of minds and spirits which had existed at Scrooby and at Leyden—was being destroyed. Or already destroyed. What comfort was prosperity in the face of this?

When he tried to explain this to Alice, she would tell him to stop worrying, or bring him a glass of wine, or laugh and tell him he was getting old and set in his ways, unable to accept change or receive with a thankful heart the prosperity God had brought them. He would try to think she was right, yet when he remembered the warmth of fellowship there had been for a sensitive orphan boy at Scrooby, or the beauty of revealed faith in Pastor Robinson's preaching at Leyden—then he would know within himself that they had strayed from the right way like lost sheep and were being swallowed up by prosperity.

There was even a market in Plymouth now every Thursday.* At least this brought people back into town, filled up the streets again, brought guests for supper and a better congregation for the mid-week meeting. To market came the local products of the several trades being practiced in Plymouth now, as the many acts regulating apprenticeship show. Plymouth had its tailor, its bricklayer, its cabinetmaker, and since 1636 its corn mill—a great comfort to housewives who in the early days had had to soak and pound their own corn. A tannery was being started in 1640, though since it took a year to prepare a hide, there would be no product yet awhile.

* Authorized in 1639, along with a May fair for Plymouth, an October fair for Duxbury.

Yes, Plymouth was prosperous with a prosperity like to prove its ruin, Bradford thought as he stepped out into the street. Behind his back a man who had been "drinking tobacco" would quickly douse his pipe and give the warning to any others who happened to be near. There was a strict law against smoking in the streets or in barns and haystacks—not out of a notion that smoking had anything to do with morals, but for fear of fire. Tobacco was a profitable crop and a pleasure in which even the saints of the church indulged. Around the market stalls a few Indians would be mingled in the crowd, nearly naked if the day was hot, nothing but a kind of fringed leather apron about their waists. Except for furs, there was little the Indian had that he could trade for the coveted white man's goods now, for even in corn-growing the white man—by superior attentiveness and persistence—excelled. The presence of Indians had long been taken for granted. Without being sentimental about it, Plymouth had been just in its dealings with them. Over and again the statute books record a fine against a white man for mistreating an Indian, or for allowing cattle to trample his corn. Still Bradford felt a twinge of conscience whenever he saw an Indian, for Robinson's reproof—"Oh! how happy a thing had it been, if you had converted some, before you had killed any" —had sunk in deep. He had intended to do something about the souls of the Indians, but there had been so many things to do. He had learned but a few words and phrases of their language, he had never had the time or the knack to know them as Roger Williams did. But something, after all, must be left to others.

Even more urgent was this problem of educating Plymouth's children. William at sixteen was past the age, and Mercy had had as much as a girl child needed, but Joseph at ten was ripe for it, as were many other youngsters in the colony. It was high time that the colony provide for its young. The men of the Bay had done far better, establishing schools soon after their arrival and now even a college. And at last it looked as though Bradford's hope was to be realized. For William Paddy, the colony's treasurer, had proposed settling at Jones River and opening an academy "to read the arts to some fit for the purpose." Settled between Plymouth and Duxbury, he would be able to draw scholars from both. It was a hopeful idea. And here was Edward Winslow, come over from Marshfield to the market—just the man to speak to.

Much to Bradford's surprise, Winslow greeted the idea with something less than enthusiasm. "Paddy run a school? It is like to destroy the congregations. His judgment is more rigid than any Separatist I ever read or knew."

No reminder of Plymouth's backwardness in providing schools for its youth could shake Winslow. Better no school than one run by Mr. Paddy. What of Paddy's gifts? Bradford asked.

"His errors go along with his gifts," Winslow replied, and there let it rest.

But when he went home that night, Winslow wrote a letter to Winthrop in Boston. Both Bradford and Reynor favor Mr. Paddy's academy, he said, yet it will be the ruination of the churches. If you conceal how you came by your information and give your Christian advice to Mr. Bradford, you may do much good.

Whether or not Winthrop gave his advice, no more was heard of the academy. And no formal school was established in the Old Colony within Bradford's lifetime. For the prosperity which Plymouth had won after twenty years of almost incredible labor and hardship was about to collapse—swiftly, decisively. Ironically, the collapse was to be due to the triumph in England of the very principles for which the Pilgrims had fought and to which they had led the way.

"Clamours and Aspertions"

THE collapse came suddenly, without warning. Within a month the price of cattle dropped to a quarter or a fifth of the market value. A cow that had brought £20 fell to £5, a goat worth fifty shillings to ten. The collapse came, moreover, just as the undertakers were making a last effort to bury the debt to London.

There is an element of irony in this collapse of values, for while it was caused at first by the frantic efforts of Archbishop Laud to stamp out Puritanism at home and in the colonies by closing the ports to emigrants, it was the triumph of their Pastor John Robinson's principles in England which put a final, effective stop to emigration and thus knocked the props out from under the cattle market. For Cromwell was an Independent, and Robinson through his well-known writings was an acknowledged leader of the Congregational or Independent way. With Cromwell and his forces achieving victory, the goad to emigration was taken away, and men began returning home from New England instead of going out to settle there. The triumph of principles for which the Pilgrims had already sacrificed homes, ease, and even lives, had now turned to destroy the basis of their prosperity.

Hardened by one crisis after another, Bradford was not to be bowled over by this. He went ahead with the negotiations to pay off the merchants though it was now an added burden to do

so and though he finally had to sell three hundred acres at
Rehoboth to meet his share of the costs. Fantastic as those costs
were, thanks to mismanagement, cupidity and the ruinously
high interest rates then prevalent, the equally astronomical
bounty of the new world fields and forests finally cleared the
debt.

But while the settlement with the merchants was still dan-
gling, another crisis suddenly blew up much closer to home.

Since 1630 Plymouth Plantation had been legally the do-
main of William Bradford. The patent issued in that year (13
January 1629/30) by the Council for New England had been
drawn in Bradford's name and signed by Ferdinando Gorges
and the Earl of Warwick. But Gorges had never given up his
dream of making himself master of New England, and if persistence could do it, he meant to see it through. Why he was willing
to sign the 1630 patent, especially after the clash over Morton
and his frequent efforts to get control of all New England for
himself, is a mystery. Perhaps he knew that without the royal
seal the patent was of little worth and easily revoked. If Allerton
actually greased as many palms as he claimed, Gorges must have
been a principal beneficiary. And if Allerton wished to put a
high valuation upon his signature, why should he depreciate it?

In 1634 Gorges began to agitate for a general governor for
the whole of New England, making no secret who it ought to be.
On June 7, 1635 the Council for New England surrendered its
charter and Gorges was appointed governor general for all New
England. At last the old knight, now sixty-nine, was to achieve
his lifetime ambition. For thirty years he had poured money and
effort into explorations and settlements of New England. Like
Captain John Smith (who had died in 1631 without achieving
his ambition of settling a New England colony) he believed in
New England with a passion amounting to religion. Now he got
a ship ready, made plans for a private army of a thousand men
and prepared to engage a whole consistory of Anglican priests.
The long, precarious independence of Plymouth was balanced
as on a cliff's edge.

Then, as Bradford would have seen it, Providence intervened
once more. Gorges' ship was damaged beyond repair. His right-
hand man died suddenly. And Gorges lacked the means to over-

come these losses. Still the doughty old knight would not give up. No vessels could leave for New England without his permission, and in 1638 eight ships which had attempted to evade him were seized. He now began to move heaven and earth to get the Massachusetts charter annulled. Then, on April 3, 1639, he obtained a royal charter for his Province of Maine—a vast area between the Merrimac and Kennebec rivers of which he was to be supreme ruler. The charter gave him feudal powers, which he quickly developed into a wonderful paper empire full of obedient subjects and loyal officials. At last his lifetime of effort was bearing fruit.

But just as he was preparing to gather in his harvest came the Long Parliament, the execution of the Earl of Strafford, the impeachment of Laud, and civil war. No one now wanted to emigrate to New England, and without settlers, Gorges' vast empire was but a waste. Loyal to Charles the First, the aging warrior lived long enough (1647) to see his world collapse and his own empire fade with that of the captured king.

Ever since the demise of the Council for New England, Plymouth's patent had been of little value. For years the Pilgrims had longed and labored for a royal charter, yet in the end their strength to survive had proved stronger than that of the royal Charles himself.

In 1639, however, Plymouth was stirring with a dissatisfaction which arose in part from the patent of 1630 to Bradford. The issue was "by what virtue the governor and assistants give and dispose of lands," and it came as near to an impeachment as Bradford was ever to get.

Discontent, apparently long brewing, broke out at the general court on March 5, 1638/9, when Bradford was challenged to explain why, ever since the patent had been issued in his name, "there hath been a cessation of grant of lands." The court constituted itself a grand jury to hold an inquest on the subject, with Bradford and the other undertakers on the carpet to defend their actions. Clearly, it was a case of the haves against the have-nots, of church members against strangers. Bradford, with his concept of the covenant-bound community, felt himself justified in any steps that would keep that beloved brotherhood from threatened disintegration. Through the dangers of starvation, invasion, economic collapse and authority imposed from without he had fought to preserve that intimate, tightly bound community based upon the law of God as he had experienced it at Scrooby and Leyden. This was his vision of the good life; this was his mission on earth as a man responsible to God. Plymouth had been planned and built by men to whom this concept of a Christian brotherhood meant everything. It was frankly a community for men who shared a religious faith and who believed that nothing short of this faith, present in all its members, could make a good community. Was this bigotry? The debunkers of Plymouth would have it so. Anyone who takes the trouble to understand what these men aimed at will not be so sure. Our own form of democracy, the nation-state, has not been so free of error that it can afford to ignore or condemn other concepts of responsibility and freedom.

The vision of this ideal community must have been in Bradford's mind as he stood up before the court to justify his course. Like many a leader grown accustomed to power, he may have felt irked by this criticism in view of the twenty years of effort by which he had kept the colony alive. He may have been angered by the sheepish faces of the ringleaders or by the frankly satisfied smirks of the hangers-on, the men sentenced or put in the stocks for past misdemeanors who now delighted to see authority called on the carpet. But there were other faces there to sustain him—Brewster to whom service and reflection had brought a look of saintly resignation and calm; Winslow whose quizzical expression showed the keen anticipation of the diplomat for the expected display of Bradford's own powers in that direction; Alden big and blond and firm of chin, ready to back any course the governor should take; Standish already glaring at the crowd to kill any disturbance before it could start, his very beard crisp with authority.

To a hushed crowd in the cold, clammy-aired, low-ceilinged fort Bradford reviewed Plymouth's history, reminding them of what it had cost to gain and keep a foothold on a cold, indifferent shore. He spoke of the hungry years, then of the agreement by which every man had grown his own corn, then of the further division of land and cattle and the voluntary act of the leaders in making every colonist a purchaser or joint owner of the colony.

The settlers had then been content to leave the debts to the undertakers, he reminded them. And the debts had been so great that the undertakers were still struggling under the burden. Yet they had been willing to disburse a large sum for the "enlargement" of the colony patent, even though this expense which they had taken upon themselves would benefit all.

Then, when he saw in the faces before him a look of contriteness and embarrassment, he made his offer—made it suddenly and without preamble and with dramatic effect. He would surrender into the hands of the whole court the patent taken out in his name. He would surrender to "the freemen of this corporation of New Plymouth all the privileges, immunities" and other benefits of the patent, asking only that the purchasers or old comers be allowed to make choice of two or three places for themselves and their heirs, and that up to £300 be paid to him and his partners if they had to dig into their personal estates in order to satisfy the London merchants.

Taken by surprise and overwhelmed by the offer, the opposition collapsed. The offer was accepted. With the surrendered patent went a personal empire which Bradford might have claimed for himself and his heirs. But Bradford was no Gorges. It was not power or wealth he wanted, but a way of life—a community of dedicated men and women, bound together as close and warm as a family is bound, by covenants sacred and inviolable.

There was still another direction in which Bradford had to keep an eye peeled for encroachments upon the liberties of Plymouth. Massachusetts, growing fast and sending out new towns all around the Bay like shoots from a poplar stump, now appeared likely to encroach upon Plymouth territory as it had once encroached upon Plymouth's trade. Rubbing against each other along the hazily defined boundary line, Bay men and Old Colony men were soon warm with anger. Friction was hottest between Hingham and Scituate. The Bradford patent of 1629/30 had established a line running from the bottom of Massachusetts Bay to Narragansett Bay. The Massachusetts patent stretched three miles beyond the southward extent of the Bay and the Charles River. Between the terms of the two patents there was plenty of room for argument. Timothy Hatherly, one of the four London partners, had come over and settled at Scituate in Plymouth Colony about 1632. A few years later men from the Bay had settled Hingham. The Hingham men were soon staking out meadows claimed by Scituate. So the Scituate men pulled up the stakes and tossed them away, laying down stakes of their own. These the Hingham men tore up. The settlers took their grievances to their respective governments, but in spite of many letters back and forth neither would give in. Then Massachusetts surveyed its line—and of course found that all of Scituate was within it. Plymouth did the same—and took in all of Hingham.

Finally each colony appointed two commissioners. Bradford and Winslow represented Plymouth, Endecott and Israel Stoughton the Bay. They met in Hingham in the spring of 1639, but stubborn old Endecott stuck to the ridiculous position that any brook or runlet flowing into the Charles was a part of the Charles River, and that as a result not only Scituate but part of the town of Plymouth itself belonged to Massachusetts.

How about the Humber? Bradford asked, provoked beyond his wont. It has the Trent, the Ouse and many other streams flowing into it and yet not counted parts of it. And still other smaller rivers and brooks (it was the Idle of his own boyhood he was thinking of) fall into the Trent and the Ouse, having their own names and divisions. But Endecott would not give in. Nor would Bradford. Even Winslow's diplomacy failed this test.

After tempers had cooled for a year the same commissioners met once again, this time at Scituate. And this time they made an agreement. It was fair and reasonable to both sides, permitting any settlement then established to remain where it was, and laying out a line from the Cohasset marshes through a body of water "which was formerly named (and still we desire may be caled) Accord pond."

It is Accord Pond to this day.

Yet this accord was scarcely settled when another problem popped up. In 1641 Massachusetts tried to claim Seekonk (now in Rhode Island) on Narragansett Bay—a point well to the south of Plymouth and long acknowledged a part of it. In 1636, in fact, Roger Williams had settled there after his flight from Massachusetts Bay, but had been "lovingly advised" by Winslow to move beyond Plymouth's jurisdiction to the other side of the bay. He had done so, thus founding Providence. Yet Massachusetts was now challenging this long-established claim. Realizing perhaps that they had overstepped themselves, the Massachusetts leaders finally withdrew. But there were increasing signs that they would have no objection to swallowing their neighbor to the south.

In 1644 Winslow made over the Penobscot trading post to Winthrop, in order to empower Massachusetts to recover it from the French. In 1650 Bradford was again involved in a boundary negotiation with Massachusetts, which ended with Plymouth making over its rights to Pawtucket and Warwick (Rhode Island) while Rhode Island howled in protest.

Meanwhile the dispersal from Plymouth continued. Duxbury had been settled as early as 1631. Marshfield, Scituate, Sandwich, Barnstable, Yarmouth and Taunton had soon followed. But now came a still more bitter blow, in the form of a proposal that Plymouth itself be abandoned, the whole town removing to Nauset on the Cape.

To Bradford the proposal, first made in 1643, seemed ruinous. Plymouth was his creation if it was any man's. He had preserved it through one crisis after another, fighting against incredible odds, buoyed up by faith when most men would have sunk in despair. To abandon Plymouth would be to abandon the dream that had led from Scrooby and Austerfield to Amsterdam and Leyden, and from Leyden to the great hazard of a settlement in an unknown wilderness.

But the opposition was firm—bent upon removing no matter what the rest of the community did. Plymouth, they said, was too barren to support a growing population. Look at Boston! Half the age of Plymouth, it was now five times its size.* Plymouth would soon be a ghost town. Better to make a new settlement than by slow attrition to lose all.

The chosen site was one of those the undertakers had reserved for themselves when Bradford surrendered the patent. This they now gave up, the colony added more land, and the Indian rights were purchased. But now a more careful survey showed that

* Plymouth colony in 1644 had 3,000 inhabitants, the Bay 15,000.

Nauset, far from being able to support an increase, was only suitable for twenty or twenty-five families. The decision for a mass removal was therefore reversed. But Thomas Prence, together with half a dozen other prominent families, went ahead anyway, renaming the place Eastham. "Neither could the rest hinder them, they haveing made some beginning." Thus one more blow was struck at Plymouth, now reduced to a population of 150—less than that of 1623.

"And thus," said Bradford, seeing the work of a lifetime slip out of his hands, "thus was this poore church left, like an anciente mother, growne olde, and forsaken of her children . . . Thus she that had made many rich became her selfe poore." It was a bitter blow, and though Bradford still had fourteen years of faithful public service ahead of him, he never quite recovered from it. For he had seen that even among those he respected, "it was not for wante or necessitie so much that they removed, as for the enriching of them selves." And if this was of more importance to a man than the beloved community which wrapped him in the warm blanket of togetherness and made him of one body with all the faithful—why then, what was there to work for? How could anything be more important than to be "admitted into the freedom of this society"?

Yet he went on working, for what else was there to do? Meanwhile the close-knit neighborly quality of Plymouth dissolved as families spread out to live on their farms. Since it was now impossible for all the colony's voters to meet, a representative form of government was set up, and in 1649 seven selectmen were chosen to tend to the town's business. One of the chief duties—and one which emphasizes the pastoral quality of the government in its attitude toward the people—was the care of cattle assigned for the support of the poor. Particularly were the selectmen to see that they should not be lost "in the summer season before the winter and times of hard things come."

Bradford's concept of government was no doubt a limited one —limited by his acceptance of the individual, separated congregation as the ideal unit. A small-town boy, he naturally thought in terms of the small neighborly community. This smallness was to him no restriction. Rather it was a framework in which the

individual could operate most happily, for it was large enough
to give him scope, small enough to give him the comforting
sense of safe enclosure. He had grown up in this sort of community. Maybe he never outgrew it. But the Congregational way
was essentially a rediscovery of local responsibility without need
or fear of any higher authority except God. This love of self-
government is living yet in many a New England community.
And Bradford was instrumental in putting it there.

Along with the breaking up of Plymouth as a community, it
seemed to Bradford, came a slump in morality and religion. It
was in 1642 that young Tom Granger was hanged for his experiments with animals. Other cases of a sexual nature were
brought before Bradford as magistrate—"Katheren Winter of
Scituate for fornication with her father-in-law," even Peregrine
White, stepson of Winslow and famous as the first English child
born in New England, for fornication with Sarah Bassett before contract and marriage. In 1648 Bradford had to take evidence in the murder of a four-year-old daughter by Alice Bishop,
upon whom he pronounced the death sentence in October.

As for the sex crimes, Bradford wisely concluded "that it may
be in this case as it is with waters when their streames are stopped
or dammed up, when they gett passage they flow with more violence, and make more noys and disturbance, then when they are
suffered to rune quietly in their owne channels." The figure
of speech was no doubt innocently Freudian, but the conclusion,
together with the recognition that sin was more closely looked
to in Plymouth than elsewhere in the world, was sensible. "These
common-sense conclusions," Samuel Eliot Morison has remarked,
"stamp the self-educated Pilgrim as a man of greater breadth
than the eminent Governor of the Bay."

Yet the conclusions did not lead to any loosening of the reins.
Disciplined himself, Bradford apparently had the intolerance of
the strong for the weak. As in morals, so in religion. When William Vassall, a resident of Scituate, introduced in 1645 a resolution "to allow and maintain full and free tolerance of religion
to all men that would preserve the civil peace, and submit unto
government," Bradford was against it, but the vote was close.
If Prence had not maneuvered for a delay, it would have passed.

Winslow sided with Bradford, as such a law—including even Turks and infidels—"would make us odious to all Christian commonwealths."

Attempts to liberalize the Plymouth church had been made much earlier than this. About 1637 Samuel Hicks had raised questions regarding infant baptism and the singing of psalms.

"If I may worship God in sperit and in truth singing out a booke," Hicks wanted to know, "why may I not worship God in praying out of a booke?"

This seemed to stump the faithful. But not for long. "Prayers are not part of Holy Scripture," the congregation finally decided. "Prayers are to God, singing to ourselves and one another." Whether the answer satisfied Mr. Hicks the church records do not say. But they indicate a sense of vulnerability and irritation in having to deal with such matters. "It is ezier for a Child yea for a foole to Cast Stones into a well then for a wise man to Gett them out," they concluded—apparently content to leave Mr. Hicks' stones where they fell.

Their efforts to redirect questioners into the right path seem on the whole not to have been too successful. They wrestled earnestly with one such person. Yet "the poor man fell yett further and further, and att last became a Quaker."

Sometimes the disputes became serious enough to threaten Plymouth's standing in England. This was the case when Samuel Gorton, with other critics, brought such charges against both Plymouth and Massachusetts that Edward Winslow was chosen in 1646 to sail once more to London, there to exercise his persuasion and charm. With Laud already dead from the executioner's axe and Cromwell in power, Winslow met a reception very different from his last when Laud had thrown him in jail. The Lords Commissioners for Plantations listened courteously and judged in his and the colonies' favor. Only Plymouth lost its ambassador. For Winslow, delighted to be in an England run by Puritans, never went back.

His failure to return was one more blow to Bradford, who now had to take upon himself the missions he had formerly passed over to Winslow. In the summer of 1647 he went up to Cambridge as Plymouth's representative to a synod of the churches, where he listened to John Eliot preach a sermon to the Indians in their own language before the whole assembly. He also listened, somewhat uncomfortably no doubt, while Ezekiel Rogers attacked the custom of private members speaking in church—an old Plymouth habit and one of the finer aspects of its faith in the priesthood of all believers. A year later he went back to Boston again, this time to help negotiate a dispute between the Dutch and the colony of New Haven which the Dutch governor had submitted to the arbitration of Winthrop and himself. But when he was asked to go to Hartford, he excused himself because of "bodily infirmities," promising to go the following summer.

This is the first sign of any physical weakness since Bradford's illness during the first winter and spring at Plymouth. Through all these years of hard physical labor, improper diet, exposure to cold, and the lack of what we would consider essential conveniences and sanitary precautions—to all of this he had apparently been immune. Devoted to his job, to his many jobs, he had been too wholeheartedly occupied to be sick. But here, at fifty-eight, is the first sign that he may be slowing down. In the seventeenth century anyone beyond fifty was old.

While Plymouth had never waged war against the Indians and had on the whole dealt fairly with them, there was always a submerged sense of the possibility of an Indian uprising. With the sea before them and the vast forests behind, the men of Plymouth lived by a precarious grace in the narrow thread of open land between the two wildernesses.

In 1642 the sense of danger had risen to the surface again because of an Indian feud between the Narragansetts and the Mohicans. A council of war was set up with Bradford at its head, the defenses on Fort Hill were strengthened, and the next year a brick watch house was put up. In 1644 the town was divided into military companies to meet an emergency and Bradford took charge of a company which included Prence (who soon after removed to Eastham), Hanbury, Lee, Howland, Cooke, Phineas Pratt, Gregory Armstrong and John Winslow. Though still in charge of the colony's military forces, Standish now lived in Duxbury.

Aroused to united action, the four colonies of Plymouth,

Massachusetts Bay, Connecticut (the settlements around Hartford) and New Haven met at Boston in 1643 to form a confederacy. According to John Quincy Adams, the idea of a confederacy originated in Plymouth and was suggested by the example of the United Netherlands, but there is no confirmation
of this in Bradford, or in other contemporary records that I
have been able to find. Whoever started it, Massachusetts dominated it from the beginning. Articles of confederation were
signed in May by all but Plymouth, whose commissioners had
to report back to their general court and to the towns before
they could commit themselves—an interesting proof of Plymouth's greater democracy even though prompted in part by the
fear of being dominated by Massachusetts. In September Winslow and Collier returned to Boston to ratify and confirm the
articles, whereupon the United Colonies of New England came
into being and English America began its first experience with a
form of government which was to be tried again a hundred and
thirty years later, and then in a strengthened form to emerge as
the United States of America.

After naming as its chief purposes mutual defense and the
propagation of the Gospel, the articles established the size of
the army to be provided in case of invasion (100 from Massachusetts, 45 each from the other three), and a commission of
eight men (two from each colony). The commissioners were also
empowered to frame agreements about civil matters in which
all the colonies were concerned, such as "the free and speedy
passage of justice," escaped criminals and servants, and residents removing from one colony to another. Roger Williams'
colony at Providence was pointedly refused admission thanks
to the influence of Massachusetts, though Williams was the man
best endowed in all New England to negotiate with the Indians.

The confederation was not aimed at the Indians alone. With
England engaged in a civil war and unable to protect its colonies, New England was afraid that France and the Netherlands
might jump at the chance to extend their American territories.
But its first activity came when the Narragansetts, after repeat-
edly breaking their promise not to war on Uncas, boasted "that
they would lay the English catle on heaps, as high as their houses,
and that no Englishman should sturr out of his dore to pisse, but

he should be kild." Standish led forty Plymouth men to Seekonk, the nearest settlement to the Narragansetts, while Boston sent forty men to aid Uncas. Another two hundred and ten soldiers were to be called immediately.

Prompt action apparently convinced the Narragansetts that the colonies meant business. War was averted, the Narragansetts agreed to pay "2000 fathome of good white wampame, or a third parte of black wampampeage," to restore all Mohican captives to Uncas, to keep the peace with the English colonies and with Uncas, to deliver up four chieftains' boys as hostages, and to "resigne & yeeld up the whole Pequente cuntrie, and every parte of it, to the English collonies, as due to them by conquest."

In the early years of the confederacy Bradford played no active part. But in 1647 he was one of Plymouth's commissioners at the July meeting held in Boston, where such matters as a custom to be levied by Hartford upon the Connecticut river trade and the condition of Harvard College were discussed. In 1648 the commissioners met at Plymouth with Bradford as president. From this time on an increasing friction with the Dutch is noticeable, and at the meeting in Boston the following year Bradford heard a good many complaints about them. They were stirring up the Indians against the English, they were selling arms, they were encroaching on English territory. Bradford was not a commissioner the next three years, but when he was elected to attend an extraordinary meeting at Boston in April of 1653 he must have had the feeling of the movie-goer, "This is where I came in." The argument with the Dutch was still going on. They were accused of "treacherous falshood against the English Collonies," and Bradford was put on a committee to summarize the grievances. The ill-feeling was heightened, of course, by the naval war which had broken out between England and Holland in Europe, and with the end of that war in 1653 the trouble in America died down, but not before Plymouth and Connecticut had declared that the colonies ought to go to war. This was at the meeting in September 1653, where Bradford had been replaced by Prence. With his warm memories of Holland, it is unlikely that Bradford would have voted for it.

Once again, on September 4, 1656, Bradford presided at the annual meeting of the commissioners, held this time at Plymouth. It was a quiet meeting. The end of the Dutch war in Europe had given a new tone to the communications from Stuyvesant in New Amsterdam. There was some wampum tribute paid in by the Pequots to be divided among the colonies, and somehow the thought of the commissioners gravely dividing the beads among themselves gives a tone of innocence and make-believe to the scene. Chiefly the commissioners were interested in discussing the propagation of the Gospel.

The very phrase brought Winslow to Bradford's mind—Winslow who had been his mainstay in affairs of state, now ten years absent from Plymouth and dead a year since. It was Winslow who in 1649 had got from Parliament a charter for the "Society for Promoting and Propagating the Gospel of Jesus Christ in New England." The charter provided for a corporation and officers, and authorized the commissioners of the United Colonies to expend the money to be sent them. The first appeal for funds was carried to every church in England and brought in £4,582.

Meanwhile, in the Bay Colony, John Eliot had already begun (1646) to preach to the Indians in their own tongue. The Indians, somewhat skeptical, wanted to know, "how it happened, if Christianity was of such importance, that for six and twenty years the English had said nothing to them about it?" Other difficulties arose. If the English God was so powerful, why did he allow English vessels to be cast away? This called for quick thinking.

"Satan wrecked the vessel, but the Lord saved the cargo."

The Gospel Society's money went largely to the support of Eliot's work. It built an Indian College at Harvard, provided presents to impressible Indians, and paid for the publication of religious works in Indian. The greatest of these was, of course, Eliot's Bible. In this, Plymouth had a part through its pastor John Cotton, who helped with the second edition. The Old Colony Indians showed no great eagerness for the Gospel, Massasoit himself standing firmly against conversion. One exception was the unique and still-existent Indian settlement of Mashpee. Thanks to the efforts of Richard Bourne (John Bradford's father-in-law), an area near Sandwich was set aside for a group of Christianized Indians where they could govern themselves and have their own church. Church and burying ground are there today, and services are still held.

The decade of the forties had tried Bradford's faith in Plymouth and in himself more than had the struggle for existence in the twenties or the commercial blows of the thirties. For the vision of the beloved community was fading, and it was this which sustained everything else. Morality and religion seemed to him at ebb tide, with men more eager for the quality of their outward estates than for the perfecting of their immortal souls. The death of Brewster in 1643 had marked, for Bradford, the end of that communion of saints which had been his mainstay since adolescence. Brewster's death was symbolic of something that had died in Plymouth, in the church, in the hearts of men. Winslow's failure to return was almost as bad.

In 1650, thinking that the purpose of his life had ended in failure, Bradford stopped writing his book.

"*Anno* 1647. *And Anno* 1648," he wrote. And stopped. He was tired, discouraged, and beginning to feel old.

"These Scribled Writings"

BRADFORD had no idea, when in discouragement he gave up writing *Of Plimoth Plantation*,* that he had fathered an American classic, the noblest narrative of American beginnings that we have. He had no idea of publishing it. He apparently did not think of it as literature. And it is only by rare good luck that the manuscript has survived.

The tale of Bradford's most important book is almost as full of hard knocks and last-minute escapes as that of the Pilgrims themselves. At his death it went to his son William. Thus, according to a note on one of the first pages of the manuscript, it was "given to his son mager William Bradford and by him to his son mager John Bradford. rit by me Samuel bradford mach 20, 1705." If Samuel's spelling is somewhat erratic, it at least shows us in "mach" that the wonderful twang of Yankee speech had begun.

From the next leaf we learn, from his own hand, that in 1726 when Thomas Prince the historian went to call on Major John,† he borrowed several octavos written in the governor's hand. Major Bradford told him that Samuel Sewall had borrowed *Of Plimoth Plantation,* and suggested that he get it from the judge. Prince asked if he might add the book to the New England Li-

---

* This is the title Bradford himself gave it; not "The History of . . ."
† The governor's grandson. Both he and his father were officers in King Philip's War.

brary of Prints and Manuscripts which he had been collecting ever since he had entered Harvard in 1703. The major, according to Prince, signified his willingness, "only that He might have the Perusal of it while He lived." Yet Prince wrote on a following leaf that John Bradford "had so high a value of it that he would never Part with the Property, but would lend it to me & desired me to get it [from Sewall], which I did, & write down this that sd Major Bradford and his Heirs may be known to be the right owners." This did not prevent Prince, however, from pasting his own bookplate in the volume. It is clear, therefore, that from the death of William Junior in 1704 until some time before 1726 * the Bradford manuscripts lay in the John Bradford house which still stands beside the Jones River, preserved by residents of Kingston as a memorial to the governor and his family.

Prince never returned the manuscripts he had borrowed, but deposited them in the library in the steeple room of Old South Church at Boston where he was pastor. When the British occupied Boston during the Revolution they used the church as a riding academy. When they evacuated the city, the library was found rifled and all the Bradford manuscripts gone. Many years later part of Bradford's letter book turned up in Halifax, to which the British fleet had sailed from Boston, but not before three hundred and thirty-eight priceless pages had been used to wrap groceries. When the history failed to turn up, it looked as though it had suffered the same fate.

Then in 1855, almost simultaneously, two writers on Massachusetts history happened to read a book by the Bishop of Oxford, the *History of the Protestant Episcopal Church in America,* which had been published eleven years before. It contained obvious extracts from the lost history—known to scholars through excerpts in Nathaniel Morton's *New England's Memoriall* and the histories of Prince and Hutchinson. Eager queries to London brought forth the fact that Bradford's manuscript was in the library of Fulham Palace, residence of the Bishop of London. Surely Bradford would have appreciated the irony of having his book preserved in the very palace where Laud had signed

---

* Not 1728 as generally claimed, as a careful reading of Prince's own notes will show.

יֶחֱזֶה מְנָת חֶלְקִי?

‏Isa: 16·5·

‏Isa: 26·5·ל· וַיְשַׁ שָׂנֵאתִי קְהַל מְרֵעִים·

A' Dialogue
Or 3. conference, betweene some
yonge-men borne in New-England;
And some Ancient-men, which came
out of Holand, and old England,
concerning the
Church

And the gouermente therof·

— yonge-men —

Gentle-men, we hope you will pardon
our bouldnes, in that we haue impor=
tuned you to giue us meeting once
more in this kind, for our Instru
on, & establishmente in the truth.
We find that many, and great are the
controuersies, which haue risen in these
later times, about the Church, and for
gouerments therof; and much trouble
and disturbance hath growne in these

Page from Bradford's manuscript, *William Bradford his Booke*, 1652. (By permission of the Massachusetts Historical Society, owner of the manuscript.)

an order putting Winslow in jail, and from which Laud himself was led out to trial and execution.

In 1856 the Massachusetts Historical Society issued the first edition, and finally after much diplomatic negotiation the original was returned to America where it is now displayed as the chief treasure of the library in the State House at Boston.

The discovery and publication of Bradford's manuscript made it possible to rewrite the history of Plymouth, and every retelling of the story since that time has leaned principally on Bradford. Written between 1630 and 1650 when he was fully occupied with the colony's business and political affairs, his book nevertheless has all the marks of conscious artistry—alliteration, paired synonyms, antithesis and balance. The rhythm of its best sentences remain in the memory like music:

"But they gathered up their spirits, and the Lord so helped them, whose worke they had in hand, as now when they were at lowest they begane to rise againe, and being striped (in a maner) of all humane helps and hops, he brought things aboute other wise, in his devine providence, as they were not only upheld & sustained, but their proccedings both honoured and imitated by others; as by the sequell will more appeare, if the Lord spare me life & time to declare the same."

Only a writer with an ear sensitive to subtle rhythms and conscious of the sound as well as the sense of words could write this, with its balance, its skillful repetition, its wonderful way of suggesting growth and space:

"Thus out of smalle beginings greater things have been prodused by his hand that made all things of nothing, and gives being to all things that are; and as one small candle may light a thousand, so the light here kindled hath shone to many, yea in some sorte to our whole nation; let the glorious name of Jehova have all the praise."

Sometimes a mere facility of grammar gives a terse dramatic effect:

"And if this had been all, it had been less, thoug too much."

Enough of Bradford's sentences have been scattered through this book to show that his skill as a writer was not limited even to these rhythmic effects, impressive as they are, but that he was capable of realism (as in the passage on smallpox), of deft and even cruel characterization (as with Lyford), of a fine elegiac tone (his lament for the church of Plymouth), and of intense drama (the separation of the Scrooby men from their families and the storm during the flight to Holland, or the leave-taking from Delft Haven). His effects range all the way from the colloquial to the stately, from the simple to the complex. And— mark of a true writer—he knows how to heighten drama by stripping his sentences of all superfluous words. The better educated Winthrop, writing under similar circumstances, cannot approach him as a writer. "As a Seventeenth Century writer," says Charles Francis Adams, "he deserves to rank with Bunyan and Camden." Yet how many Americans have read Bradford? *

As an historian Bradford is frankly partisan. Yet no one has disproved his statements of fact, and his sense of the importance of documentation has led him to a laborious copying of pages of letters and other source materials. His book, like that of Thucydides, is not merely history, but a work of art composed by one who played one of the chief roles. As Churchill is proving today, there is scarcely a more fascinating kind of history. And Churchill shares with Bradford a fine sense of the drama, destiny and duty which make history what it is.

Something should be said of the physical appearance of the manuscript. The volume, bound in vellum or heavy parchment, was obviously purchased and set aside for this one purpose since the peculiar, rather bell-shaped watermark with a five-petaled flower appears throughout. His other writings Bradford kept apart in a number of small books. The beauty of the handwriting is in marked contrast with the crabbed scrawls of most contemporary manuscripts, and when one or two minor differences of orthography have been learned, it can be read today as easily as a printed book. Clearly, here is a man who takes pride in his work.

Yet when Bradford dictated his will from his death bed it was not this masterpiece he mentioned, but a group of quite different works.

"I comend unto youer Wisdome and Descretions," he said, "some smale bookes written by my owne hand to bee Improved

---

* Fortunately a new edition of his history in modern spelling, edited by Samuel Eliot Morison, is planned for early publication.

as you shall see meet; In speciale I comend to you a little booke with a blacke cover wherein there is a word to Plymouth a word to Boston and a word to New England with sundry usefull verses."

Among the small books were three dialogues, the second of which has since been lost—presumably beyond any such remarkable resurrection as happened to the history. The title of the first, written in 1648, shows well enough what Bradford was aiming at: *A Dialogue, or the Sum of a Conference betweene some Yonge-men, born in New England, and sundry Ancient-men, that came out of Holand and Old England.* The failure of the beloved community, he felt, was partly due to the fact that the young men born in New England had no contact with the rich heritage of suffering, sacrifice and scholarship out of which it had grown. He therefore set out to describe the Scrooby congregation and its antecedents, their early trials in England, the persecutions, the flights into Holland, the straitness of their lives there, and some of the principal saints—Ainsworth, Robinson, Smyth, Clyfton. He makes no mention, to be sure, of the Johnson scandal. But he was not writing history now. When he did write it, he spared nothing. He was writing here to pass on a precious heritage, to make the new generation conscious of the martyrdoms which were the bedrock of their present security. He was writing to inspire, if he could. He was writing with the desperate tenderness of the old to whom the past is warm and alive, and who have been shocked to see in the indifferent eyes of the young that it is cold if not already dead. He wanted to make that past live so that the knowledge of it would strengthen the moral fibre of Plymouth which, to his aging eyes, was growing weaker with each passing year.

Yet to do these things he must be interesting, he must say things a young man would want to hear. And he is interesting. Choosing the dialogue form already long sanctified in literature, he packs it with anecdotes, descriptions, people. When he says that Henry Ainsworth knew the Scriptures "as if the book of God had been written in his heart," you do not forget the phrase, or Ainsworth. And when he praises the same reverend gentleman for his ease at quoting Scripture "without tossing and turning of his book," you suddenly see what many a Puritan preacher with his two-hour sermon must have been like. The young men no doubt saw it too, and smiled.

Yet he also manages to inject sound doctrine. When the young men ask whether Browne was the beginner of the Congregational way, Bradford replies that it was the prophets, apostles and evangelists who laid the groundwork, "and upon that ground is their building reared up and surely settled." The Pilgrims always resented being called Brownists, though they never found a good name for themselves, and Bradford here jumps at the chance to say: "It is very injurious to call those after his name, whose person they never knew, and whose writings few if any of them ever saw, and whose errors and back-slidings they have constantly borne witness against."

The *Third Dialogue* takes a wider scope. It discusses the Roman Catholic, the Anglican, the Presbyterian and the Congregational forms of church faith and government. It can hardly have surprised the young men that Bradford finds flaws in all but the last. Yet here again, though he is dealing with a subject which could have been deadly, he makes it interesting— partly by his attack on the worst excesses of Mariolatry and the moral deviations of the more spectacular pontiffs. (For money the popes and prelates "make as good marchandise of women's . . . .* as the gould-smith doth of gilded plate.")

In his argument for the Congregational way Bradford shows again his essential democracy, for it is the freedom and self-government of the church as a separate community, uncontrolled from above, that appeals to him. The early Christian church, he argues, was "almost like a popular government." The spirit of true Congregationalism is this: "We shall desire the Lord to make his word to be a lampe unto our feete and a light unto our pathes; that we may walk in his ways and make choyse of his statutes." And here, echoing back from a reading of the psalmist long, long ago as he struggles now to impart all that the church has been to him—here from his youth to theirs he tries to pass on to Plymouth's young men an intimation that the true church, the true community and fellowship, is a feeling in which a man's whole spirit is wrapped.

"We have the rather noted these thinges," he concludes, "that

---

* Thus in manuscript.

you may see the worth of these things, and not necligently loose what your fathers have obtained with so much hardshipe . . . Yee have been caled unto liberty; only use not liberty for an occassion to the flesh, but by love serve one another."

Did the young men of Plymouth ever hear these dialogues read? Or did Bradford lay them aside in his study after passing them around among his own young men? Though one of the three works is embalmed in the Plymouth Church Records, there is nothing to show that it was ever read in public. In fact Nathaniel Morton himself, who wrote it into the record, seems never to have seen it until long after his uncle's death. What a touching modesty this argues in the author!

The writings for which Bradford had the greatest affection were not the dialogues and not *Of Plimoth Plantation*. They were the "sundry usefull verses" in the little black book. On these, it seems, Bradford was content to rest his literary reputation. The choice shows how dangerous it is for an author to judge his own works. Bradford's poems—and there are seven of them, ranging in length from twenty-two lines to forty-seven pages —are his poorest work. They are interesting because they are by Bradford and because he also wrote *Of Plimoth Plantation* and was a great man, and this is about the worst thing you can say of a poet. To us they are also interesting because of some incidental information they contain about Plymouth, because they prove once again how different the arts of prose and poetry are, and because Bradford cherished them.

The best of the shorter poems is "A Word to New England":

> O New England, thou canst not boast;
> Thy former glory thou has lost.
> When Hooker, Winthrop, Cotton died,
> And many precious ones beside,
> Thy beauty then it did decay,
> And still doth languish more away;
> Love, truth, good-men, mercy and grace,
> And wealth and the world take their place.
> Thy open sins none can them hide,
> Fraud, drunkenness, whoredom and pride.
> The great oppressors slay the poore,

But whimsie errors they kill more.
Yet some thou hast who mourne and weep,
And their garments they unspotted keep;
Who seek God's honour to maintaine
That true Religion may remaine.
These doe invite and sweetly call
Each to other, and say to all,
Repent, amend, and turn to God
That we may prevent his sharp rod,
Time yet thou hast, improve it well,
That God's presence may with you dwell.

Here, despite the halting meter, the sudden absence of that felicity of rhythm we are accustomed to in his prose, he does manage the elegiac tone with some success. It is not very good, to be sure, but it is much the best of the "words," and much, much better than "Some Observations." "A Word to New Plymouth" is far less effective than his prose passages on the forsaking of the beloved community, but "Of Boston in New England" ends on a note of prophetic warning which has a certain earnest and convincing strength:

The trade is all in your own hand,
Take heed ye doe not wrong the land,
Lest he that hath lift you on high,
When, as the poor to him do cry
Doe throw you downe from your high state,
and make you low and desolate.

"Some observations of God's merciful dealing with us in this wilderness, & his gracious protection over us this many years. Blessed be his name"—this is the title of Bradford's worst poem so far as verbal felicity is concerned, though it tells us a few interesting things about Plymouth, reviews the search for a harbor, the night assault, the hungry years, then the coming of plenty, then of prosperity, then the sudden collapse of the cattle market, the falling off of true godliness, the criminal arming of the Indians with its attendant dangers. In the early part of the poem, despite the hampering effect of having to stay within the metrical straitjacket, we can feel the youthful energy stirring in Bradford as he tries through the magic of the bard, the minstrel to recapture the heroic days and deeds of his youth. But the mood is not long sustained. The elegiac tone soon dominates him again.

Bradford's longest and most vigorous poem is virtually unknown. It has never been reprinted, was long dismissed (on no apparent evidence) as not his, and has to be read in a manuscript copy, in a hand less clear than Bradford's though still not a bad one. Since the beginning is lost it lacks a title, but its subject is similar to that of the dialogues—a discussion of various heresies and a praise of the true, the Congregational way. The first lines land us in the midst of a blast against Henry Nicols and his followers.* Thereafter we are in for some forty pages of spirited invective and satire which in meter, gusto and content (though not in point of view!) is so like Samuel Butler's *Hudibras* that we would be sure Bradford was copying—except that he was dead before *Hudibras* (1663–1678) appeared.

Of the Ranters he says:

> They shun the nature of man kinde
> And blot out reason in the mind.

Of the Seekers:

> For new apostles they still expecte
> but doctrines of the old rejecte . . .

> Singes [signs] and marakls [miracles] they woulde see
> but leave those truths that confermed be . . .

> As children with their ratls play
> what now they like straight throw away.

Of the Quakers:

> And well they doe diserve the whip
> even at a cartes arse to skipe . . .

> As though their branes bee but muddy
> Yet they can preach without study
> One [on] any theame they will assey
> Even for to teach extempore.

* Nicols or Nicholas (Henrick Niclaes, fl. 1502–1580) was the founder of the "Family of Love," an Anabaptist and mystical sect whose chief principle was a love of humanity. The sect spread from Holland to England, where it was especially active around 1645 under a man named Randall.

Answering the argument of the Anabaptists against infant baptism:

> But shure they either dreme or slepe—
> because the'ar lambes are they not she[ep]? . . .
>
> Jaacob's shepe and lamb[s] mad[e] out one floke
> and soe doe those of Jaacob's stocke.

After demolishing all other sects and gloating over the fall of the Anglican bishops, Bradford comes to the Presbyterians whose stubbornness in the present struggle in England is preventing perfect peace and harmony. Again, as he criticizes the classis, the provinces, the synods, the courts and the Great General Council, Bradford's mistrust of delegated authority and hierarchy comes out. The true church, the church of the Bible, is to be found in the autonomous congregation, in the beloved community of the faithful.

> Let fall your plum[e]s and lowly bee
> And with your brethren doe agree.

Let Presbyterian give way to Independent and together they can stamp out heresy. It is as simple as that!

The poem ends on a noble plea for unity—on the Independent's terms.

> . . . for God his truth will advance high
> when all errours in the dust shall lye
> But keepe ye truth in puriety
> and walke in all humility
> take heed of pride & contention
> for that will bring distruction
> Seeke love & peace & unity
> and preserve faith, & sanctitie
> and God will blesse you with his **Grace**
> and bring you to his resting place.

Not great poetry, certainly. Yet when read as a whole the poem has a pleasing strength of line and a vigor of spirit which raises it quite above the rest of Bradford's verses. Running through it like a refrain, though not always expressed in the same words, is the idea:

For Gods most holy truth will stand
when all erours shall then be damd.

This pedal point of faith, set against the successive attacks on
the various religious "errors," gives the poem an effective tension
and dramatic contrast—the work of an artist who knows what
he is doing. Here if anywhere Bradford the poet is guided by the
same instinct which makes his prose great.

The epitaphs on John Robinson and on himself are formed
out of phrases so custom-worn as to wash out personality. In
those days a man was apparently expected to leave an "Epitaphium Meum" in a convenient pocket when he died. Ex-
Governor Thomas Dudley of Boston did it in 1653, and did a
better job than Bradford.

Keeping almost exclusively to the four-foot iambic couplet,
Bradford rarely if ever escapes the prose writer's sense of con-
striction, and the results show it. Yet how could a prose writer
with an aptness for figures of speech fail to write poetry instead
of mere verse?

One answer lies in the intent of the verses. They were warnings, they were appeals, they were memorials. They were satires
and they were sermons. Bradford sought to convince rather
than to move, to state rather than to suggest, to define rather than
to wipe out boundaries. When he praises the fertility of Plymouth he names, one after the other, twenty-eight products of the
soil. Poetry is not written that way. Poetry lets us look over the
horizon; Bradford pulled down the curtains and climbed into
the pulpit. Even on his death bed he knew that what he had
written were "usefull verses." We may let it go at that.

Bradford was forty when he began *Of Plimoth Plantation,*
fifty-eight when he wrote the first of the dialogues, probably in
his sixties when he wrote most of his poems. He abandoned his
history because he was too heart-sick over the dispersal of the
Plymouth congregation and community to go on, taking to
the more literary forms of dialogue and verse in the search for
an instrument with which to save Plymouth if it could be saved.
An active man, a creative man, Bradford had labored with hands
and brain and wealth for the thing he believed in—the small,

self-managed community of believers. This was the vision to which he had dedicated his life, and now it looked as if the vision would never be realized.

Yet he could not entirely give up, for surrender was not in his nature. The urge to build, to create, still troubled his mind. So he began to build again with words, though he probably had no idea that the name of poet itself means one who makes. And as he wrote, he found a wonderful release from emotions, frustrations, disappointments that had been souring within. Uncorked in this way, they began to have the savor of wine. And so a double purpose was served—saving instruction to those who stood in need of it, sweet, unexpected relief to the heaviness within himself. No wonder if Bradford, like many a writer before and since, mistook the relief within himself for deathlessness in the product.

In addition to writing, he was finding another outlet in study. Ever since Brewster had first introduced him to the world of books and ideas, Bradford had been a reader. His reading was not limited to the religious controversies of his time. He had studied Calvin, Beza, Zwingli, Peter Martyr and Luther. He knew Erasmus, Foxe's *Book of Martyrs,* the early dissenters of England. Of the classic writers he could quote Ovid, Pliny, Seneca, Marcus Aurelius, Plato. The dialogues are full of references to religious and historical works, ancient and modern.

Bradford's own library contained a good many books on religious and general history, and of course he had access to Brewster's larger library too, from which he may have inherited or purchased at the Elder's death.

"He was a person for study as well as action," said Cotton Mather, and his works show it. Both poems and dialogues have quotations in Latin, Greek and Hebrew. The beautiful little manuscript which contains the *Third Dialogue* opens with a hand-lettered title page headed "William Bradford his Booke, A[nn]o 1652" followed by a quotation from Proverbs, first in Hebrew letters and then in English translation. There follows a page of "the untimly, and strang deaths of many of the heathen poets & comedians" which shows an acquaintance at least with all the Greek and Roman dramatic writers. Then come eight pages of Hebrew words and phrases, with translations. The manuscript of the poem, "Some Observations," contains a collection of Latin sentences.

But most affecting of all Bradford's studies was his pursuit of the ancient Hebrew. As early as 1632 Winthrop had remarked on Bradford's knowledge of Hebrew, but it was not until the last years of his life that he was able to devote himself to it. The evidence of this labor is still visible in his own hand, for written on the blank leaves at the beginning of the history are eight pages of Hebrew. The first two are in Roman letter. Still Bradford was not satisfied. Turning to the next page he wrote, shaping his words to the form of an inverted triangle:

"Though I am growne aged, yet I have had a longing desire, to see with my owne eyes, somthing of that most ancient language, and holy tongue, in which the Law, and oracles of God were write; and in which God, and angels, spake to the holy patriarks, of old time; and what names were given to things, from the creation. And though I cannot attaine to much herein, yet I am refreshed, to have seen some glimpse hereof; (as Moyses saw the land of Canan afarr of) my aime and desire is, to see how the words and phrases lye in the holy texte; and to discerne somewhat of the same, for my owne contente."

Then follow five and a half pages of Hebrew words and phrases with translations, carefully wrought in his beautiful hand. Enough so that Bradford had his wish, enough so that he was ready for the last of his pilgrimages as he had proven competent to those before, his eyes and ears prepared to greet in the most beloved of all communities the voice and countenance of his God.

"Called unto Liberty"

ALTHOUGH William Bradford left off writing *Of Plimoth Plantation* in 1650, he was still a busy man, and remained so until his death. In trade, farming, governing, and as an active member of the church he was still Plymouth's leader. Every month the court of assistants continued to meet at his home, dining at his expense until 1651 when the colony finally saw fit to defray the costs. The year before, he had dined a guest whose presence at Plymouth was almost as unexpected as if the king should walk in. This was Father Gabriel Druillettes—a Roman Catholic priest! He had come down from Kennebec with John Winslow who was then in charge of the trading post there and who had apparently taken a fancy to the good father, a missionary among the near-by Abenaki Indians. After inviting him to dinner, Bradford recalled that the day was Friday. Perhaps there was a hurried conference with Alice, for when the main dish was served, it was fish. Would the Wilsons and Dudleys of Boston have been capable of this kind of gracious consideration? Bradford, though he knew what he believed, was no bigot. There is something very touching about that dinner of fish, the two men sitting across from each other at the trestle table with wooden trenchers before them, each leaning forward as he struggled—perhaps in a mixture of French and English and Latin—to seize hold on the other's mind. Bradford, perhaps, has put on the lead-colored suit with silver buttons, while Father

Gabriel is wrapped in the long, coarse, dark-colored robe of
the Jesuit order. After dinner Bradford no doubt showed him
his library—managing perhaps to draw attention to the silent
argument of Luther and Calvin and Peter Martyr on the shelves
—those good Catholic priests who had seen the light and become
Protestants. Perhaps he walked him up Fort Hill. (Not until
long after his death was it known as Burial Hill, though death
rather than the Indians had proved the stronger enemy after
all, the fort having never yet been needed as a refuge nor exercised in the town's defense.) They may have climbed to the
roof where the unneeded cannon still stuck defiant muzzles out
over the solid oak walls. Here was the best view of Plymouth
Harbor, and from this location Bradford could indicate the out-
lying towns. Descending the hill again, they must certainly have
gone into the meeting house where Father Gabriel was no doubt
as polite as he could be in the face of this distressingly barren
barn of a building—so forbidding and colorless a place in which
to conjure up the joys of the spirit!

Druillettes, arriving late in 1650, stayed until the following
February, being welcomed by John Eliot at Roxbury, his peer
in work with the Indians, but chiefly trying to persuade New
England to join the French and the Abenakis in an alliance
against the Iroquois. He was, in fact, successful in his mission.
Only as soon as he left, New England changed its mind.

As for work with the Indians, Bradford came closest to real
achievement in this direction when, in 1652, he served as one
of the commissioners for the Society with the long name, dis-
bursing £28 "which is for an Indian whose scull & Jaw bone was
broke by the fall of a peece of timber as he was sawing the meeting howse, sorely bruised & wounded lying senseless many daies
for which Cure the Chirurgeon hath 20 pounds & his diett &
attendance 8 pounds he is, as Mr. Elliott saith, no looser by this
Affliction there being great hopes of his Convertion and hath
dilligently followed that Imployment ever since." If conversion
required such a jolt to the system, it is small wonder the Indians
fought shy of it.

In 1654 Pastor Reynor quit, leaving Plymouth without a minister for thirteen years. Yet every Sunday there were two services,
sometimes with visiting ministers, sometimes without. With one

of Bradford's young men, Thomas Cushman, as ruling elder the congregation kept to its established ways. To those who truly practiced the Congregational way the lack of a minister, though regrettable, could be overcome so long as there were brethren to prophesy, "prenciple whereof were our then Surviveing & much honored Govr. Mr. William Bradford and his son in law Captaine Thomas Southworth." Southworth, of course, was another of Bradford's young men who combined religious with military skills. The latter he had learned from Standish. That doughty old warrior finally had retired to his farm at Duxbury in 1653, after he and Thomas Willet had been sent westward in an action against the Dutch. He died a year before his friend Bradford. Both men of action, with courage answerable to the demands made upon them, they had worked well together and Bradford missed him greatly.

The lack of a minister greatly troubled Bradford. In 1655 when the court again tried to elect him governor, he balked. The people showed no will to maintain a minister, he said. The deputies were unwilling to vote a tax for the purpose. Bradford believed in a tax on the community for the support of religion, though he also believed that it was up to the church alone to choose its minister and determine religious matters—a scheme familiar to him from the practice in Holland. He was unhappy over the unwillingness of other men to share the burdens of government and he complained that the people were refusing to pass laws for the suppression of error. Here at last is a sign of age, for Bradford during most of his life had shown the tolerance of Robinson rather than the rigidity of the Bay leaders. When men begin to rely on legislation instead of persuasion they have begun to admit the weakening of the cause.

In the end, of course, he agreed to go on. He had probably been too long in harness to be altogether happy in an open field.

The following March (1655/6) he signed articles of agreement with Prence, Willet, William Paddy and Josiah Winslow which continued their partnership in the Kennebec trade for seven years, all the towns having agreed.

By the time the commissioners for the United Colonies met that same year, so many churches in Plymouth Colony were without ministers that Massachusetts brought the matter up for action, citing "our dear brethren" of Plymouth for failing to encourage the ministers of the Gospel. To Bradford, presiding at the meeting, it was a bitter blow, the crown of thorns pressed down upon his aging head. For he had warned, he had chided, he had written dialogues and poems, he had done his best to preserve that wonderfully sweet sense of community, that bond and covenant with the Lord which had been the chief purpose of Plymouth Plantation.

"I have been happy," he wrote in one of his most eloquent passages, "in my first times to see, and with much comforte to injoye, the blessed fruits of this sweete communion, but it is now a parte of my miserie in old age, to find and feele the decay and wante therof (in a great measure), and with greefe and sorrow of hart to lamente & bewaile the same."

Sitting in his study he had taken up the big volume of his history, turning back the pages to find in the glowing past a comfort he could not find in the present. And there he had come upon the words which brought back to him memories of forty years ago, memories of the congregation at Leyden which were sharper and clearer—such was the nature of old age—than those of yesterday. Had there really been such a sweet communion, he mused, or was it only that the warmth of youth and hope and the bright colors beyond the horizon had now departed? Was his beloved community only a dream, after all, or had he once known the mother-warmth of it in reality?

Yes, he had known it. Of that he was certain. But he could not have known that the impact it had made on him, at Scrooby, at Leyden, and then at Plymouth was due in part to its providing the mother he had never known. For as surely as Brewster had become his father, the church community had become his mother, wrapping him in its protective, inclusive, nourishing arms. By breath and by heartbeat rather than by the colder knowing of the brain Bradford understood that a community must be the mother of its members and the community's leader their father. His orphanage had made him know this and feel it more keenly than other men. It had shaped his vision—the vision of the community so closely bound that it was to each of its members like an extended personality, an enlargement of self. This was Bradford's greatest gift to his people. Like most visions of worth it was too much for most of them to grasp. And so, like all men of vision, Bradford had to suffer the supreme tragedy of failing to communicate his idea though he had tried every act, every service, every device he knew. "The old men shall see visions, and the young men shall dream dreams." His dreams had sharpened into vision, into vision refined by experience. The vision was inside; it was a part of him and it was beautiful but he had failed to implant it in other hearts. Yet despite this beauty within, on the outside—he must have known it—he began to seem like a crotchety old man.

Bradford's westering years were not all dark. He was one of the most honored and respected men in all New England, and even Plymouth's decline did not alter the esteem for his person. Then there was his writing. Most men write poetry in their youth; Bradford wrote it in his old age. This argues a continuing energy and expansiveness quite in keeping with what we know of him. Also there was Alice, his helpmeet—a "godly matron" about whom we know so little that we must infer what we can from blanks rather than from knowledge. No one ever spoke ill of her. Nathaniel Morton loved her more than he loved his own mother. Making her will three years after Bradford's death (she lived another ten years beyond that) she prayed that she might be buried as near him "as conveniently may be." The many children, her own and others, raised under her roof grew up to be a credit to her, to Bradford and to the community. This tells a great deal. She was the kind of wife he had needed—dependable, a good manager, able to soothe him when he was angry and to buoy him up when he was discouraged. Perhaps she even liked his poetry!

As for the boys she had raised, they developed into a quite exceptional group of young men—Thomas Cushman who succeeded Brewster as ruling elder; Nathaniel Morton, secretary of the colony and of the church, town clerk and author; Constant Southworth, treasurer and assistant governor; Thomas Southworth, agent at Kennebec, captain, assistant governor, commissioner; William Bradford the younger, treasurer, assistant governor, major in King Philip's War, commissioner, and councillor under Andros. Their achievements helped to make Bradford

feel that his work had not been fruitless after all—helped also
to ease his sense of loss as the leaders of Plymouth and Boston
departed from the scene—Winthrop in 1649, Cotton in 1652,
Dudley the next year, Winslow in 1655 and Standish the year
following.

Yet as the old departed the young filled up the ranks. His
daughter Mercy, marrying in 1648, must have given him grandchildren before his death, though no record of them has been
found. William married in 1650, and two or three of his fifteen
children came onto the stage before Bradford left it. Interest-
ingly enough, he named his first for Dorothy's son and his half
brother—an act which must have touched his father, stirring an
old chord of memory, an aching, wistful memory of what it was
like to be young.* John himself had no children, and Bradford's
youngest child Joseph did not marry until 1664. But the numerous children of the other young men were also like grandchildren to William and Alice. He could scarcely go out of doors
without bumping into a parcel of them, and their piping voices
often trailed into the study as he was busy with the language
God spoke to the patriarchs and would one day soon, he confidently believed, speak to him. He was a patriarch himself these
days, he would reflect, leaning back for a moment to rest his
eyes. Yes, like a patriarch of the Old Testament with his flocks
and herds, his sons and his sons' sons about him. Well, he was
ready, ready to be called when his time should come. Yet that
piping from outside the window—it drew a man back to youth
that was gone, except in recollection . . . Austerfield and his
first memory—the loss of some treasured trifle, perhaps, in the
rushes deep on the floor; retrieved for him by some unknown
hand, bestowed with the caress of a half-remembered voice . . .
school and the feel of the hornbook in his hand . . . the bitter
cast-out realization of orphanage, the long sickness, the friend,
the walk across the fields to Babworth. Fragments of the past
came back without will or purpose: a sweet inflection in Robin-

* William Junior named his second child William, and the fact was proudly
entered in the colony records in the governor's own hand: "William Bradford,
and sonne of William Bradford, Junior, was borne the 11 of March, 1654[5],
and was baptized the 25 of March, 1655." As no other baptisms are noted, the
governor's eagerness to set his namesake upon the right path is, under the circumstances, at once staunch, pathetic and charming. William Junior's third child,
Thomas, was born in 1657, month not known.

son's voice as he read from the Bible, the shame of being led a prisoner through the streets of old Boston, the innocent bud of Dorothy's child-face when first he had seen her, the finger motions of weaving, the hell of sea storm and seasickness, then the first sight of the golden, sun-stricken beach.

Strange how the images grew hazier as they grew nearer in time. Age must be truly a backward motion—into weakness like that of a child, at last into nothingness again.

Was his time near? Throughout the winter of 1656–1657 he had been unwell, on and off. He was unable to preside at the March court—the second one he had ever missed (he had been absent from the May court in 1653). He was not a man accustomed to sickness and it was irksome to him. Yet he was not made helpless and fretful by it like most strong men, for he loved books and he was still very imperfect in the language of God and the patriarchs. As spring came on he had felt a stirring in him like that of the trees outside his window, as of sap rising, as of new vigor. And he had thought, perhaps not yet.

But then, with spring blowing and caroling and smelling all around him, on May seventh he had taken to his bed. It has come, he thought, a little surprised with himself that the knowledge could strike so lightly. And in the night, though he slept little, he was refreshed rather than exhausted by his wakefulness—borne up by visions and sensations he could not have put into words. The feelings were of light and of warmth, and it seemed to him that he had in him the light of all knowledge and the warmth of—what was it?—the warmth of a whole people living as in one body, the warmth of a mother's breast, of a child's hand in a father's hand, the warmth of the gathered congregation, of the people bound firm by covenant to God. This warmth and this light were from one source, and together they made faith. They were from the beginning—for had not God first of all things made light?—and so would they be to the end.

When Alice looked at him in the morning she gave no sign, but she knew. During the day his young men dropped in to see him as they were in the habit of doing, to ask his advice or to bring him news. He tried to tell them what had happened to him during the night. "God has given me a pledge of my happiness in another world," he said. They tried to pass it off. They spoke reassurances they did not feel. And not entirely for his sake but for their own, because he had been their shield and buckler and they could not conceive of Plymouth without him. But he was not deceived.

The next day he asked to make his will. He spoke with a clear mind, knowing exactly what he wanted to do with his various lands and trading accounts, not forgetting the little books which were to carry on his influence after he was gone. But of his great book he said never a word.

He died that evening at nine o'clock.

He was buried on the hill overlooking the community which but for him might not have been, escorted by a company of soldiers and lowered into the grave with loud volleys of shot— the only service Plymouth permitted to a soulless body. All of Plymouth was there. All of Plymouth knew that an era had ended. Outside Plymouth, throughout New England, the loss was felt, for Bradford, as Cotton Mather put it, was "lamented by all the colonies of New England as a common blessing and father to them all." Even Nathaniel Morton, a good but unimaginative man, wrote an elegy with one couplet which sticks in the mind.

> Now blessed, holy Bradford, a successor
> Of blessed, holy Bradford, the Confessor

had joined the other saints of the Lord.

As the inventory of his estate soon proved, Bradford had been able to combine saintliness with sound business principles, for he died the richest man and the largest property holder in the colony. His estate was valued at about £900—no great amount nowadays, worth about $67,000 (spring, 1951) but large for the times. Yeoman that he was, the possession of lands and flocks gave him good content. The selling of his English lands, followed by the loss of some at least of the money derived from them, had been a hard blow in his youth. It had made him all the more eager for land in the new world. And at his death he had land in abundance, proving himself worthy of his yeoman heritage, worthy even of good old Peter's bequest of those ewe lambs.

Bradford had already given half of the Stony Brook farm to William at his marriage, together with a stock of animals. To John too he had given land. Now in his will he asked that his other son Joseph be made equal with them. Alice was to live on the stock of the Kennebec trade, valued at £256. There were £153 due from the Dutch account at Manomet and over £151 in cash in the house. There were bequests to other members of the extended family.

Three of his young men were with him when he dictated his wishes—Thomas Cushman, Thomas Southworth, Nathaniel Morton. He still thought of them as young, though Cushman was fifty, the other two forty-one. Supervisors of his will were to be Thomas Prence, elected governor to succeed him at the June court a month afterward, Thomas Southworth, and Thomas Willet. Willet had come over from Leyden in 1629 on the second *Mayflower* as a lad of nineteen, had quickly proven himself a capable and resourceful trader, stayed a while at New Amsterdam as agent for Peter Stuyvesant, and when the English seized that town in 1664, became the first English mayor of New York.* As for Alice Bradford, if any doubt exists as to the admiration Bradford had for her, it is sufficient to say that he made her executrix. She lived thirteen years longer, continuing to entertain the court of assistants as she had done for William all these years, though now she was paid for it at last—£10 a year. Then at eighty she was carried the short, steep distance from her house to the burial ground behind it.

Though Dorothy May's line died with her son John in 1678, the descendants of William and Alice are many and distinguished. A grandson and two great-grandsons were counsellors of Massachusetts. A great-grandson was Senator of the United States from Rhode Island. Colonel Gamaliel Bradford commanded a regiment in the Revolution, and since that time the number of Bradfords who have distinguished themselves, down to the recent Governor of Massachusetts, Robert Bradford, are numbered in the thousands while all those who can trace descent back to him would fill a large city.†

* In 1653 the Dutch, fearing an attack, had built across Manhattan the wall which gave Wall Street its name. This was then the northern boundary of the town. But the wall failed to keep the enemy out.

† For genealogical information, see Bibliography.

As for Plymouth after Bradford's death, it struggled on until 1692 when it finally succumbed to the inevitable—an inevitable aided and abetted by the machinations of paid agents —and was merged with Massachusetts Bay. Thomas Prence, who followed Bradford as governor, immediately asked for and got a man to attend him at the colony's expense. There was none of this in Bradford's time. Nor had there been such persecutions for conscience as now began. In June 1657, the very month after his death, a law against Quakers passed the court. In this, Plymouth was following the lead of Boston where in 1656 two Quaker women were seized the moment they stepped off the ship and, though no law against Quakers had been enacted, were thrown into jail where no one was allowed to speak to them and where they were nearly starved. By official order the two women were stripped naked so that the reverend magistrates could examine them for witch marks.* The first law against Quakers was enacted in October and Boston was soon stripping Quaker women to the waist, tying them to the tail of a cart, and whipping them through the streets until the blood ran down their backs and breasts. When the executioner whipped Ann Coleman "he split the nipple of her breast, which so tortured her that it had almost cost her life." Bradford was spared, at least, this degradation of the Christian spirit.

He might have been amused, however, if he could have known that in 1689, thirty-two years after his death, the inhabitants of Rehoboth, Taunton and many other towns suddenly discovered that their lands were still under the patent of 1629/30 given to William Bradford and his associates. They hastened to get quit-claim deeds. But it now appeared as if a large part of Cape Cod was still legally Bradford's, and as no deeds are known to exist, many of the Cape towns may still be.

Though Massachusetts Bay managed to swallow up Plymouth Colony, the victory in the long run was Plymouth's. For it was the principles of Plymouth which ultimately triumphed over those of Massachusetts theocracy in American life. The Plym-

* What this examination involved is revealed by the following excerpt from Winthrop's *Journal* in which he describes the examining of Margaret Jones: "She had (upon search) an apparent teat in her secret parts as fresh as if it had been newly sucked." (Vol. 2, page 344.)

outh idea was basically democratic, as that of Boston was aristocratic or theocratic. The Plymouth idea offered a complete formula for living to all who would receive it. It used the instrument of contract or voluntary association to regulate all the relationships of life—God and the church, an earthly government, livelihood, marriage and ownership of land. The purpose of these contracts was to create a harmonious community, to perfect the human link in the great chain of being which God had forged. God's plan was perfect, but man had failed to fulfill his part. The pattern of that perfection was to be found in the Bible, and in the close-knit voluntary community of the primitive churches. This was the origin of the Congregational way, the Plymouth way.

To Bradford the hazardous pilgrimages, the struggle to get a foothold in the wilderness were but incidental to this main purpose—to build a like-minded, peaceful community dedicated to the service of God. His arguments against Christian sects other than the Congregational and his attempts to maintain the Congregational way were not undertaken out of any bigoted sense of infallibility, but simply from the conviction that a true community must be a like-minded one. Though this falls short of the modern ideal, it is worthy of respect for the emphasis it places upon harmony and what we nowadays call community spirit.

The men of Plymouth, who had to get with their own labor every bit of food, shelter, heat and clothing they enjoyed, still had time to put God at the center of their lives, to regard the community as His vehicle, and to sacrifice personal convenience and comfort to the common good and goal.

"They were in journeyings often, in perils of waters, in perils of robers, in perils of their owne nation, in perils among the heathen, in perils in the wildernes, in perils in the sea, in perils among false breethren; in wearines & painfullness, in watching often, in hunger and thirst, in fasting often, in could and nakednes. What was it then that upheld them? It was Gods vissitation that preserved their spirits." Only the community which did God's will could expect His aid.

Part of a much wider movement which was inevitably working toward democracy and humanitarianism, the Pilgrims had the humanest laws of their day, far more lenient than England or Massachusetts. They were a bridge between the medieval and the modern world, and they brought to America many of the basic concepts and freedoms we now take for granted. Organized first as a voluntary community of the faithful, they extended the basic democracy of this organization to include the political, economic and social order. With them, Independency had already grown beyond the ecclesiastical into all the departments of life. They brought the freehold tenure of land which wiped out any possibility of a landed aristocracy and led toward the wider liberalism of the eighteenth century, making a fuller realization of democracy inevitable. They established the Congregational way in religion. They instituted the civil marriage.

They believed so firmly and practiced so vigorously the art of local government that it is with us yet—in the town meeting, in the intense local pride of American communities, in the habit of organizing a voluntary association to get things done. This last, by the way, is so ingrained in us that we are surprised when it is mentioned as an American trait. Yet it is a habit we can be proud of, and far more impressive to foreigners than our much-praised individualism. We could use more of it, for only through maintaining that hard core of local pride and local action can democracy sustain the heavy weight of a great nation with world-wide responsibilities. So Plymouth still has something to offer us here. It suggests that an urban civilization must somehow find ways to tie all of its people to small, vital community units where they can learn what democracy is by serving it, and where they can recapture the deep satisfaction, absent in many Americans today, of being responsible, contributing members of a responsive, useful community: where they can experience that enlargement of personality which comes from giving more than they take—and thus paradoxically gaining more than they had dreamed. This was Bradford's vision of the beloved community.

Nor must we forget that other gift of Plymouth to the American way—Thanksgiving Day. How like Plymouth it is, with its religious basis, its rediscovery of the importance of such simple basic things as food, family and home.

"Thus out of smalle beginings greater things have been prodused by his hand that made all things of nothing, and gives being to all things that are; and as one small candle may light a thousand, so the light here kindled hath shone to many, yea in some sorte to our whole nation." Prophetic words indeed, William Bradford of Plymouth.

Yet at his death, it seemed to him as if Plymouth had failed to live up to its vision, to his vision of the ideal community. He did not see how it could have failed, if it had only been tried. For the rigidity and lack of equality in the Massachusetts idea Bradford had no sympathy, nor for their attempt to maintain the aristocracy of a class of ruling magistrates, nor yet for their dangerous tendency toward Presbyterianism no matter what they called it. Yet on the other hand he could not accept Roger Williams' idea of complete toleration. Not because he opposed tolerance in itself, but how could a man pretend to true religion and be a Seeker? A Seeker had no church, was a law to himself. And without the congregation, without the beloved community gathered together in a united faith, without the mother warmth of the group and the fatherly guidance of the experienced, how could a man—weak and alone—hope to reach God?

In his last years Bradford had to confront the tragedy that overtakes every man who has been a radical in his youth. He does not change, but the world does. The very liberalism he has fought for has been passed by and he finds himself a conservative. Something like this happened to Bradford so far as his ecclesiastical views are concerned, yet his vision of the beloved community is as good today as it ever was—and as far from being realized.

Bradford was not a great originator of basic principles. But like Franklin he knew an idea when he met one and was full of the practical wisdom, the persuasiveness, the tenacity and the energy to put it into practice. He fell victim to none of the superstitions and delusions of his day. No poor women were persecuted as witches within his jurisdiction. He ascribed no occult significance to the occasional eccentricities of nature which excited other men. Of great integrity, he worked well with men because he loved and honored them as God's creatures, the end and purpose of the divine scheme. Yet this sense of the largeness and dignity of man made him neither pompous nor humorless. Those who knew him spoke of his cheerful disposition, and his books themselves reveal his sense of humor.

Yet great as his achievement was, Bradford felt that the major work of his life was ending in failure, that all he had fought for was being lost. He could not know that in the end Plymouth would triumph over Boston and that—possibly in ways he would not approve—the underlying idea of voluntary association and self-government would win out.

In William Bradford it is possible to see the making of the first American, the pattern of the self-made man. The other New England colonies were run by university men, Virginia by men of the court. But Bradford was homespun. He was yeoman, he was self-educated, and with neither birth nor wealth behind him he had made his way to the top. He had the intense local pride, the shrewdness in dealing with people that goes with this American type. Where many had failed, he clung to his toe hold on the new continent and he forced the riches of its forests, if not of its waters, to yield to him. And he died well to do.

Samuel Eliot Morison calls him "a genuine Christian and a consummate politician." George Willison says, "Talented and indefatigable, passionately devoted to the welfare of New Plimoth, Bradford was unquestionably the greatest of the Pilgrims, one of the greatest figures of seventeenth century New England— indeed, of our whole colonial period." Yet the thousands of Americans who every year make the pilgrimage to Plymouth scarcely know his name. They see Standish dominating the countryside from his tower on Captain's Hill. They visit the Howland house. They look eagerly about them for signs of John Alden and Priscilla. But they go into the drug store or the bakery on Main Street with never a thought for the fact that they are standing where Bradford's house once stood. Then they go down to the shore where a replica of an early plank house now greets them and where, under a pile of masonry, Plymouth Rock rests upon the sand. Here is the summit of their pilgrimage, for Plymouth Rock in some vague and yet satisfying way represents what we are and what we mean as Americans. Yet the real rock on which Plymouth was built is not this boulder but Bradford himself. He has never had his monument, for with a strange perversity Americans have preferred to do honor to a stone. It is high time he had a place in every American heart. For he still has a great deal to say to us, not only in what he has written but in what he was—"a lampe unto our feete and a light unto our pathes." And across the distance of three hundred years the sound of his voice comes with the clarity of a vision still negotiable, still worth our pursuing when he tells us:

"We have the rather noted these thinges, that you may see the worth of these things, & not necligently loose what your fathers have obtained with so much hardshipe."

Notes and Sources

The chief source for the story of Bradford and Plymouth is Bradford's own book, *Of Plimoth Plantation*. Unless otherwise identified, all quotations in the text are from this book. Where *Mourt's Relation* and Winslow's *Good Newes from New-England* (often called Winslow's Relation) are referred to in the text, they are not further identified here. These three basic source works should be read entire by anyone who wants to get the Pilgrim story direct from those who lived it.

To cite a source for every fact and opinion in this book would require an apparatus far too cumbersome to be worth its weight, since my own notes and researches would make another volume easily the size of this. Instead, I have assembled here whatever notes are necessary to identify direct quotations or to warn the reader of points in dispute, following them with a discussion of sources.

For complete bibliographical information for books listed in these notes, see the section on sources.

Chapter 2
Page 24. Quotation from Mildred Campbell, *The English Yeoman*.
Chapter 3
Page 47. From R. H. Tawney, *Religion and the Rise of Capitalism*.
Page 48. Quoted in Mary Caroline Crawford, *In the Days of the Pilgrim Fathers*.
Page 49. From Bradford's *First Dialogue*.
Page 51. From David Hume, *History of England*, Albany, Packard, 1816, vol. 3, chap. 40, p. 76.

Page 53. From Robert Browne, *A Booke which sheweth the Life &
Manners of all True Christians.*

Page 59. Robinson, *Works,* vol. 2, p. 278.

Page 61. Same, vol. 1, p. 42.

Page 61. From Robinson's *A Justification of Separation from the
Church of England. Works,* vol. 2, p. 153.

Chapter 5

Page 76. From Motley, *Rise of the Dutch Republic,* vol. 2, p. 571.

Page 78. Motley, *History of the United Netherlands,* vol. 4, p.
571.

Page 80. Quoted in Frederick A. Noble, *The Pilgrims,* Boston, Pilgrim Press, 1907, p. 107.

Page 83. Quoted in Arber, *The Story of the Pilgrim Fathers,* p. 143.

Pages 85, 95. Cotton Mather, *Magnalia Christi Americana.*

Chapter 6

Page 106. For the argument that Bradford was in London, see
Charles Edward Banks, *Proc. Mass. Hist. Soc.,* vol. 61, p. 57. For a
contrary view see Samuel Eliot Morison's essay in the same volume, p. 34.

Chapter 7

Page 131. The reader who enjoys nautical detail should read W. S.
Nickerson's *Land-ho! 1620,* a tightly reasoned reconstruction of
the landfall and exploration of the *Mayflower.*

Page 133. John Quincy Adams' essay on "The New England Confederacy of 1643," *Coll. Mass. Hist. Soc.,* 3rd series, vol. 9, 1846,
p. 200.

Page 137. For an interesting discussion of the geology of the Old
Colony see Albert Perry Brigham: *Cape Cod and the Old Colony.*

Chapter 8.

Page 146. *Mourt's Relation,* in Young's *Chronicles,* p. 174.

Page 151. *Mourt's Relation,* in Young's *Chronicles,* p. 194.

Page 163. The military commands are taken from Hexham, *Principles of the Art Military,* 1637.

Page 165. Sir Ferdinando Gorges, *Briefe Narration,* 1658. Reprinted in *Coll. Mass. Hist. Soc.,* 3rd series, vol. 6, 1837, p. 73.

Chapter 9

Pages 174, 175, 180, 191, 192. From Winslow's *Good Newes.*

Page 186. The date of Southworth's death has never been exactly
determined.

Chapter 10

Page 195. From William Wood, *New England's Prospect,* 1635.

Page 202. The estimates of Bradford come from Winthrop. Roger

Williams, the *Plymouth Church Records*, p. 110; and Hubbard's *General History of New England*, p. 556.

Chapter 11

Page 217. Perry Miller, *The New England Mind*, p. 378.

Page 218. R. H. Tawney, *Religion and the Rise of Capitalism*, p. 102. Second quotation is from G. P. Gooch, *History of English Democratic Ideas in the Seventeenth Century*, p. 67.

Page 219. Fynes Morison, *Itinerary*, vol. 4.

Page 220. The declaration of liberty is in *Plymouth Colony Records*, vol. 11, p. 6. For a highly interesting evaluation of Plymouth's legal code, see Julius Goebel, Jr., "King's Law and Local Custom," *Columbia Law Review*, vol. 31, no. 3, 416–48.

Page 226. The *Plymouth Church Records* give the date of the first meeting house as 1648, but William T. Davis, whose *History of the Town of Plymouth* and *Ancient Landmarks of Plymouth* are highly trustworthy, is positive that the meeting house was built in 1637. The music on this page is taken from Waldo Selden Pratt's *The Music of the Pilgrims*. On town meeting, see A. B. Maclear, *Early New England Towns*.

Page 227. Quoted in John Fairfield Sly's *Town Government in Massachusetts*. Sly, incidentally, regards Plymouth as of little importance in America's political development, for reasons which are not clear to me.

Chapter 12

Page 243. Winslow, *Hypocrisie Unmasked*, London, 1646.

Chapter 13

Page 252. The Bradford letter is in the *Mayflower Descendant*, Jan. 1907, p. 1.

Page 252. Winthrop's *Journal*, p. 93.

Page 261. Robert C. Winthrop, *Life & Letters of John Winthrop*, Boston, 1867, vol. 2, p. 200.

Chapter 14

Page 277. Winslow's letter is in *Coll. Mass. Hist. Soc.*, 4th series, vol. 6, p. 162.

Chapter 15

Page 286. Samuel Eliot Morison, *Builders of the Bay Colony*, p. 99.

Page 289. John Quincy Adams' essay on "The New England Confederacy of 1643" is in *Coll. Mass. Hist. Soc.*, 3rd series, vol. 9, pp. 189–223.

Page 291. For the missionary society and related quotations see *The New England Company of 1649 and John Eliot*, p. xxxv; Nathaniel Morton, *New England's Memoriall*, p. 162 n.; Joseph

Dillaway Sawyer, *History of the Pilgrims and Puritans,* vol. 3, p. 124.

Chapter 16

Page 304. The Dudley poem is quoted in *New England's Memoriall,* p. 168.

Chapter 17

Page 309. *Plymouth Church Records,* vol. 1, p. 109.

Page 316. For the Quaker persecutions see Richard P. Hallowell, *The Quaker Invasion of Massachusetts,* and George Bishop's *New England Judged by the Spirit of the Lord,* 1667, from which the quotation is taken, p. 430.

Page 320. Morison, article on Bradford in *Dictionary of American Biography.* Willison, *Saints and Strangers,* p. 340.

SOURCES

To list the hundreds of magazine articles, books from which but a fact or a phrase was taken, and volumes which had to be read for the sake of thoroughness though they produced no new information—to list all this would be out of place in a work of this kind. Instead, I have drawn up a bibliography which I hope may be of some help to a reader desiring to go farther along some of the paths opened up in this book. There is an excellent bibliography, moreover, in George Willison's *Saints and Strangers,* listed below—a work so excellent that I long hesitated to go ahead with a life of Bradford. The Boston Public Library also issued a useful bibliography in 1920: *The Pilgrims, a selected list of works.*

First, a list of Bradford's own works:

A Relation, or Journall, of the Beginnings and Proceedings of the English Plantation settled at Plimoth, in New England. London, 1622. Though this appeared under the name of G. Mourt, it was actually written by Bradford and Edward Winslow. Available in Arber (see below).

Of Plimoth Plantation, written 1630–1650, first published in full by Mass. Hist. Soc., 1856. New edition edited by Samuel Eliot Morison scheduled for 1952.

A Dialogue, or the Sum of a Conference betweene some Yonge-men, born in New England, and sundry Ancient-men, that came out of Holand and Old England. 1648. Printed in Young's *Chronicles* and *Plymouth Church Records* (see below). This is the First Dialogue. The second is lost.

William Bradford his Booke, 1652. Manuscript in Bradford's hand, in Mass. Hist. Soc. library. Contains the *Dialogue or Third Con-*

ference, printed in *Proc. Mass. Hist. Soc.,* 1869–70, p. 407. Also contains pages in Greek and Hebrew and a page of "the untimly, and strang deaths of many of the heathen poets & comedians."

Poems:

An epitaph on John Robinson, *Plymouth Church Records,* vol. 1, p. 62.

A satire on heresies, with a praise of the Congregational way. Never printed. Ms. in hand of John Willis in Mass. Hist. Soc. library. Dated 1657.

"A Word to New Plymouth," and

"Some observations of God's merciful dealing with us in this wilderness, & his gracious protection over us this many years. Blessed be his name." These two poems are printed in *Proc. Mass. Hist. Soc.,* 1869–70, vol. 11, p. 465.

"Of Boston in New England," and

"A Word to New England." Both printed in *Coll. Mass. Hist. Soc.,* 3rd series, vol. 7, 1838.

"Epitaphium Meum," in *New England's Memoriall* (below), p. 173.

Letter-Book. Coll. Mass. Hist. Soc., series 1, vol. 3, 1794, p. 27.

Miscellaneous Bradford letters appear in the *Mayflower Descendant,* vol. 9, p. 1 (Jan. 1907); *Coll. Mass. Hist. Soc.,* 4th series, vol. 6, p. 156; *American Historical Review,* vol. 8, p. 295. The Pequot Library of Southport, Conn., has the letter printed in *Coll. Mass. Hist. Soc.,* 4th series, vol. 2, p. 119.

Bradford's will and inventory are in the *Mayflower Descendant,* vol. 2, 1900, p. 228.

SELECTED READING LIST

Ainsworth, Henry. *The Book of Psalmes.* Amsterdam, 1612.

Arber, Edward. *The Story of the Pilgrim Fathers.* Boston, Houghton Mifflin, 1897.

Bacon, Leonard. *The Genesis of the New England Churches.* New York, Harper, 1874.

Banks, Charles Edward. *The English Ancestry and Homes of the Pilgrim Fathers.* Boston, 1929.

Baxter, James Phinney. *Sir Ferdinando Gorges.* Boston, 1890.

Baylies, Frances. *An Historical Memoir of the Colony of New Plymouth.* Boston, 1830.

Bible. Bradford's Bible was the Geneva version, 1592, from which quotations in this book are taken.

Bishop, George. *New England Judged by the Spirit of the Lord.* London, 1667.

Brigham, Albert Perry. *Cape Cod and the Old Colony*. New York, Putnam, 1920.

Brown, John. *The Pilgrim Fathers of New England*. New York, Revell, 1896.

Browne, Robert. *A Treatise of Reformation without Tarying for Anie*. Middleburgh, 1582.

———. *A Booke which sheweth the life and manners of all True Christians*. Same.

Browne, William Bradford. "The Ancestry of the Bradfords of Austerfield," *New England Historic & Genealogical Register*. October, 1929, p. 439. Carries the Bradford line back to William's great-great-grandfather Peter.

Burgess, Walter H. *The Pastor of the Pilgrims. A Biography of John Robinson*. New York, Harcourt, 1920.

Campbell, Douglas. *The Puritans in Holland, England & America*. New York, Harper, 1892.

Campbell, Mildred. *The English Yeoman*. New Haven, Yale, 1942.

Channing, Edward. *Town and County Government in the English Colonies of North America*. Baltimore, 1884.

Chronicles of the Pilgrim Fathers. Everyman, 1910. Convenient source for Morton's *New England's Memoriall*, Smith's *New England's Trials*, Winslow's *Good Newes*, and others.

The Compact with the Charter and Laws of the Colony of New Plymouth. Boston, 1836.

Crawford, Mary Caroline. *In the Days of the Pilgrim Fathers*. Boston, Little Brown, 1920.

Davis, Ozora Stearns. *John Robinson, the Pilgrim Pastor*. Boston, Pilgrim Press, 1903.

Davis, William T. *Ancient Landmarks of Plymouth*. Boston, 1883.

———. *History of the Town of Plymouth*. Philadelphia, 1885.

Dexter, Henry M. & Morton. *The England and Holland of the Pilgrims*. Boston, Houghton Mifflin, 1905.

Dow, George Francis. *Every Day Life in the Massachusetts Bay Colony*. Boston, 1935.

Drew, Thomas Bradford. *The Ancient Estate of Governor William Bradford*. Boston, 1897.

Earle, Alice Morse. *Home Life in Colonial Days*. New York, Macmillan, 1898.

Eekhof, A. *Three Unknown Documents*. The Hague, 1920. Contains the power of attorney Bradford gave to William Jepson and John Keble to collect 100 guilders due on the house he had sold Jan des Obrys.

Foxe, John. *Actes & Monuments (Book of Martyrs)*. Many editions.

Fussell, G. E. "Social and Agrarian Background of the Pilgrim Fathers," *Agricultural History*, vol. 7, no. 4, Oct. 1933.

Gooch, G. P. *History of English Democratic Ideas in the Seventeenth Century*. Cambridge, 1927.

Goodwin, John A. *The Pilgrim Republic*. Boston, Houghton Mifflin, 1920. (First ed. 1888)

Gorges, Sir Ferdinando. "Brief Narration . . . Plantations in America," 1658, *Coll. Mass. Hist. Soc.*, 3rd series, vol. 6, 1837.

———. "A Briefe Relation of the Discovery and Plantation of New England," 1622, *Coll. Mass. Hist. Soc.*, 2nd series, vol. 9, p. 1.

Griffis, William Elliot. *The Pilgrims in Their Three Homes*. Boston, Houghton Mifflin, 1931. (First ed. 1898)

Hall, Ruth Gardiner. *The Descendants of William Bradford*. Ann Arbor, Edwards Bros., 1951. A genealogy containing 11,000 descendants of the first seven generations from the Governor.

Hallowell, Richard P. *The Quaker Invasion of Massachusetts*. Boston, Houghton Mifflin, 1887.

Harrison, William. *Description of England and Scotland* (1577–87). London, Trubner, 1877.

Hubbard, William. *A General History of New England* (1680). Boston, Little Brown, 1848.

Hunter, Joseph. *Collections Concerning the Church or Congregation of Protestant Separatists formed at Scrooby*. London, 1854.

Hutchinson, Thomas. *History of the Province of Massachusetts Bay*. London, 1765–1828. Modern reprint by Harvard University Press.

Jantz, Harold S. "The First Century of New England Verse." *Proceedings of the American Antiquarian Society*, 1943.

Leyden Documents relating to the Pilgrim Fathers. Leyden, 1920. Contains the marriage entries of William and Dorothy.

Lord, Arthur. *Plymouth and the Pilgrims*. Boston, Houghton Mifflin, 1920.

Maclear, Anne Bush. *Early New England Towns*. New York, Columbia, 1908.

Mason, Thomas W. *New Light on the Pilgrim Story*. London, 1920.

Massachusetts Historical Society. Both the *Proceedings* and the *Collections* are so full of rich materials that it would take a separate bibliography to list them all. The more important have been indicated elsewhere.

Mather, Cotton. *Magnalia Christi Americana* (1702). Various editions.

Meyer, Isidore S. "The Hebrew Preface to Bradford's History," *Pub. of Amer. Jewish Hist. Soc.*, no. 38, part 4, p. 289.

Miller, Perry. *The New England Mind.* New York, Macmillan, 1939.

Morison, Fynes. *Itinerary.* New York, Macmillan, 1908.

Morison, Samuel Eliot. *Builders of the Bay Colony.* Boston, Houghton Mifflin, 1930.

———. *The Puritan Pronaos.* New York University Press, 1936.

Morton, Nathaniel. *New England's Memoriall* (1669). See *Chronicles* entry.

Morton, Thomas. *New English Canaan* (1637). Reprinted Boston, 1883.

Motley, John Lothrop. *History of the United Netherlands.* New York, Harper, 1879.

———. *Rise of the Dutch Republic.* New York, Harper, 1898.

Mourt's Relation (1622). In Arber's *Story of the Pilgrim Fathers.*

New England Historic and Genealogical Register. Its pages are full of useful leads and facts.

New Plymouth Colony. *A Declaration of the Warrantable Grounds and Proceedings of the First Associates of the Government of New Plymouth.* Boston, 1773.

Nickerson, W. S. *Land-ho! 1620.* Boston, Houghton Mifflin, 1931.

Orr, Charles. *History of the Pequot War.* Cleveland, 1897. Contains the contemporary accounts of Mason, Underhill, Vincent, Gardener.

Parrington, Vernon Louis. *The Colonial Mind.* New York, Harcourt, 1927.

Perry, Ralph Barton. *Puritanism and Democracy.* New York, Vanguard, 1944.

Plumb, Albert H. *William Bradford of Plymouth.* Boston, Badger, 1920.

Plymouth Church Records (1620–1859). Boston, *Publications of the Colonial Society of Massachusetts,* 1920.

Plymouth Colony Records, 12 volumes, Boston, 1861.

Plymouth Town Records (1636–1783). Plymouth, 1889–1903. These three sets of records are crowded with facts from which the life of Plymouth can be deduced.

Pratt, Waldo Seldon. *The Music of the Pilgrims.* Boston, 1921.

Robinson, John. *The Works of John Robinson.* Boston, 1851.

Sawyer, Joseph Dillaway. *History of the Pilgrims and Puritans.* New York, Century, 1922. Somewhat thrown together, but well illustrated.

Shepard, James. *Governor William Bradford & His Son Major William Bradford.* New Britain, 1900.

Sly, John Fairfield. *Town Government in Massachusetts* (1620–1630). Harvard, 1930.

Smith, Captain John. *Description of New England.* London, 1616.

———. *New England's Trials* (1622). See *Chronicles* entry.

———. *Generall Historie of Virginia.* London, 1624. Smith's *Works* have been reprinted by Edward Arber, Birmingham, 1884.

Steele, Ashbel. *Chief of the Pilgrims, or The Life & Times of William Brewster.* Philadelphia, Lippincott, 1857.

Straus, Oscar S. *Roger Williams, the Pioneer of Religious Liberty.* New York, Century, 1894.

Tawney, R. H. *Religion and the Rise of Capitalism.* New York, Harcourt, 1926.

Taylor, Ellery Kirke. *Welcome Englishmen.* A Bradford genealogy to be published in 1951 or 1952, Haddonfield, N.J. Contains fourteen generations.

Thacher, James. *History of the Town of Plymouth.* Boston, 1832.

The New England Company of 1649 and John Eliot. Boston, Prince Society, 1920.

Tillyard, E. M. W. *The Elizabethan World Picture.* New York, Macmillan, 1944.

Usher, Roland. *The Pilgrims and Their History.* New York, Macmillan, 1918.

Waddington, John. *Congregational History, 1567–1700.* London, Longmans Green, 1874.

Webb, Beatrice and Sidney. *English Local Government.* London, Longmans, 1906–29.

Willison, George F. *Saints and Strangers.* New York, Reynal & Hitchcock, 1945.

Winslow, Edward. His *Good Newes* may be found in *Chronicles of the Pilgrim Fathers* or in Arber's *Story of the Pilgrim Fathers.*

———. *The Glorious Progress of the Gospel amongst the Indians in New England.* London, 1649.

Winsor, Justin. *Narrative and Critical History of America.* Boston, Houghton, 1884–89. Vol. 3, part 1, pp. 257–94. Shows autographs of Dorothy and William.

Winthrop, John. *Journal.* New York, Scribner, 1908.

———, Robert C. *Life and Letters of John Winthrop.* Boston, Ticknor and Fields, 1867.

Wood, William. *New England's Prospect.* London, 1635. Wood found the prospects excellent.

Wright, Thomas Goddard. *Literary Culture in Early New England.* New Haven, 1920.

Young, Alexander. *Chronicles of the Pilgrim Fathers.* Boston, Little Brown, 1844. Contains Bradford's *First Dialogue, Mourt's Relation,* Winslow's *Good Newes,* and other Pilgrim items.

Index